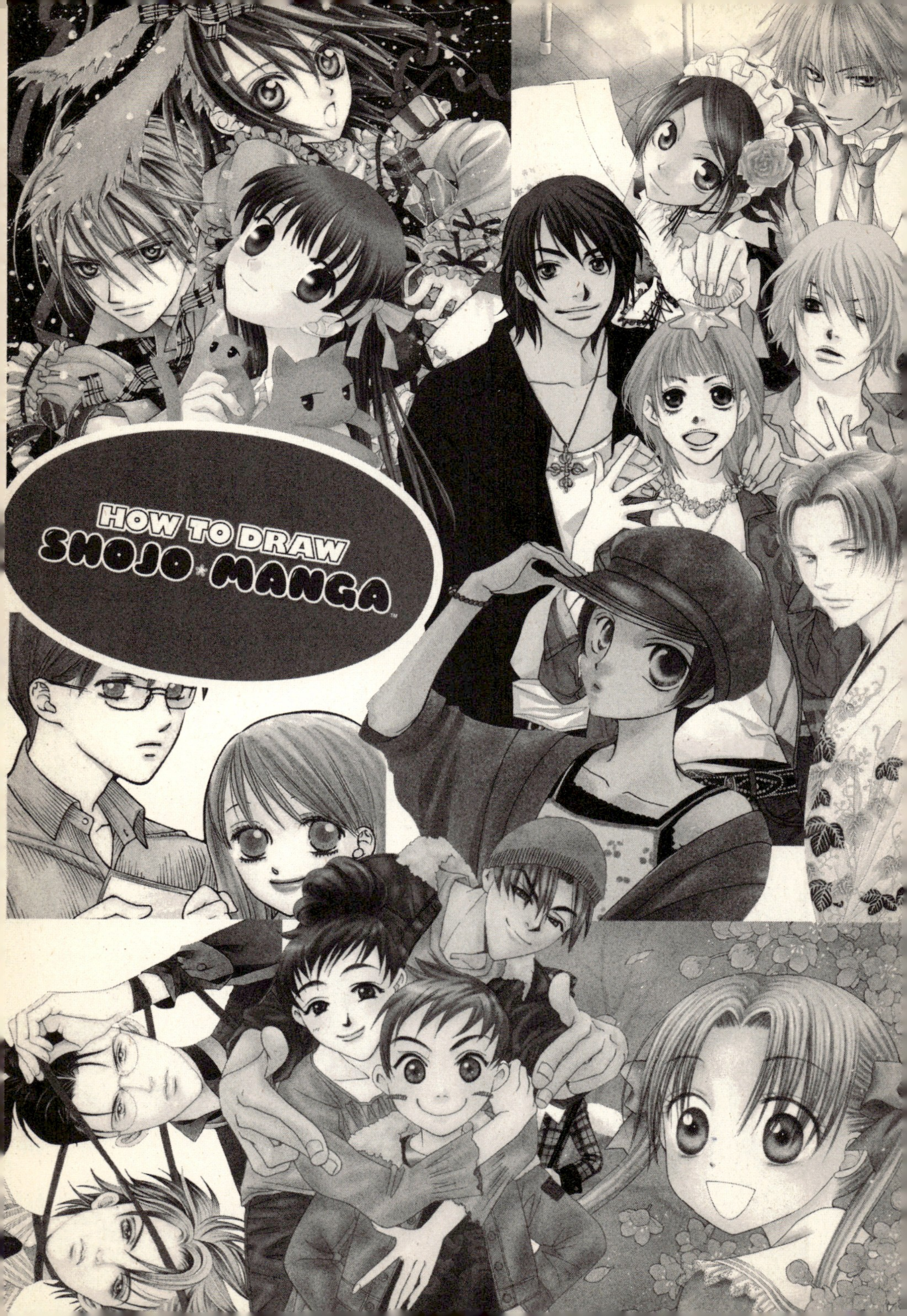
HOW TO DRAW
SHOJO MANGA™

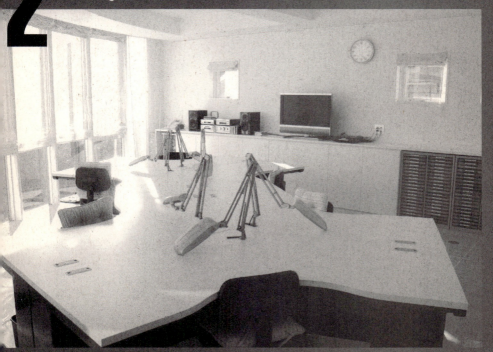

INSIDE THE ARTIST'S STUDIO WITH REIKO SHIMIZU

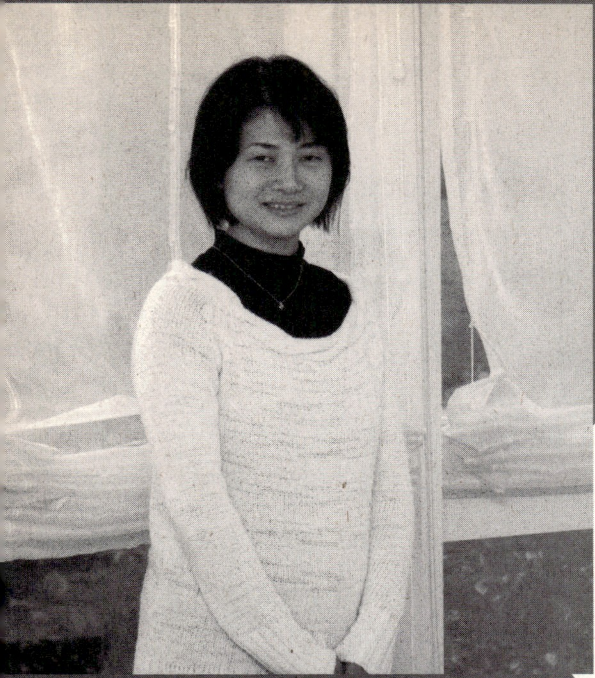

1

We have stormed the work-place of manga artist Reiko Shimizu, best known for creating *Kaguya-hime* and *Himitsu: Top Secret.*

2

The assistants' desk. Its unique design is both elegant and functional.

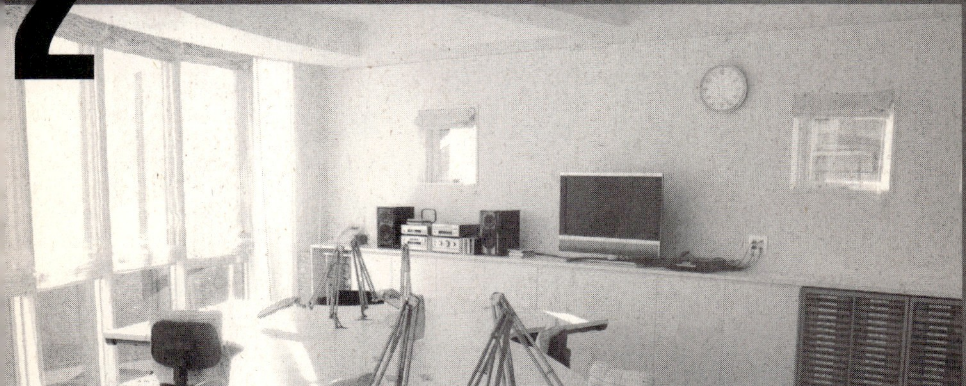

3

Reference shelves, chock-full of scrapbooks stuffed with magazine clippings and other helpful things.

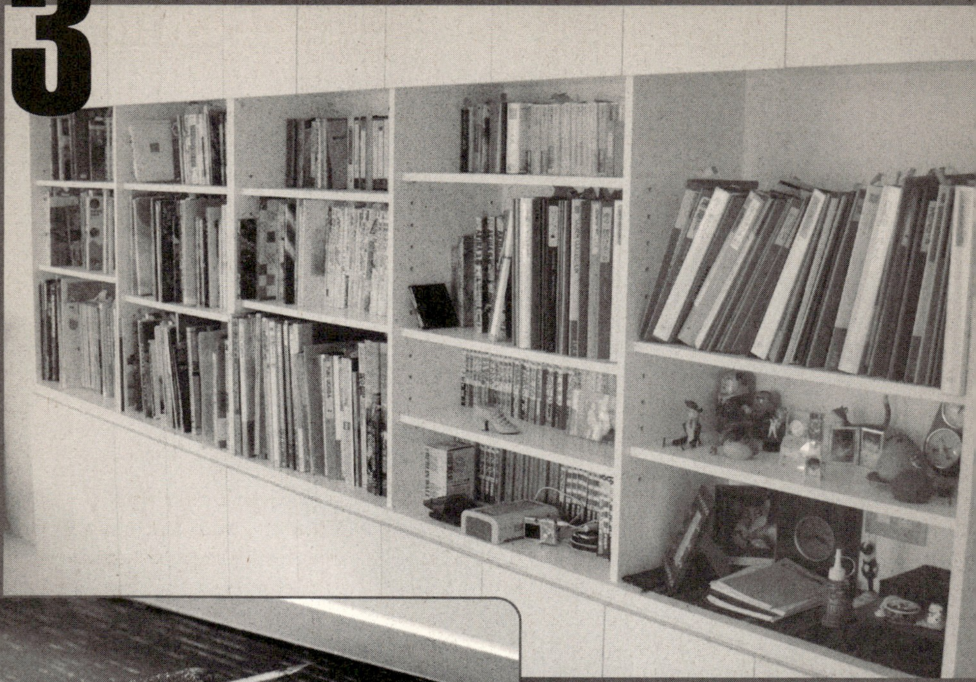

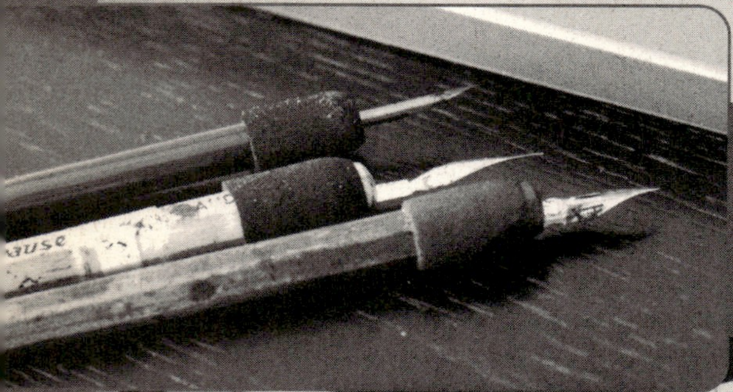

4

Shimizu's favorite pens, which have brought countless masterpieces to life.

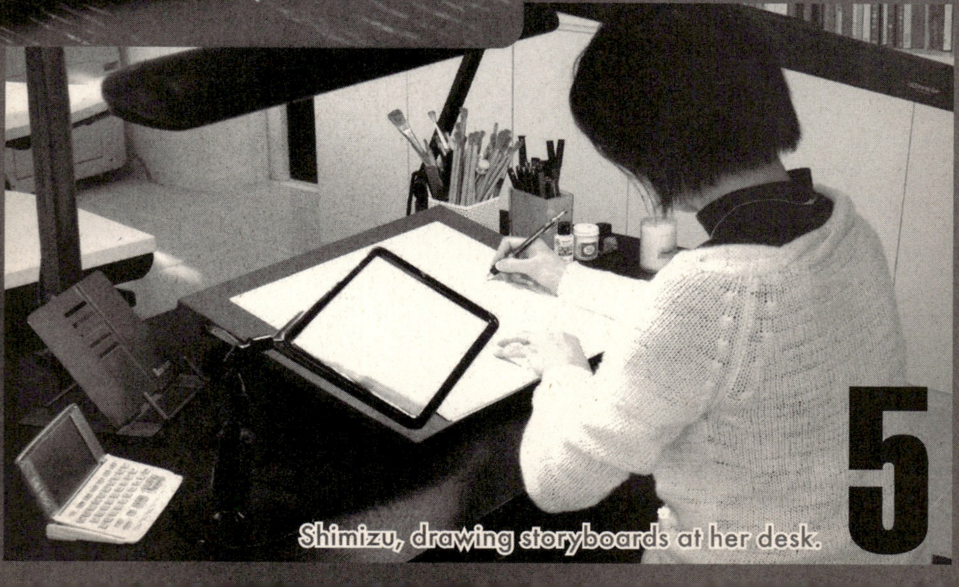

5

Shimizu, drawing storyboards at her desk.

INSIDE THE ARTIST'S STUDIO WITH REIKO SHIMIZU

6 Shelves for storing tones.

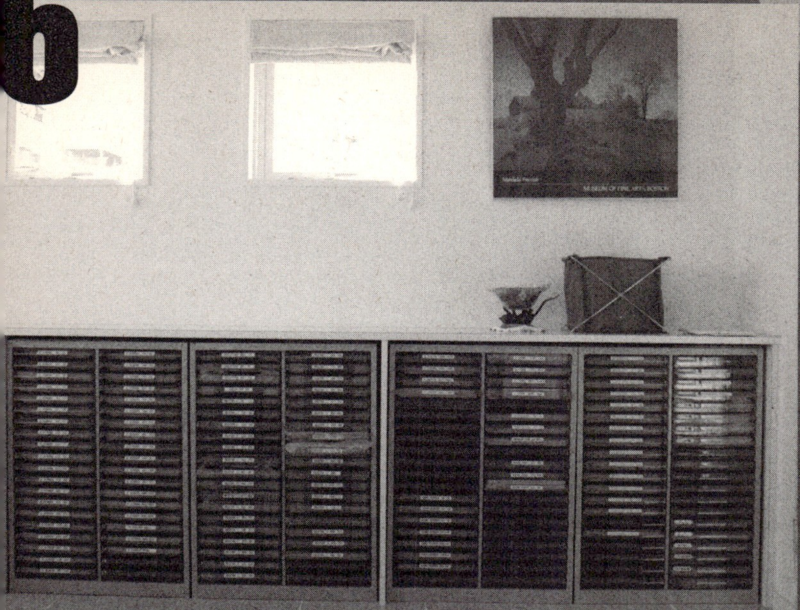

7 The depths of the studio, where more reference materials and sample publications lurk.

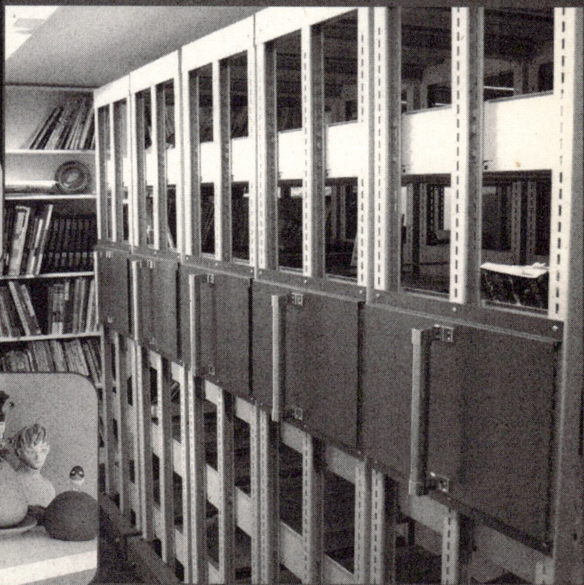

8 he brushes that bring hose beautiful color lustrations to life.

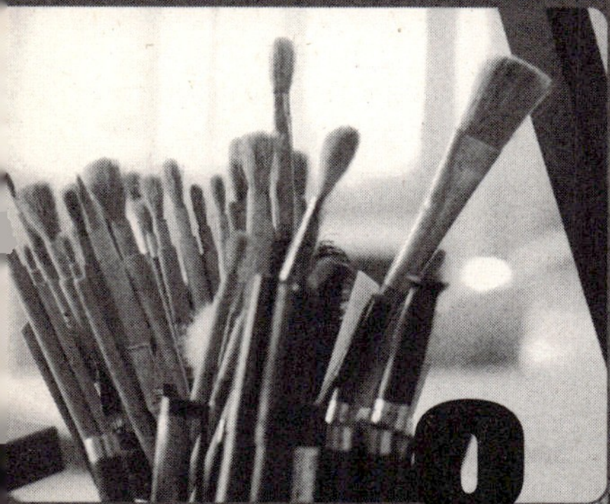

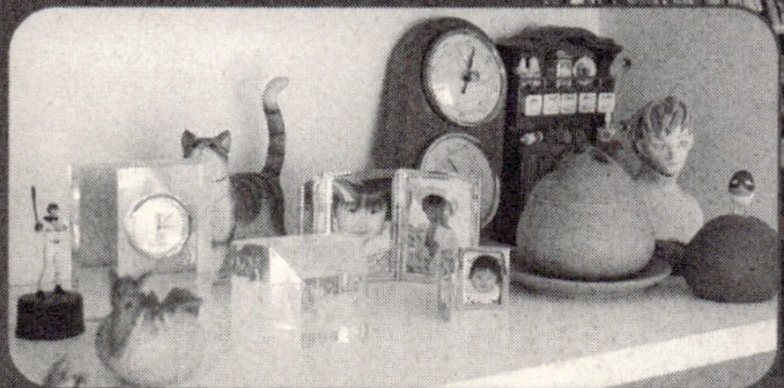

9 We found Shimizu's favorite knick-knacks, too. (Can you spot Ichiro?)

Thanks for the tour, Reiko Shimizu-sensei!

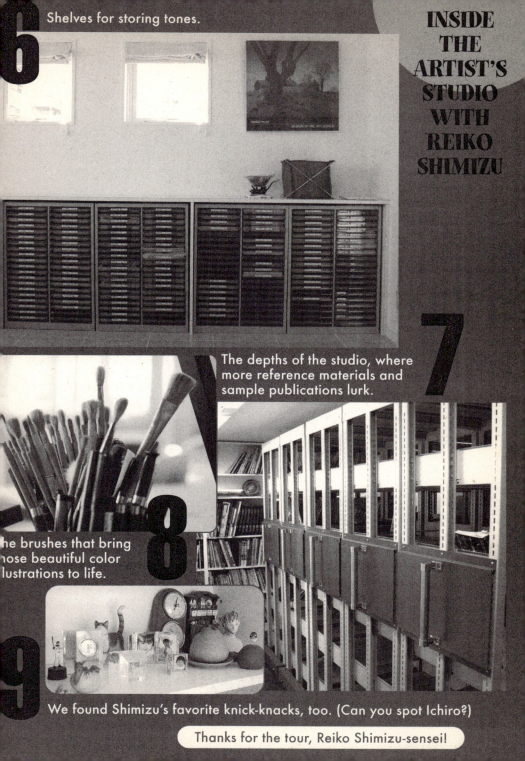

HOW TO DRAW
SHOJO ☆ MANGA

HAMBURG // LONDON // LOS ANGELES // TOKYO

How to Draw Shojo Manga
by Collaborative editing of Hana to Yume,
Bessatsu Hana to Yume, LaLa, and Melody editorials

Translation - Alethea & Athena Nibley
English Adaptation - Hope Donovan
Layout & Lettering - Lucas Rivera
Graphic Designer - Maureen McGovern

Editor - Lillian Diaz-Przybyl
Print Production Manager - Lucas Rivera
Managing Editor - Vy Nguyen
Senior Designer - Louis Csontos
Art Director - Al-Insan Lashley
Director of Sales and Manufacturing - Allyson De Simone
Associate Publisher - Marco F. Pavia
President and C.O.O. - John Parker
C.E.O. and Chief Creative Officer - Stu Levy

A  Manga

TOKYOPOP and 👁 are trademarks or registered trademarks of TOKYOPOP Inc.

TOKYOPOP Inc.
5900 Wilshire Blvd. Suite 2000
Los Angeles, CA 90036

E-mail: info@TOKYOPOP.com
Come visit us online at www.TOKYOPOP.com

SHOJO MANGAKA NI NAROU! by HAKUSENSHA, INC
Collaborative editing of Hana to Yume, Bessatsu Hana to Yume, LaLa, and Melody editorials. © 2006
by HAKUSENSHA, INC. All rights reserved.
First published in Japan in 2006 by HAKUSENSHA, INC., Tokyo English language translation rights in the United States
of America and Canada arranged with HAKUSENSHA, INC., Tokyo through Tuttle-Mori Agency Inc., Tokyo

JOINT COMPILATION : HANATOYUME, BESSATSU HANATOYUME, LALA, MELODY
MANGA, ILLUSTRATION: YUI SHIN
COVERAGE COOPERATION: REIKO SHIMIZU, RIN SAKURAZAWA, CELSYS, INC.
ILLUSTRATION: MIKOTO ASOU, IZUMI KAWAHARA, MIZUHO KUSANAGI, REIKO SHIMIZU, YUI SHIN, SHIGERU TAKAO,
NATSUKI TAKAYA, BISCO HATORI, TACHIBANA HIGUCHI, MATSURI HINO, SAKI HIWATARI, HIRO FUJIWARA,
TOMO MATSUMOTO, NANPEI YAMADA, FUMI YOSHINAGA

ISBN: 978-1-4278-1665-8

First TOKYOPOP printing: November 2010
10 9 8 7 6 5 4 3 2 1
Printed in the USA

HOW TO DRAW SHOJO MANGA™

How To Draw
Japanese MANGA For Girls

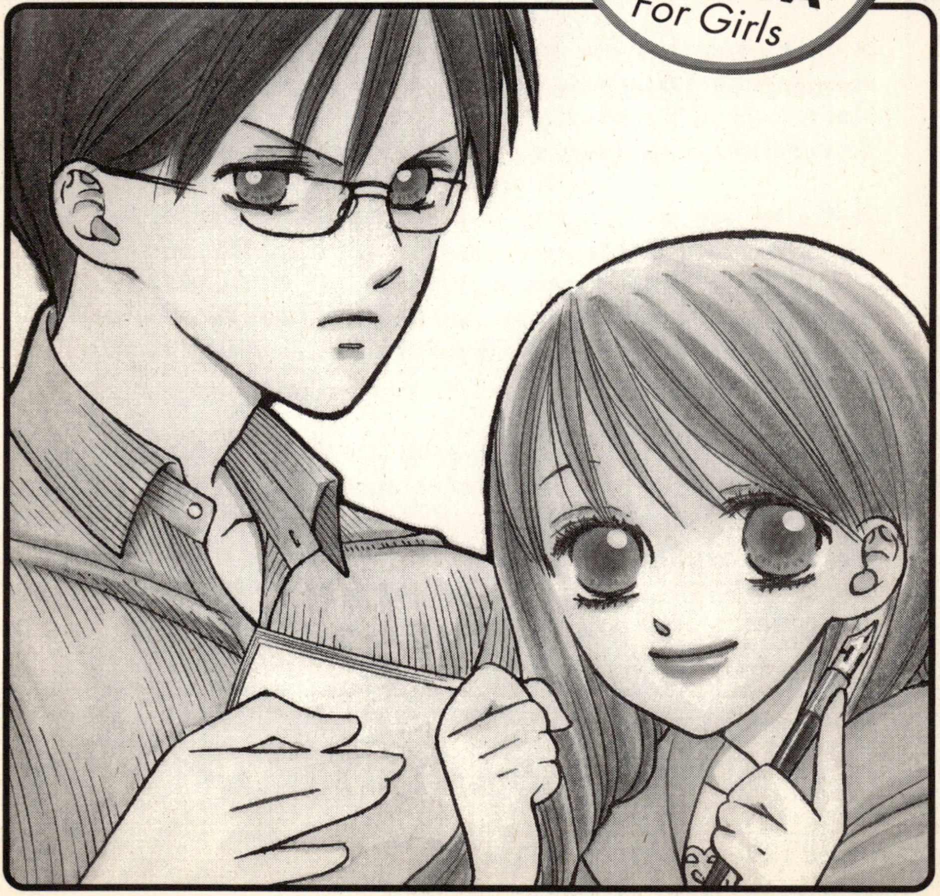

BEFORE YOU BEGIN
The Purpose of This Book

To the person holding this book:

Do you enjoy reading shojo manga? Do you have a passion for drawing characters and making up stories? If you do, then let's draw some shojo manga together! Follow along with us, work hard, and you will find yourself transformed into a professional shojo manga artist!

Creating art and developing stories isn't as scary as you think it is. The important thing is to actually do it. Many people think at some point, "I'd like to be a manga artist," but most give up before they ever draw anything.

If you've flipped through a "How to Draw Manga" book in a bookstore, looked at the pages that explain character designs and perspective and thought, "I have to learn all this hard stuff to be a manga artist?" then you are exactly the person who we want to read this book. Go ahead, take a seat.

First, draw. You can't get good at manga without drawing anything. The more you draw, the more improvement you'll see in your work. If you're already farther along the path to becoming a published manga artist, we welcome you to read this book, too. This book is of particular value to those who have submitted their work to Japanese publishers and are still waiting for their work to be recognized.

Manga artist Yui Shin will be your guide through the process of creating manga. We asked her to take on the role of aspiring artist, creating a manga from scratch. The manga she eventually created was then reviewed by the editors who judge the Hana to Yume and LaLa manga contests. Whether you're a beginner or a pro, this book contains something to help you step up your game.

Ready? Because it's time to throw open the door to your dreams and walk into the future!

Okay, let's become shojo manga artists!

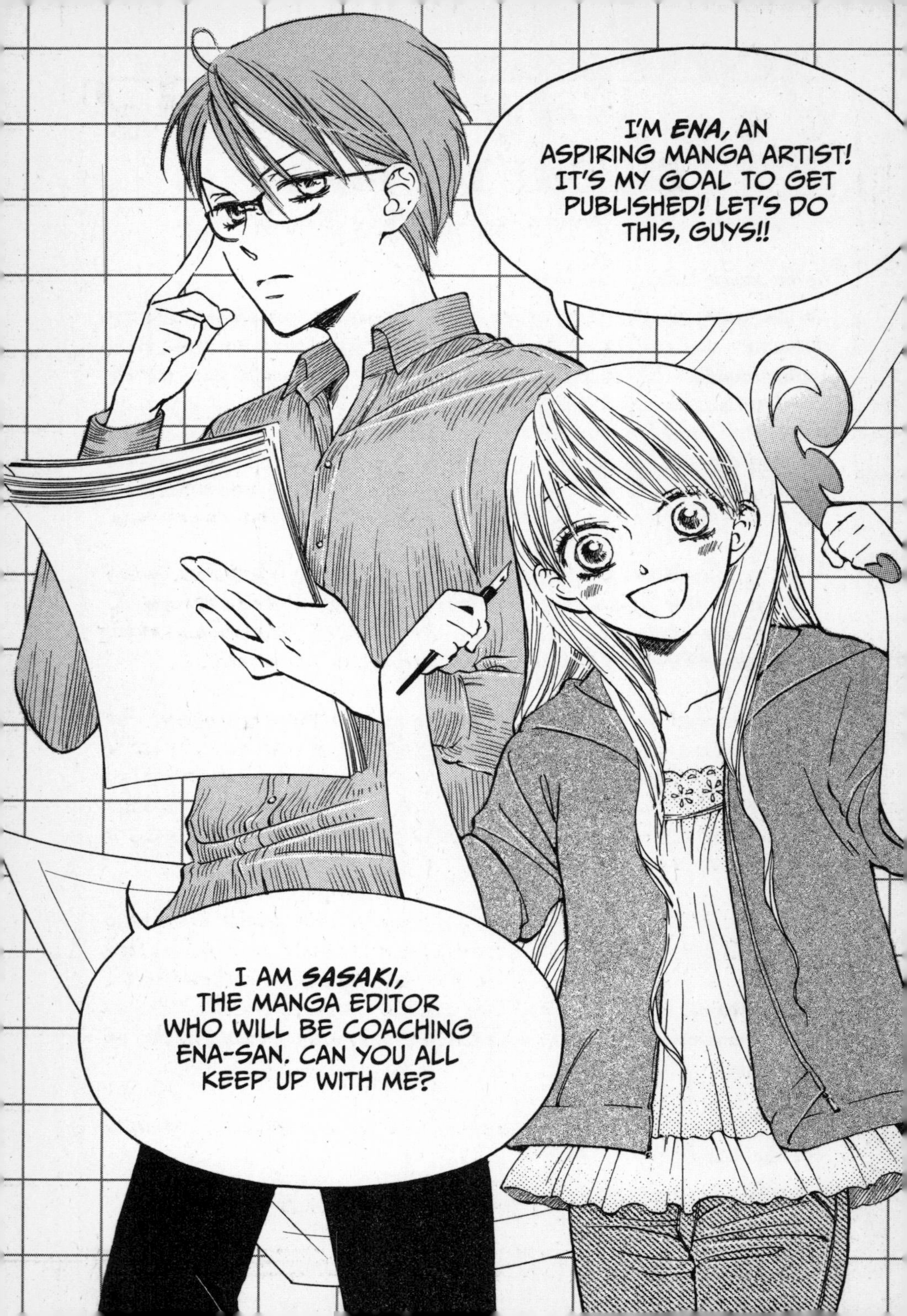
I'M ENA, AN ASPIRING MANGA ARTIST! IT'S MY GOAL TO GET PUBLISHED! LET'S DO THIS, GUYS!!
I AM SASAKI, THE MANGA EDITOR WHO WILL BE COACHING ENA-SAN. CAN YOU ALL KEEP UP WITH ME?

CONTENTS

CONTENTS CONTINUED

BUYING SUPPLIES

First, we better buy all the tools we need. You can purchase almost all of these items at any art supply store, and some at an office supply or stationary store. Here's a list of the bare minimum supplies you'll need:

- Manga Paper (size B4, submission size—that's 270x360mm)
- Pen Nibs (G pen, saji or spoon pen, maru or mapping pen)
- Nib Holders (two normal holders, one maru holder)
- Fine-Tip Brushes (one for black, one for white)
- Ink (pen ink, and sumi or caligraphy ink for filling in blacks)
- White (white poster paint or white-out)
- Fine Felt-tip Pen for Panel Lines (size 0.8-1.2mm)

You will need everything on the above list. Pen nibs wear out quickly, so it will be helpful to have a lot of them. At least a half dozen is good for starters. Your manga paper should be size B4—you can use any high quality paper with a weight of about 110kg-135kg, but beginners will find it helpful to buy manga-specific paper. Paper made for manga artists already has rulers and panel guidelines printed on in! But A4 paper (for doujinshi) also comes with pre-printed lines, so be careful not to get the wrong size.

- Eraser
- Pencil (mechanical)
- Ruler (with a protruding edge)
- Containers for brush-cleaning (one for black, one for white)
- Tissue paper
- Scratch Paper

You might have some of these things around your house or at school already. For pencils, if you're the kind of person who presses hard, you'll want HB-2B grade pencils, which don't leave as much of a mark after they've been erased. It will be helpful to have both a long ruler and a short ruler. The scratch paper is for storyboards and miscellaneous drawings—it doesn't matter what kind of paper you use for your storyboards, even lined notebook paper will do.

If it's in your budget, consider adding these items to be used for finishing touches:

- Tone
- X-acto Knife
- Tone Scrubber
- Tracing Paper
- Scotch Tape

● Pen Nibs, Nib holders

Top to bottom:
G pen, saji pen,
maru pen

*Some nib holders work with all nib types.

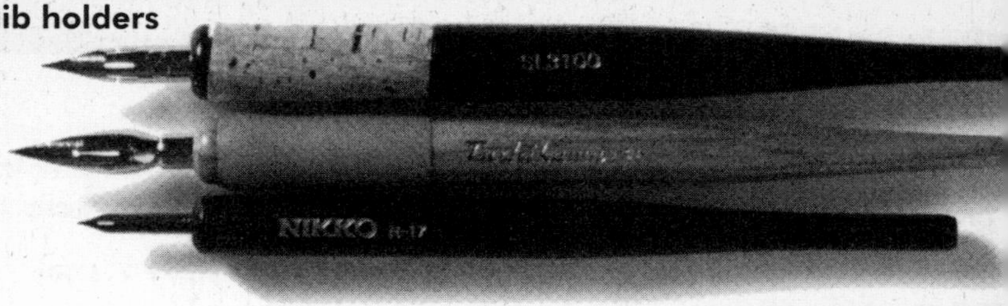
NIKKO

● Fine-Tip Brushes

Superfine tips are the easiest to use. Brush-tip marker pens are also handy.

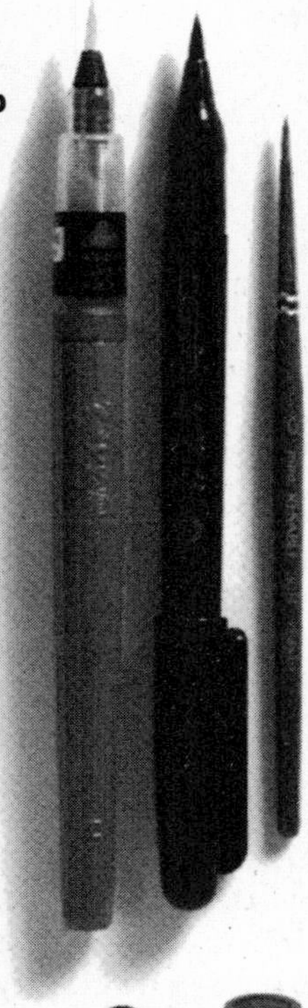

● Manga Paper

135kg, 40-sheet set. Buy a lot of them.

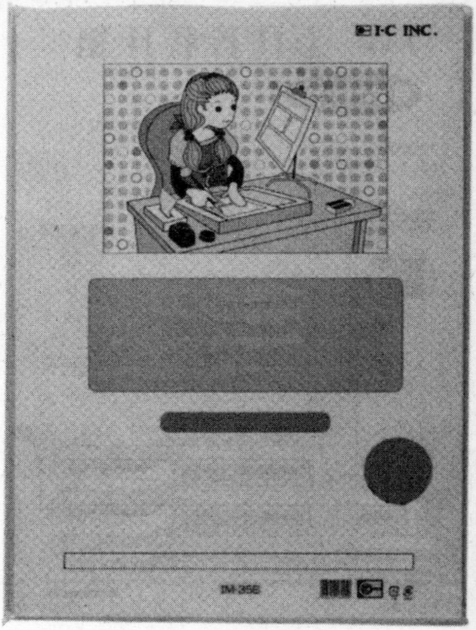
I-C INC.

● Ink, Sumi/ Bokujuu

Many artists use drafting ink for linewor
and sumi ink for filling in large black ar
The two on the right are sumi inks.

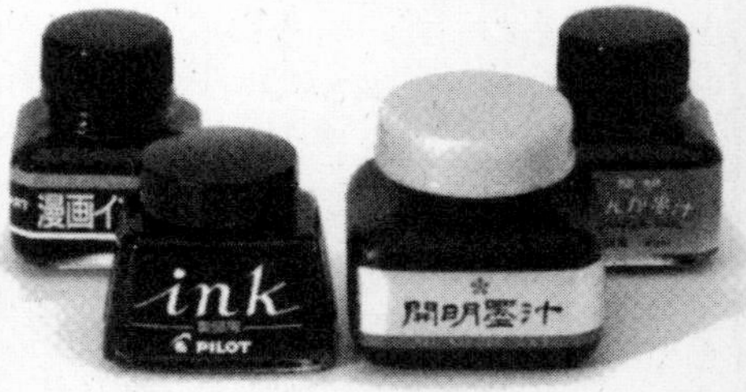
ink
PILOT
開明墨汁

● White

Both poster paint and correction fluid will work.

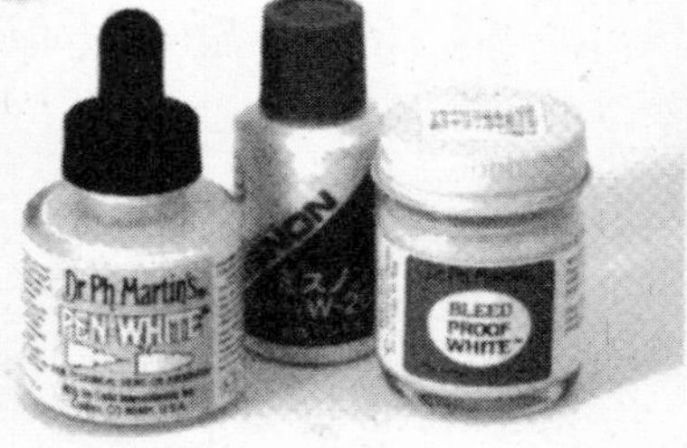
Dr.Ph.Martin's
PEN-WHITE
BLEED PROOF WHITE

● Felt-tip Pen

An inexpensive micron pen will work fine. A lot of manga artists love drafting pens, too.

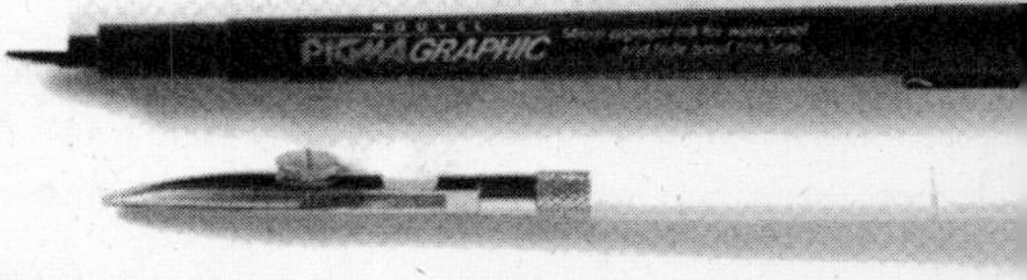
PIGMA GRAPHIC

Gathering all the supplies you see here will cost around $50.
(Includes purchase of three nib holders and six each of the three types of nibs.)

Here's some other tools that can aid you in drawing:

- Template
- French Curve
- Feather Brush

A template is an elaborate stencil for artists. This plastic, ruler-like tool with various shapes carved out of it is useful for drawing precise elliptical shapes. Some even come with word balloon shapes! The French curve is, as the name suggests, a curved ruler that can be used to draw curved lines. The feather brush is for brushing eraser droppings and/or tone shavings off your drawings.

- Tone Knife
- Cutting Mat

Unlike a utility knife with its retractable blade, a tone knife holds interchangeable blades like a nib holder holds pen nibs. The angle of the blade is different from a utility knife's, so you'll notice it feels different. The cutting mat is so you don't slice up your desk with the aforementioned knives.

- Tracing Table (light box)

This illuminates your page from behind, making it a useful tool for tracing or for laying lots of layers of tone. There is no need to buy all of the above items when you're starting out. Just try them out when you feel you're ready.

What brands do the pros use?

Nibs...
Only Nikko maru nibs. (*Bisco Hatori, Matsuri Hino*); Only Zebra maru pens. (*Natsuki Takaya, Hiro Fujiwara*); Zebra G pens, maru pens. Tachikawa or Nikko maru pens. (*Saki Hiwatari*)

Ink, Sumi...
Sumi no Hana for both linework and filling in blacks. (*Reiko Shimizu*); Just Kaimei Bokujuu. (*Tachibana Higuchi*); Kaimei Drawing Sol. (*Mikoto Asou*); Pilot drafting ink. (*Bisco Hatori*)

White...
Dr. Martin's Bleed Proof White. (*Bisco Hatori, Matsuri Hino*); POSCA white. (*Tachibana Higuchi*)

Panel borders...
Rotring Rapidograph. (*Hiro Fujiwara, Mikoto Asou*); Deleter Neopico Line. (*Saki Hiwatari*)

Other recommendations...
Kneaded eraser and drafting brush. (*Matsuri Hino*); Mint-blue vanishing mechanical pencil lead for pencils and for blocking out tone areas. (*Saki Hiwatari, Hiro Fujiwara*)

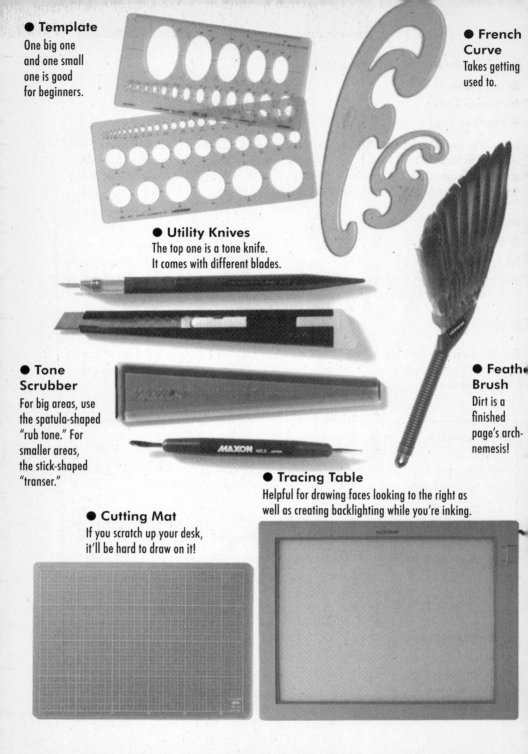

● Template

One big one and one small one is good for beginners.

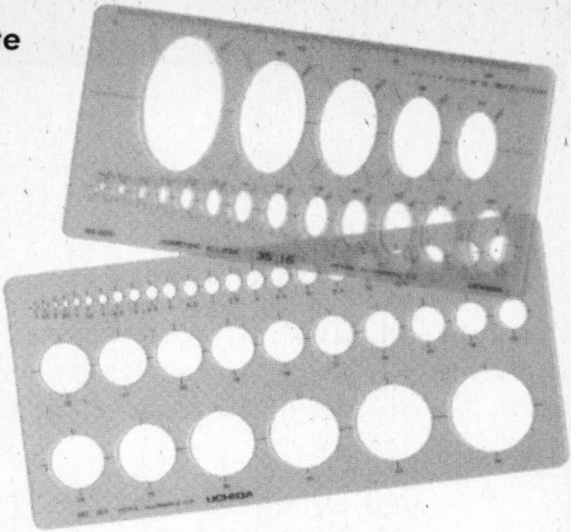

● French Curve

Takes getting used to.

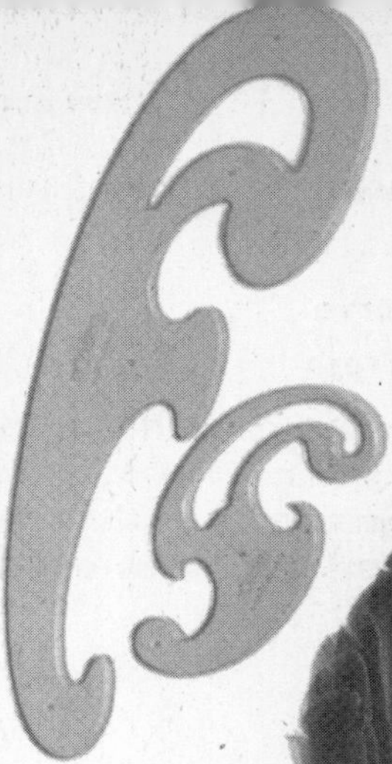

● Utility Knives

The top one is a tone knife. It comes with different blades.

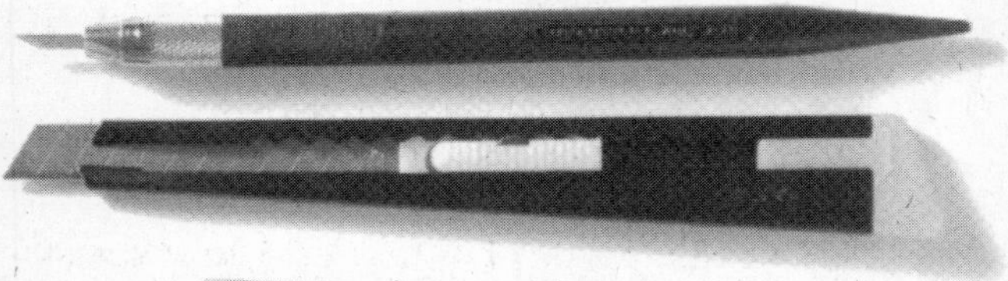

● Tone Scrubber

For big areas, use the spatula-shaped "rub tone." For smaller areas, the stick-shaped "transer."

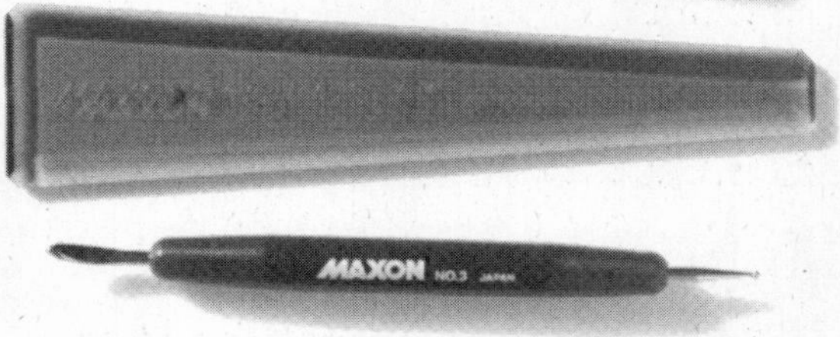
MAXON NO.3 JAPAN

● Feath Brush

Dirt is a finished page's arch-nemesis!

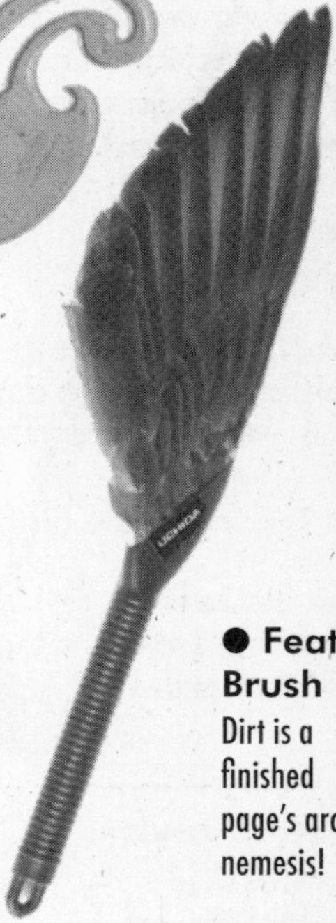

● Tracing Table

Helpful for drawing faces looking to the right as well as creating backlighting while you're inking.

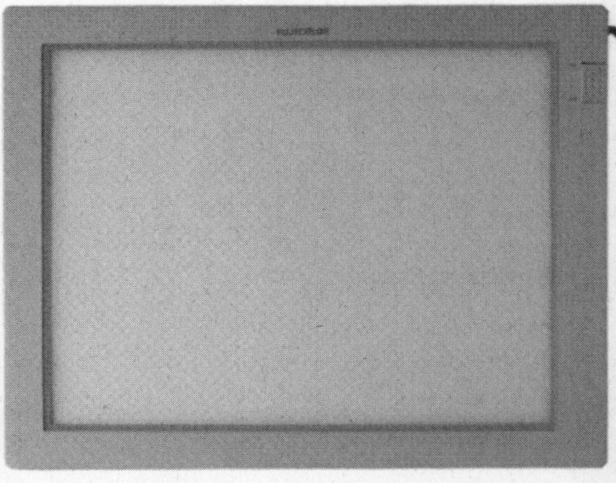

● Cutting Mat

If you scratch up your desk, it'll be hard to draw on it!

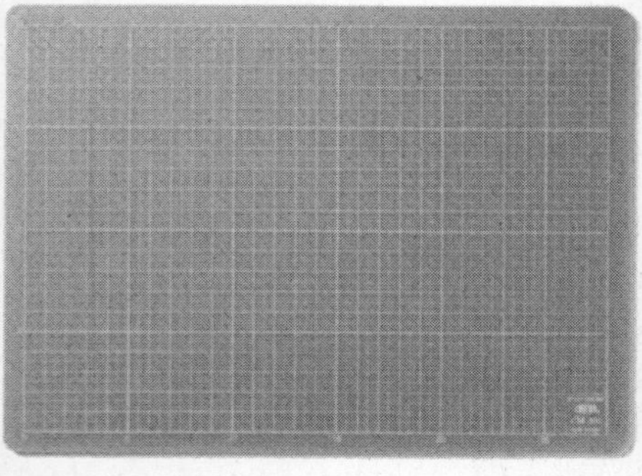

Pens

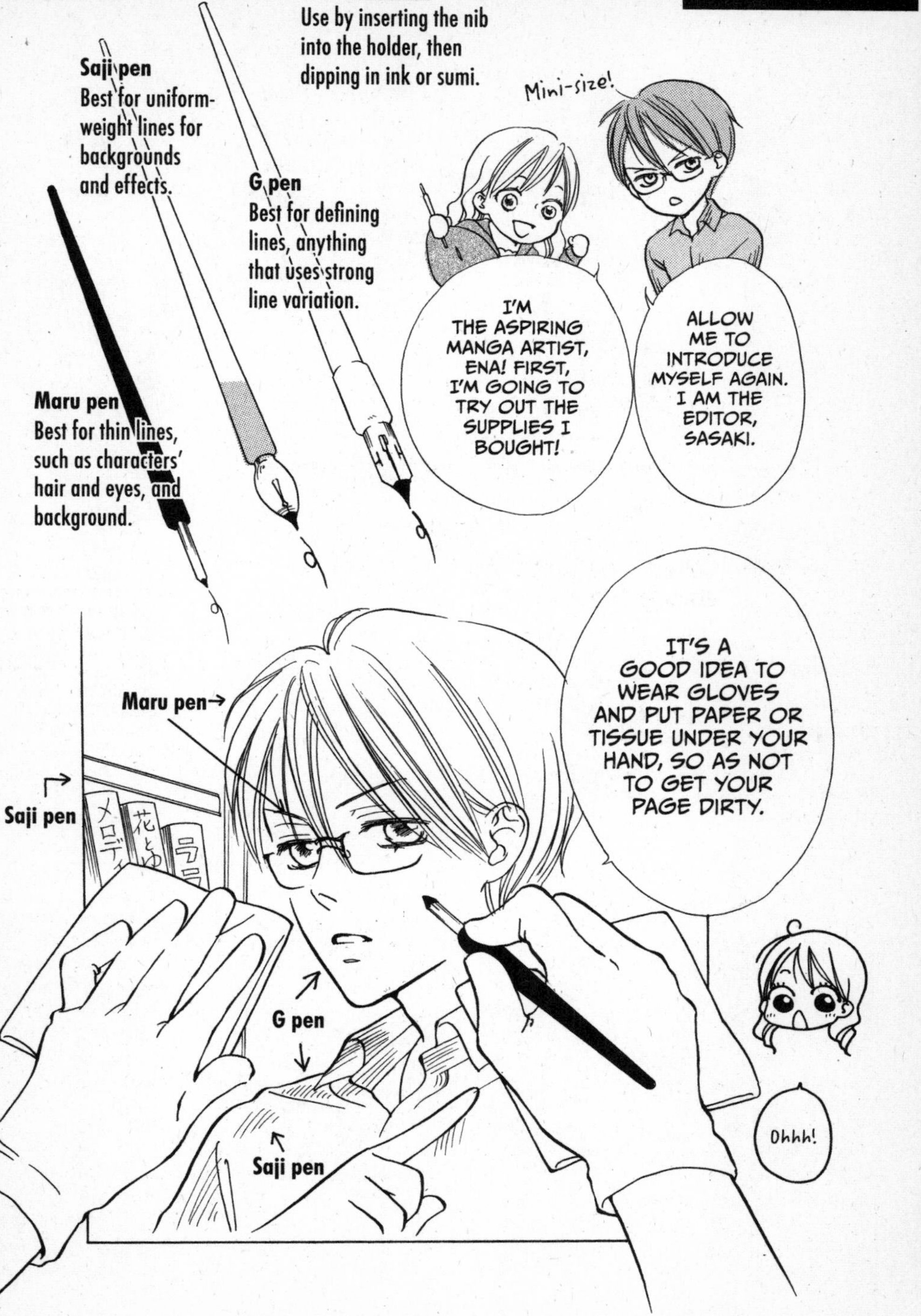
Use by inserting the nib into the holder, then dipping in ink or sumi.
Mini-size!
ALLOW ME TO INTRODUCE MYSELF AGAIN. I AM THE EDITOR, SASAKI.
I'M THE ASPIRING MANGA ARTIST, ENA! FIRST, I'M GOING TO TRY OUT THE SUPPLIES I BOUGHT!
G pen
Best for defining lines, anything that uses strong line variation.
Saji pen
Best for uniform-weight lines for backgrounds and effects.
Maru pen
Best for thin lines, such as characters' hair and eyes, and background.
IT'S A GOOD IDEA TO WEAR GLOVES AND PUT PAPER OR TISSUE UNDER YOUR HAND, SO AS NOT TO GET YOUR PAGE DIRTY.
Ohhh!
Maru pen→
Saji pen
G pen
Saji pen

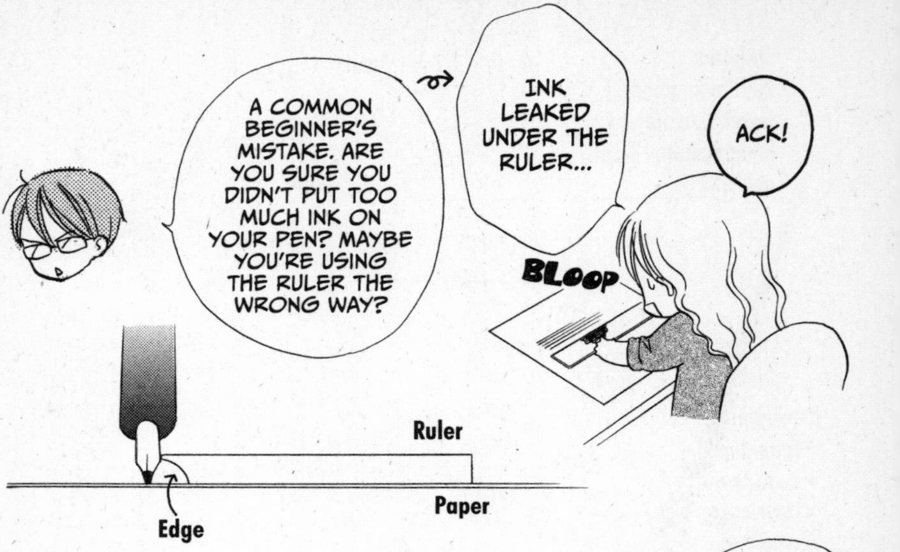
ACK!
BLOOP
INK LEAKED UNDER THE RULER...
A COMMON BEGINNER'S MISTAKE. ARE YOU SURE YOU DIDN'T PUT TOO MUCH INK ON YOUR PEN? MAYBE YOU'RE USING THE RULER THE WRONG WAY?
Ruler
Paper
Edge

MAKE SURE THE PROTRUDING EDGE IS ON TOP.

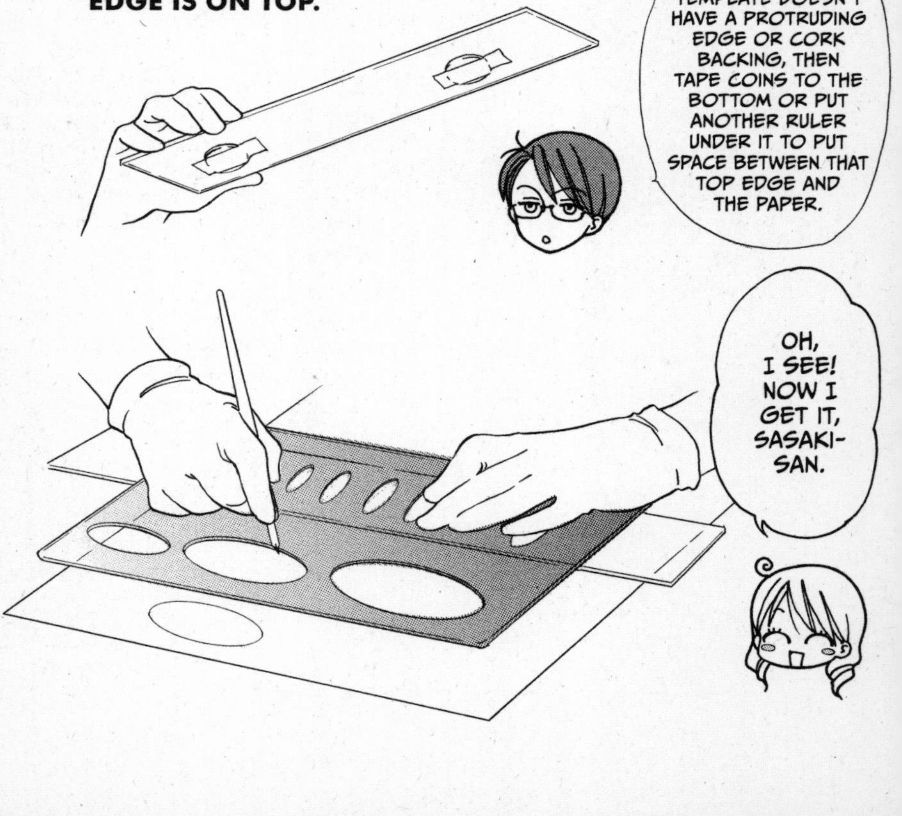
IF YOUR RULER OR TEMPLATE DOESN'T HAVE A PROTRUDING EDGE OR CORK BACKING, THEN TAPE COINS TO THE BOTTOM OR PUT ANOTHER RULER UNDER IT TO PUT SPACE BETWEEN THAT TOP EDGE AND THE PAPER.
OH, I SEE! NOW I GET IT, SASAKI-SAN.

Felt-tip pens

1.2

1.0

0.8

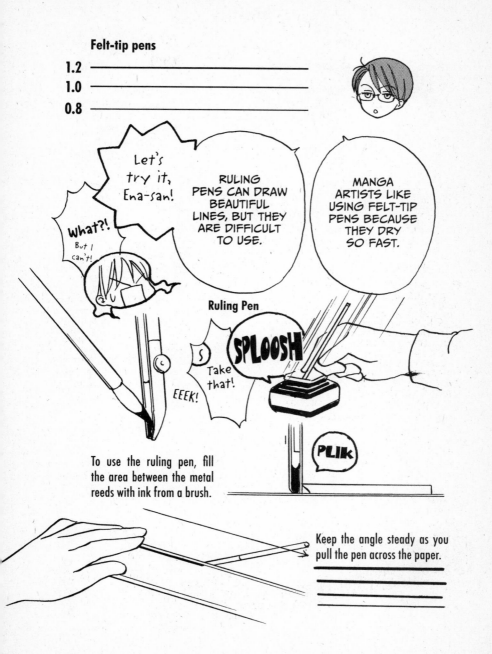

MANGA ARTISTS LIKE USING FELT-TIP PENS BECAUSE THEY DRY SO FAST.
RULING PENS CAN DRAW BEAUTIFUL LINES, BUT THEY ARE DIFFICULT TO USE.
Let's try it, Ena-san!
What?!
But I can't!
Ruling Pen
SPLOOSH
Take that!
EEEK!

PLIK

To use the ruling pen, fill the area between the metal reeds with ink from a brush.

Keep the angle steady as you pull the pen across the paper.

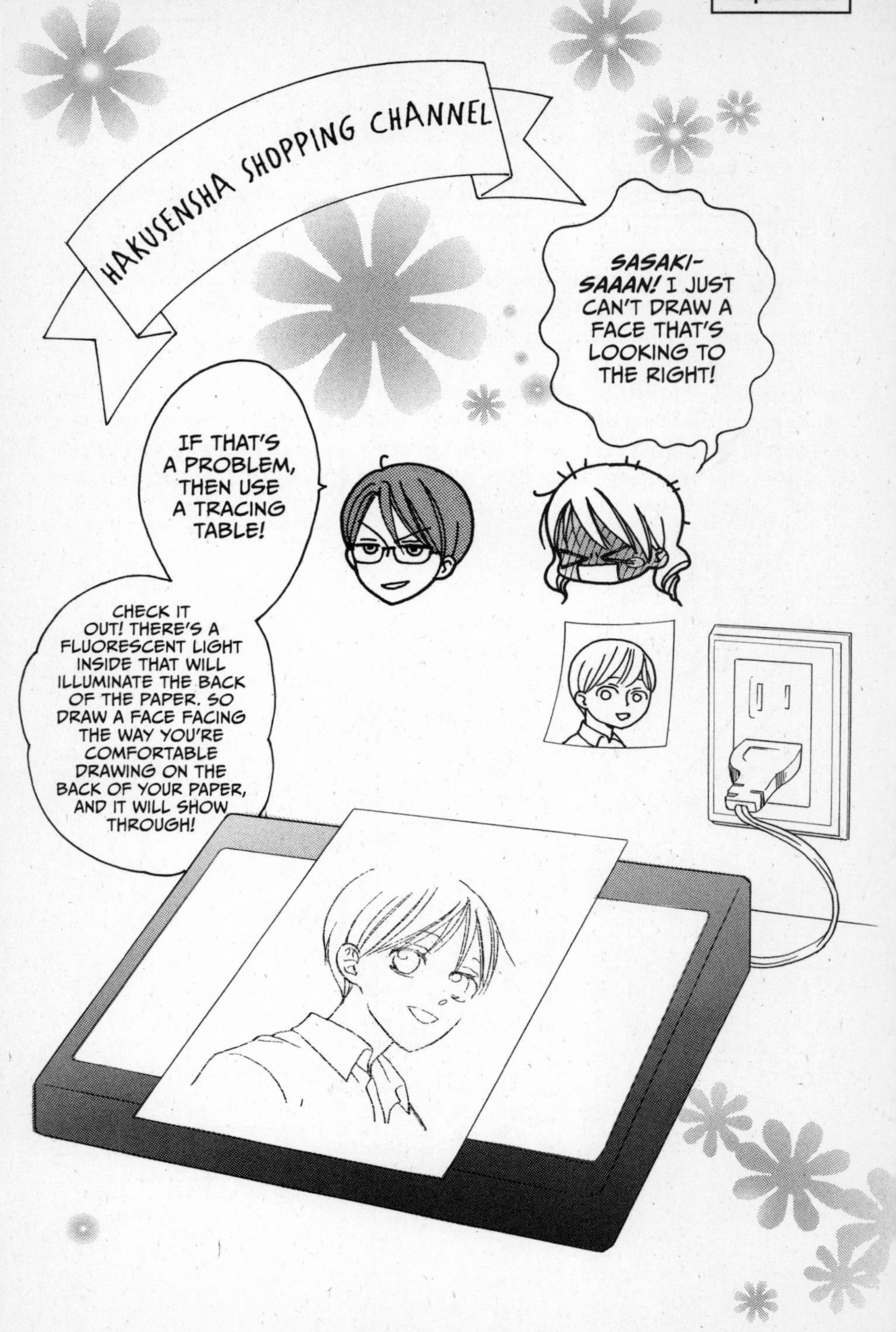
HAKUSENSHA SHOPPING CHANNEL
SASAKI-SAAAN! I JUST CAN'T DRAW A FACE THAT'S LOOKING TO THE RIGHT!
IF THAT'S A PROBLEM, THEN USE A TRACING TABLE!
CHECK IT OUT! THERE'S A FLUORESCENT LIGHT INSIDE THAT WILL ILLUMINATE THE BACK OF THE PAPER. SO DRAW A FACE FACING THE WAY YOU'RE COMFORTABLE DRAWING ON THE BACK OF YOUR PAPER, AND IT WILL SHOW THROUGH!

Drawing People

Let's explore how to draw a shojo manga character. There are plenty of books out there that go into pretty heavy detail about manga character design. Some of them even explain how to create a character with 3D modeling. Reading these books will help you build a knowledge base, but they are not necessary.

Faces and bodies in manga obey a visual shorthand--some parts are left out, other parts are exaggerated. You deliberately deform your characters, so to speak. Once you've got a sense of how real people look and move, you can exaggerate that to create your own shojo manga style.

Now, if you don't exaggerate enough, then your people will look too realistic—too harsh, too life-like and absent of the beauty of shojo. On the other hand, it looks strange if characters don't adhere to realism at all. A character's dimensions should be consistent every time they show up, and they can't be posed in unbelievable ways. And if they're rendered too flat, then you'll have difficulty showing movement or depth in your manga.

Basic Design: Body

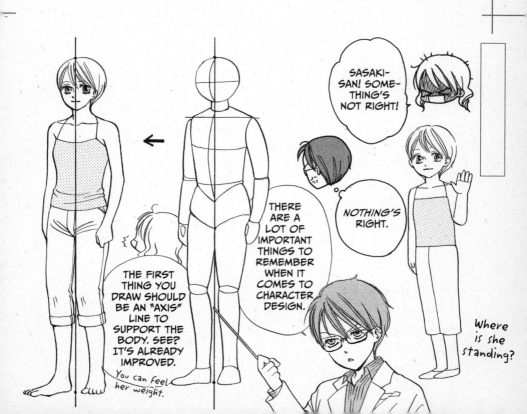

SASAKI-SAN! SOME-THING'S NOT RIGHT!
NOTHING'S RIGHT.
Where is she standing?
THERE ARE A LOT OF IMPORTANT THINGS TO REMEMBER WHEN IT COMES TO CHARACTER DESIGN.
THE FIRST THING YOU DRAW SHOULD BE AN "AXIS" LINE TO SUPPORT THE BODY. SEE? IT'S ALREADY IMPROVED.
You can feel her weight.

Drawing People cont'd.

First, sketch a skeletal frame that represents your character. After you've posed the frame, add flesh and clothing. If you normally only draw easy-to-draw poses and close-ups, draw the face first, or only draw clothes that fit your character's pose, then you need to practice more.

Challenge yourself to draw your characters in poses from photographs. It will be pretty hard at first. You'll have to work at mastering it so that you can successfully draw any pose in a shojo manga style. It's important to remember that if you draw your character having the same proportions as the person in the photograph, unless you have a very skinny model, your character may look too stout. There are exceptions, but shojo manga characters are generally far more slender than real people.

When you draw your manga, your character will need a dynamic pose in every panel. Start getting flexible with your poses now!

Basic Design: Poses

YOU'LL BE ABLE TO DRAW FASTER WITH PRACTICE.

Eeep!

EVENTUALLY, YOU CAN FORGO THE SKELETAL FRAME STEP.

People can stand on one leg, too.

Wide stanc

Drawing People cont'd.

Next is the face. As you might expect, readers focus on faces. If the facial design is wacky or unappealing, then readers won't enjoy your manga. Also, to get your characters to act how you want them to, you'll need a lot of practice drawing basic expressions.

The first thing people often try when they want to draw manga is drawing faces. But do you find yourself always drawing faces from the same angle—the one that's easiest for you to draw? "I'm good at drawing three-quarters left-facing faces, but any other angle I draw turns out bad. It doesn't even look like the same person." This is a weakness we see in an awful lot in manga contest submissions from beginners. It's important to practice drawing a variety of angles.

In shojo manga, the face is the most highly stylized part of the person's anatomy. Because of that stylization, it's impossible to make the face beautiful and shojo-like at every camera angle. On the other hand, if the range of expressions and angles you can draw is limited, your manga will seem flat. Think of the design process this way: instead of a single design, you're actually making multiple designs that differ depending on where the character is looking.

Basic Design: Faces

Left

Up

Right

Down

More

I hope I never need to draw anything that smiles like that!

Tee hee! Look, look! Here's your reference material!

Drawing People cont'd.

To draw a face, first sketch out a general oval-shaped sphere. Next, sketch a horizontal line to mark the position of the eyes, and a vertical line to indicate the center of the face. You'll be using these axes to move your character.

Move that sphere up, down, and side-to-side. Then draw in the details (eyes, nose, mouth), using the horizontal and vertical guidelines. Were you able to draw a face without anything feeling off about the horizontal or vertical placement of features?

Since the shapes of manga facial features are not very realistic, you won't get to a point where you can draw all of them from any angle. Instead, you will need to decide what you're going to draw, to deform, or to omit at each new challenging angle. As long as the reader can still tell it's the same character, it doesn't matter if the nose or mouth is even there. This is where shojo manga differs greatly from photos or computer generated images.

Remember, stylization is key!

Basic Design: Expressions

Happiness

Anger

Sadness

Joy

You're always crying, Ena-san.

Sasaki-san's only expression is anger.

Drawing People cont'd.

A whole host of characters may show up in your manga. Practice drawing all kinds of people—old and young, male and female, main characters and supporting characters. Often, beginners submit manga in which the characters all look the same: their physical builds and faces are so similar, the only way to tell them apart is by hairstyle or by if they wear glasses. In a school setting, where everyone is in uniform, it's impossible to tell who's who...

When designing your characters, use gender, age, build, face shape, hairstyle, clothing, glasses, props, and more to make each one distinct. A reader should be able to tell who the character is at a glance. Also, you can even use different line weights and stylizations to set characters apart.

Gender is one tool at your disposal while designing characters. Generally, women are made up of curvy lines and men are made up of straight lines. Using that basic form, adjust your character by modifying their proportions, such as shoulder width, bust size, waist size, and whether their figure nips in at the waist. It's worth noting that in shojo manga hyper-masculine characters don't tend to be very well-liked, so use moderation.

Age can be expressed through face, build, and posture. Basic eye placement is the center of the head; if the top half of the head is big, the character looks younger, and if the top half is smaller, the character looks more mature. Most people think to add wrinkles to the sides of the mouths of middle-aged and elderly characters, but if you go farther and add hollow cheeks, sagging skin (to give the impression that the skin is giving in to gravity) and thinning or receding hair, the drawing will become more convincing.

You can age a character by making them taller as they grow. Conversely, you can represent old age by dragging the character's posture and center of gravity downward.

If you're drawing something where almost all the characters are the same age (like at a school), differences in physique, hairstyle, and glasses are important, but also use tricks like slight differences in posture (such as square shoulders, sloping shoulders, etc). Also, it would be a good idea to make a habit of always differentiating similar things—for example, if everyone is wearing the same uniform, there can be differences in the way each character wears it, and how loosely or tightly it fits. *& Tucked in shirts / accessories*

Be a good observer—watch people on TV and around you. Hopefully no one will think you're a creep! *& Too late xD*

(from
Ghost C
Restau
for Gho

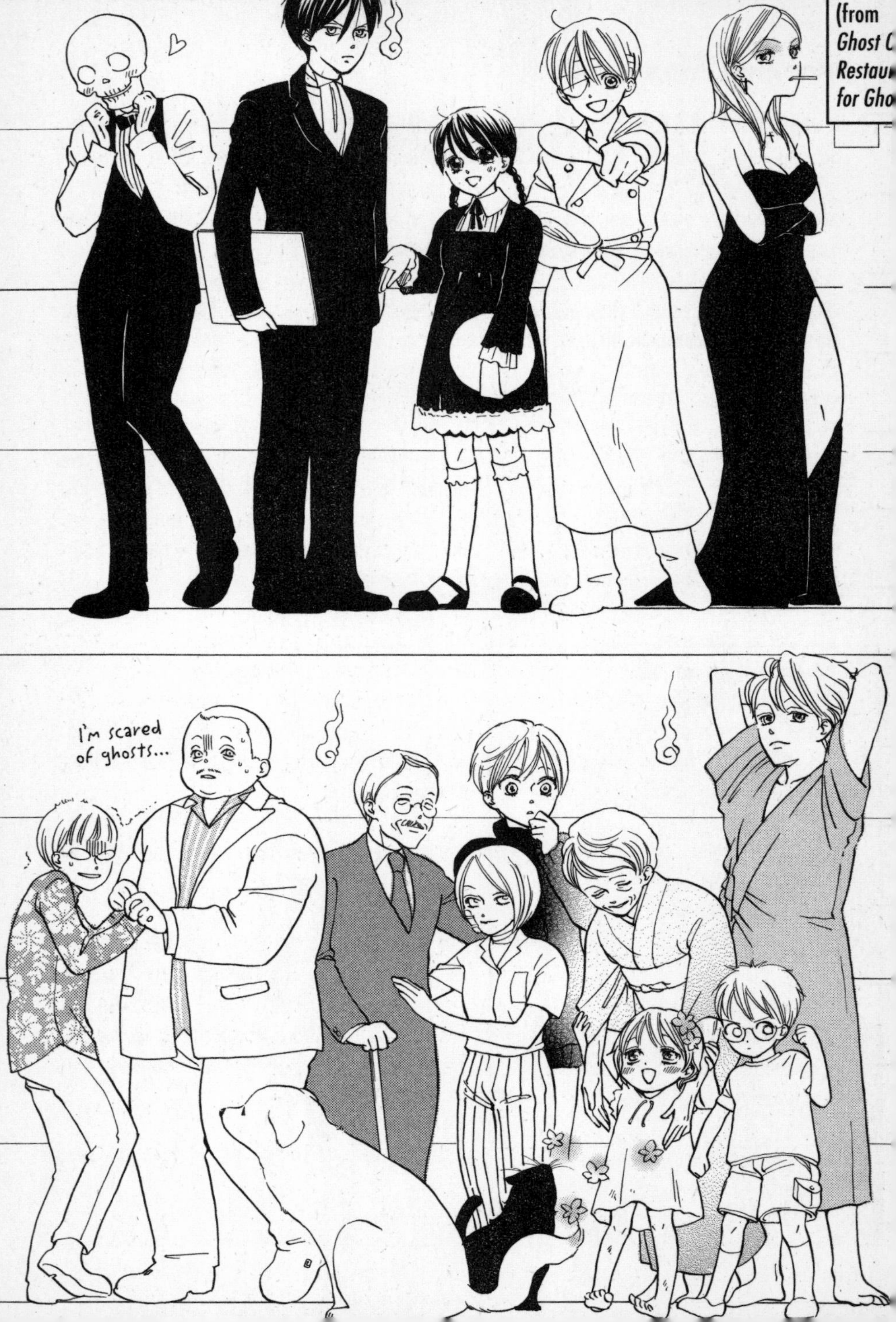
I'm scared of ghosts...

Drawing People cont'd.

Clothing and hairstyles are crucial in telling characters apart. Additionally, a character's clothing and hairstyle tells a story about who they are and where they're from. However, there are things that are difficult to draw without a certain level of knowledge and reference material at your disposal. Constant people-watching and research helps immensely.

For example, if you don't see them in your everyday life, drawing traditional Japanese outfits would be pretty impossible. How is an outfit made? What is it made of? How does someone put it on? How do people normally wear them? What makes them look bad...? Drawings based on your imagination or memories alone don't usually cut it.

This is doubly so for manga set in historical times or overseas—drawing from your memory or imagination would be unthinkable. Do at least some general research on the clothing and hairstyles of the era or world that your story will be set in. Giving your characters Edo-era clothes and hair when the story takes place in the Heian era is just plain wrong. The way the people of that era did their hair, the way they held their swords—every detail is subtly different.

Ouran High School Host Club
(by Bisco Hatori, from *LaLa*)

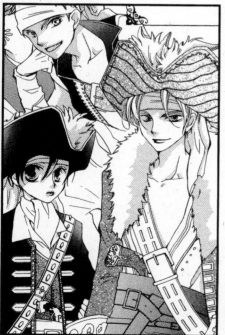

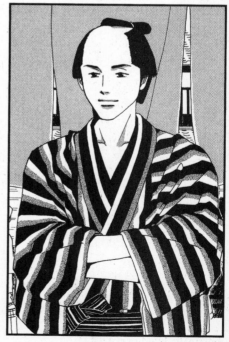

↑ Pirate cosplay. Look at all that detail!

Ooku: The Inner Chamber
(by Fumi Yoshinaga, from *Melody*)

↑ An Edo-era merchant's top-knot and kimono.

Drawing People cont'd.

Maybe this goes without saying, but you'll have to become a fashionista! If a character who is supposed to be "stylish and attractive" doesn't look stylish and attractive to your readers, that will affect their opinion of the whole manga.

Even a simple pair of jeans can express a lot about a character—in how they wear them, and what style they wear. For an extreme example, let's say a character is supposed to be a stylish, cosmopolitan young man, and yet he's walking around with jeans hanging down below his boxers. That'll get your readers thinking he's a slob or a thug! Always enrich your design sensibilities by looking through fashion magazines. A manga artist coordinates her characters' clothes to match parts of their personalities.

This also should be pretty obvious, but manga is almost always printed in black and white. It's not easy to express the colors and textures of clothes with tone and ink. Take a really close look at professional manga artists' work and use trial and error to find ways to dress your characters up!

English Tutoring School Wars
(by Tomo Matsumoto, from *LaLa*)

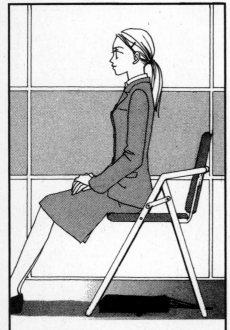

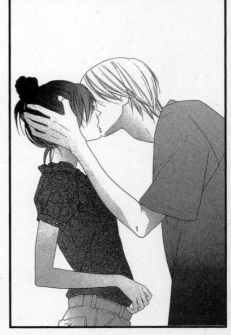

↑ What a cute shirt! Fitted, but with puffed sleeves!

Go! Hiromi, Go!
(by Mikoto Asou, from *Melody*)

↑ Very realistic depiction of a suit you'd wear to a job interview.

Creating Your Own Style

Have you ever been told that your art style looks like someone else's? Most likely, many of you who have submitted work to a manga contest have been told by the judges, "Your work looks a lot like XX artist's work."

It's only natural for artists to start out imitating the works that inspired them in the first place. But in order to stop drawing fan art and someday present your own original work to readers, you'll have to tap into your own individual style.

Beginners often tend to be inconsistent with the application of their style and it shows: the panels that resemble a particular established professional's work are well-done, but the other panels still show a lot of room for improvement.

Shojo manga lives and dies by the face. So, your first priority is practicing drawing your characters' faces. Each time, try to fractionally change their facial features. How can you tweak the eyes to make them more your own? What about the nose? The mouth? The eyebrows? Try all kinds of things. The way you draw eyes plays a big role in what people think about your art.

Once you've nailed the face, try drawing it turned up, down, and side-to-side. Were you able to move it without too many problems? If you had a hard time, then try altering the features again to make it easier.

Rather than mimicking professional manga artists' works, keep playing with your own designs until you've reached an attractive, natural style that's all your own.

Maid-sama!
(by Hiro Fujiwara, from *LaLa*)

Her sharp expression is very attractive.

Four Variations on Ena

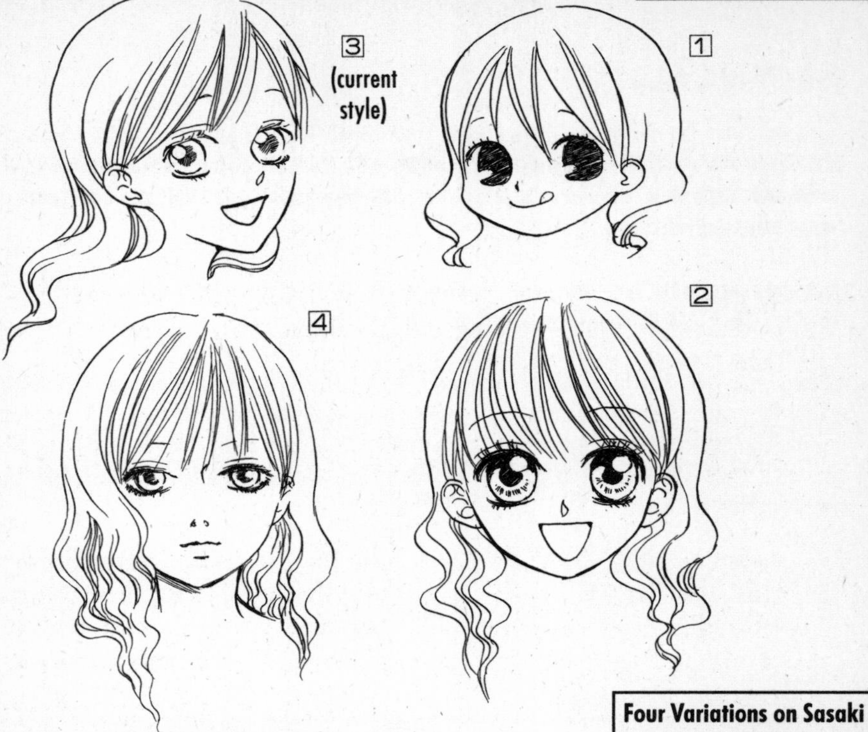
1
3
(current style)
2
4

Four Variations on Sasaki

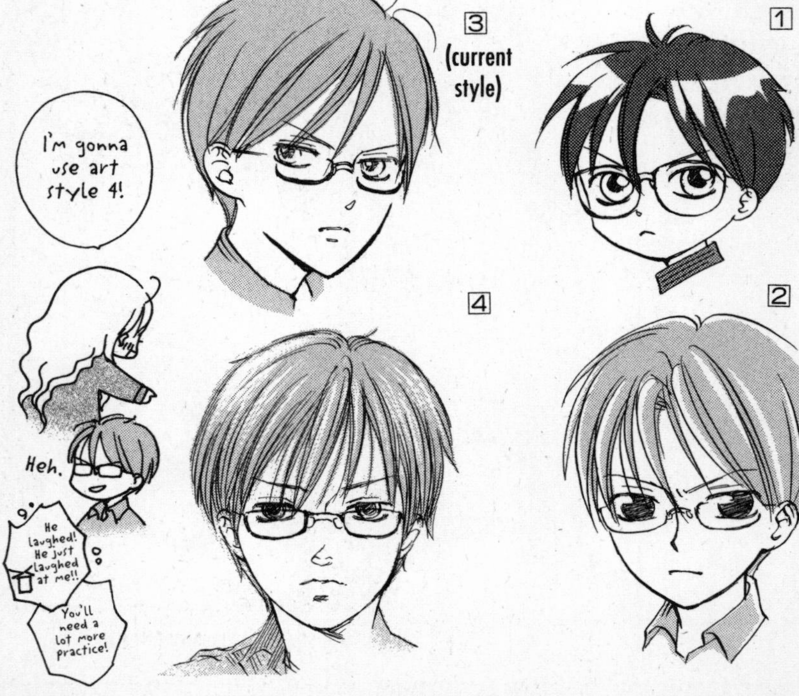
1
3
(current style)
I'm gonna use art style 4!
2
4
Heh.
He laughed! He just laughed at me!!
You'll need a lot more practice!

Drawing Objects

Explore drawing the objects you'll see a lot in your manga. It's very important to draw them from observation. Too often, aspiring manga artists will try to draw something from memory, when drawing from observation would have been a piece of cake. Unfortunately, a little bit of laziness makes a manga look totally cheap.

Here's an experiment: Try drawing your phone at home, just from memory. Then compare it with the real thing. See? Your memories aren't really all that reliable, are they?

Although, you can't look at a real version of *everything* that shows up in your manga. It's important to exercise your imagination and memory, too. But thanks to the internet and catalogs, it has become remarkably easy to obtain reference material these days. Draw from observation as much as possible, and you'll double the accuracy of your manga. Even if you're designing original objects, real things can still provide the base.

Koucha Ouji no Himegimi ("The Tea Prince's Princess")
(by Nanpei Yamada, from *Bessatsu Hana to Yume*)

Musical instruments are among the more difficult objects to draw.

World of Texture

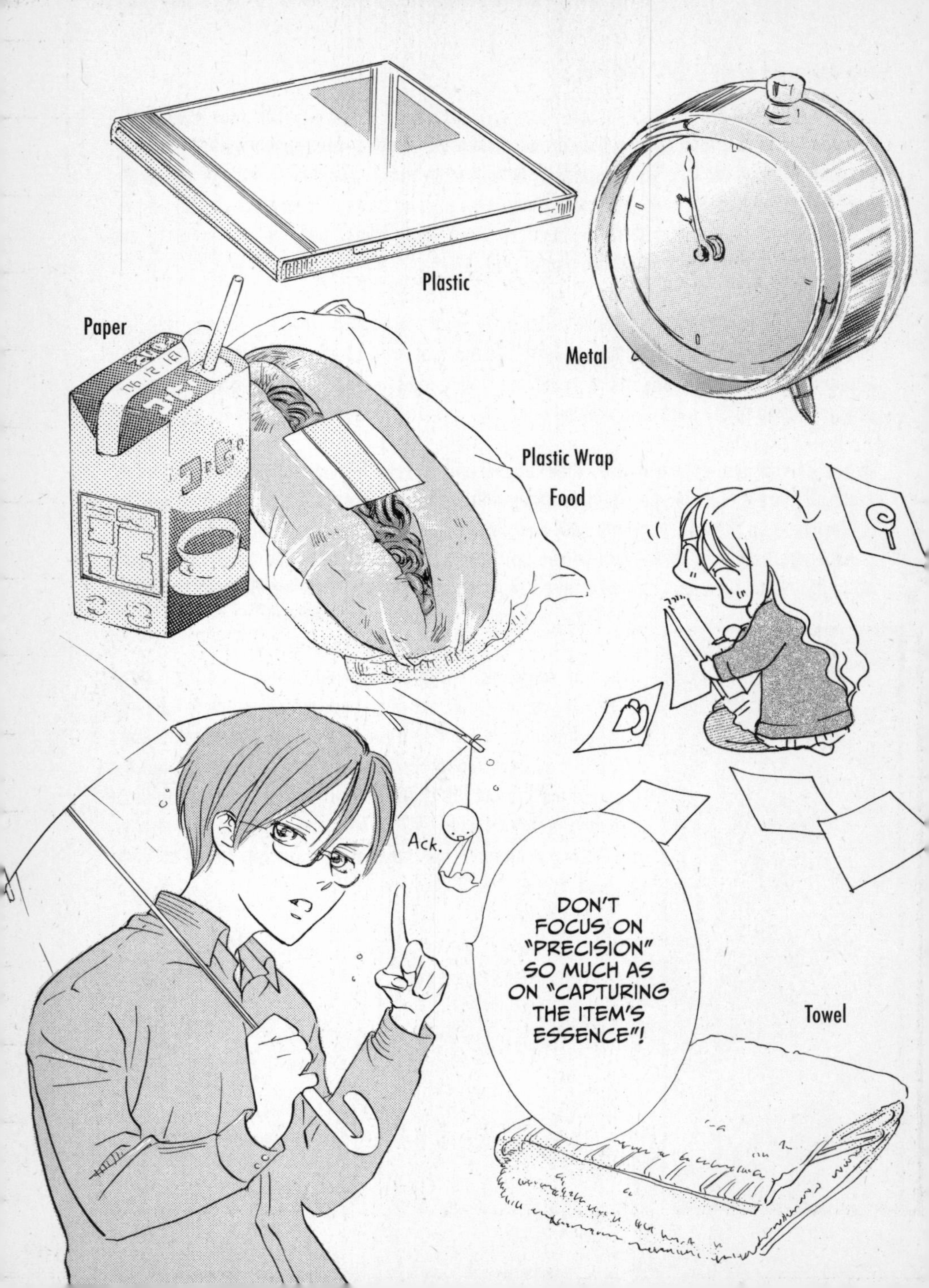

Plastic
Metal
Paper
Plastic Wrap
Food
Ack.
DON'T FOCUS ON "PRECISION" SO MUCH AS ON "CAPTURING THE ITEM'S ESSENCE"!
Towel

Drawing Backgrounds

Are you the kind of person who only draws characters, or fills every panel's background with effects? Without realistic backgrounds, how will your readers know where your characters are? Effective backgrounds not only show where your characters are, they also impart your character's mental state to the readers. Once again, reach beyond your memory and imagination to draw from reference photos and sketches.

If you can't find convenient reference material for what you want to draw, try using perspective to create your own backgrounds (see left). It's not that hard at all! There are manuals that explain perspective in depth, and it would help you to read them, but there's no need to go out of your way to spend a lot of money on one.

To the human eye, objects nearby look bigger, and objects that are far away look smaller; that's all there is to it. Perspective drawings put that principle to work. Single-point perspective is illustrated on the left. To create two- and three-point perspectives accurately, you'd need a much longer ruler and desk. Once you've practiced a few times and gotten a feel for it, you'll be able to draw perspective well enough that you won't need to define an exact vanishing point. You'll find it's not really that daunting!

When it comes to backgrounds, you should prioritize stage direction over precision. Never let your main characters fade into the background. It's standard practice to make background lines thinner than foreground lines, but use tricks like fading out the background around the characters, or putting a white highlight around the characters to make them stand out. Instead of striving for perfect draftsmanship, make it your goal to create an easy-to-read image.

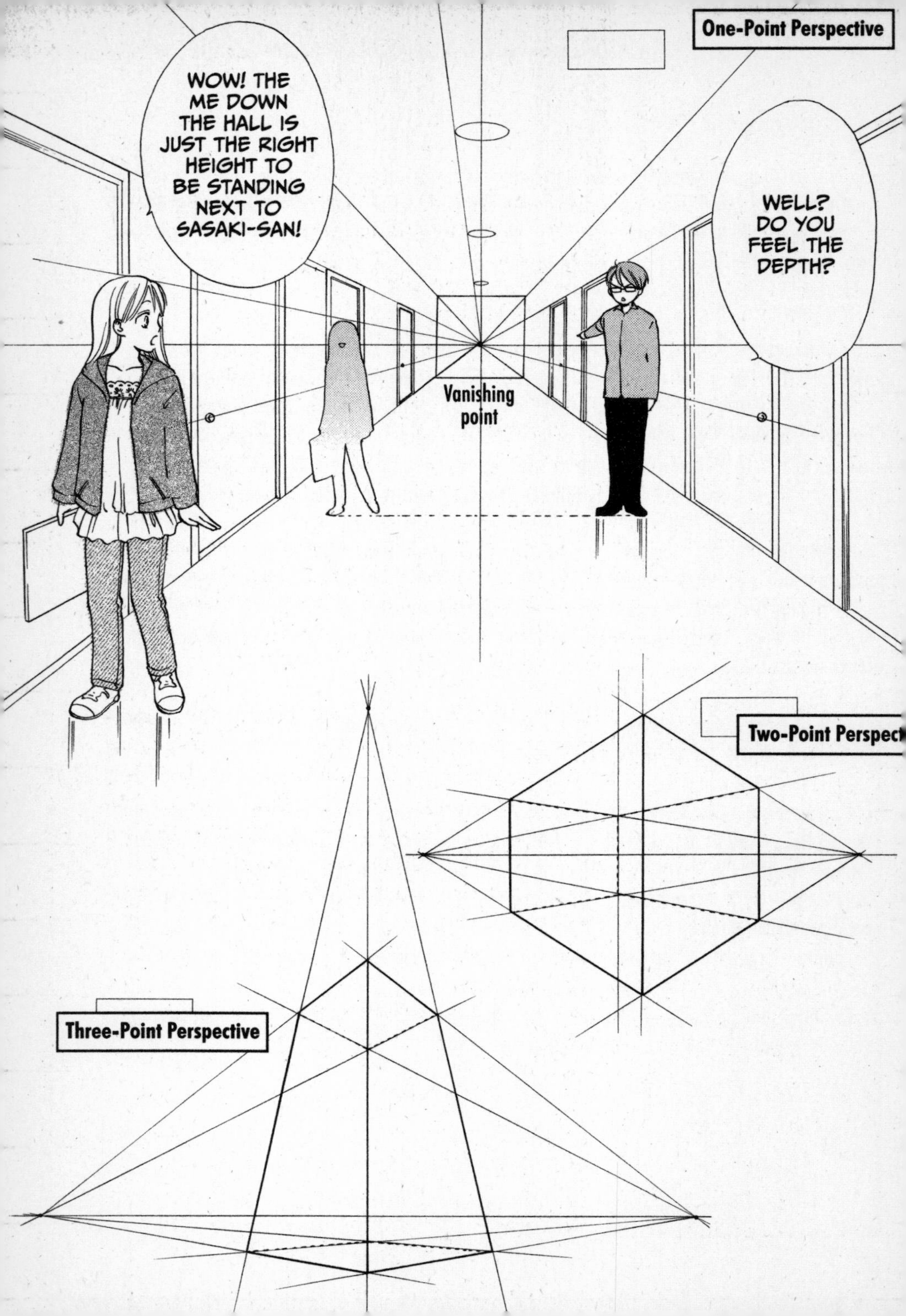
One-Point Perspective
WELL? DO YOU FEEL THE DEPTH?
WOW! THE ME DOWN THE HALL IS JUST THE RIGHT HEIGHT TO BE STANDING NEXT TO SASAKI-SAN!
Vanishing point
Two-Point Perspect
Three-Point Perspective

Finding existing photographs of backgrounds that work perfectly for your story is usually challenging. Also, don't forget that photographs in magazines or photo collections are protected by copyright laws, so it's illegal to trace or copy them without permission. In particular, copying rare photos or copying diagrams painstakingly reconstructed by historians is frowned on as the worst kind of plagiarism.

Due to the above reasons, we recommend that you hunt down your own locations, take your own pictures, and make your own sketches as often as possible. However, there are some places where you won't be allowed to take photos, or you'll need permission to do so, so it's important to check the rules before you go. It's becoming more and more common to have to get permission to photograph schools or school events. Even if you're only taking pictures for backgrounds, you could get sued by someone who happens to be in the picture, so be careful.

Nevertheless, the best reference materials are photographs you've taken yourself. Plenty of manga artists carry their camera at their hip, so that they'll never miss a chance. Apparently, when manga artist Mikoto Asou was sick in the hospital, she thought, "Maybe I'll need pictures of this someday," so she got permission from the hospital to take photos in the building. Touching, isn't it?

Even if you can't take pictures there, it's worth visiting places similar to the setting you're going for if only to get a feel for the atmosphere.

Once you've got a pool of reference photos, you can re-combine them to create new places, or change the season or time of certain places. In fact, the background is a great place to express the passage of time or what is going on in your characters' minds. It's always a good idea to simplify your drawing from the original photo too, since transferring the photo "as is" into the background can often be too visually busy. Use only what you need, hide unnecessary parts of the photo with plants or the like, or fade out parts of the background into negative space.

Speaking of hiding things, it's a good idea to remove or alter product names that appear on billboards, and erase names from buildings and signs.

Drawing Backgrounds from Your Own Photos

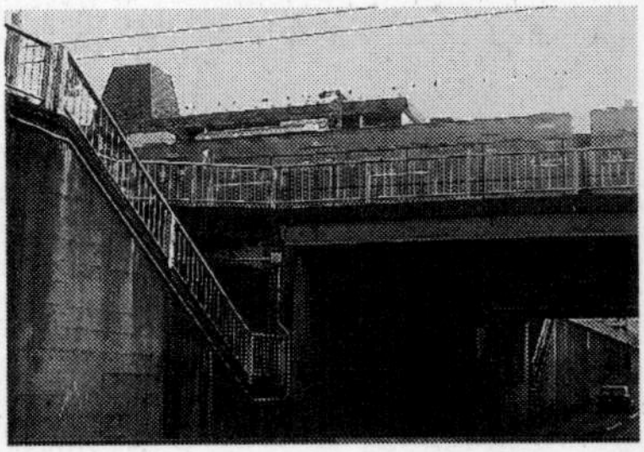

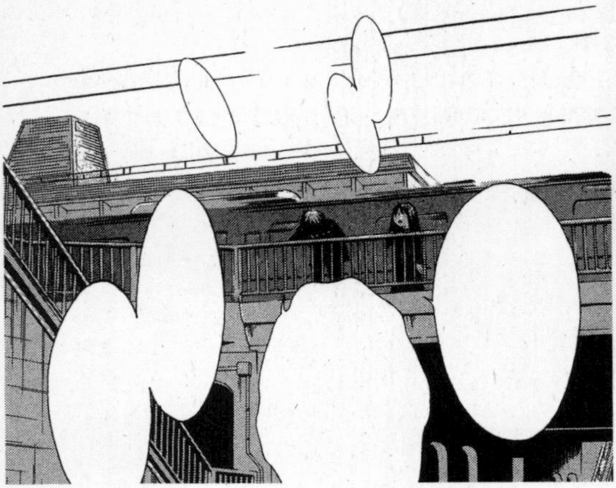

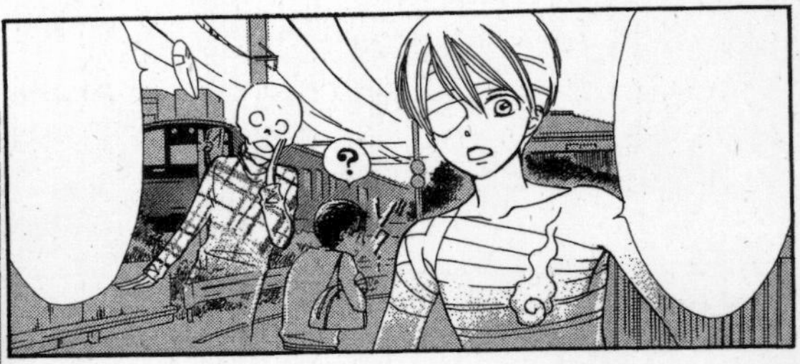

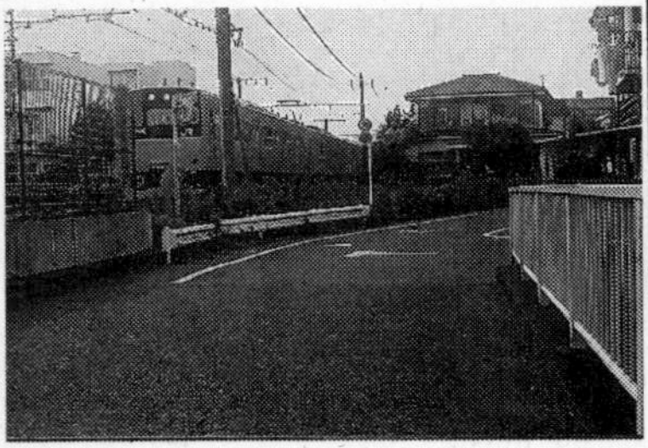

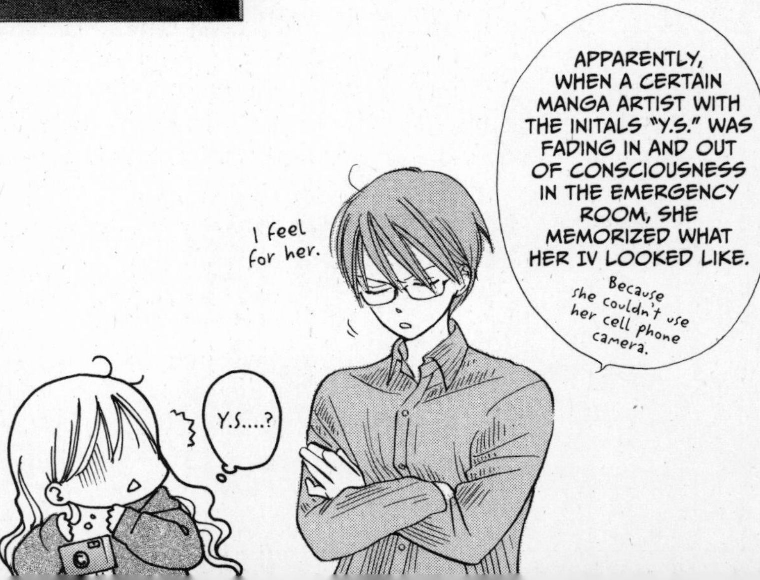
APPARENTLY, WHEN A CERTAIN MANGA ARTIST WITH THE INITALS "Y.S." WAS FADING IN AND OUT OF CONSCIOUSNESS IN THE EMERGENCY ROOM, SHE MEMORIZED WHAT HER IV LOOKED LIKE.
Because she couldn't use her cell phone camera.
I feel for her.
Y.S....?

BACKGROUND GALLERY

Backgrounds have the power to convey emotions.

1 Train Station Platform

A train station at night, drawn in one-point perspective. We know it's night because the sky is black and the platform is illuminated. There's a sense of solitude in the air.

Wild Cats (by Reiko Shimizu, from *LaLa*)

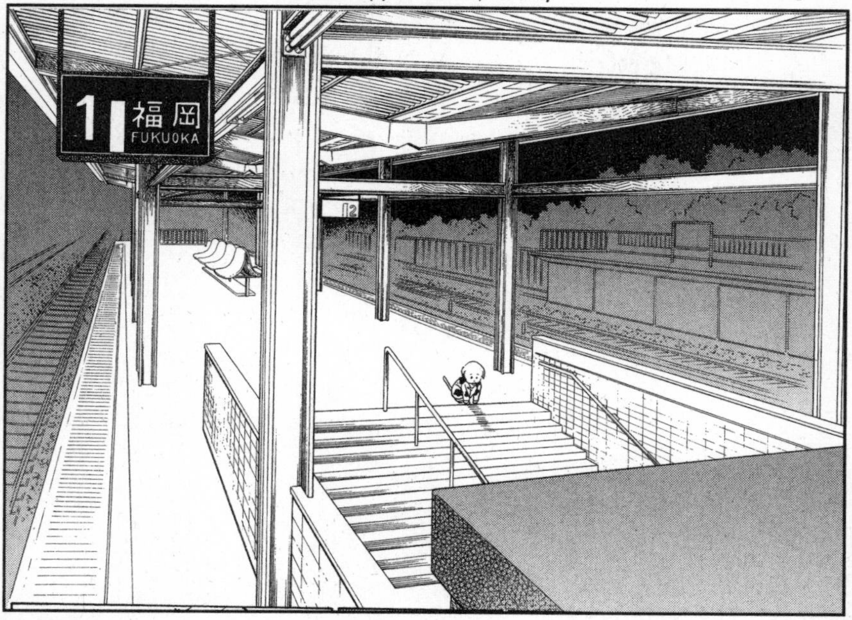
1 福岡
FUKUOKA

2 School Campus

The "There Are" series always starts with this scene. Does that make the background one of the main characters?!

Renaado Genshou ni wa Wake ga Aru
("There are Reasons for the Leonard Phenomenon") (by Izumi Kawahara, from *Melody*)

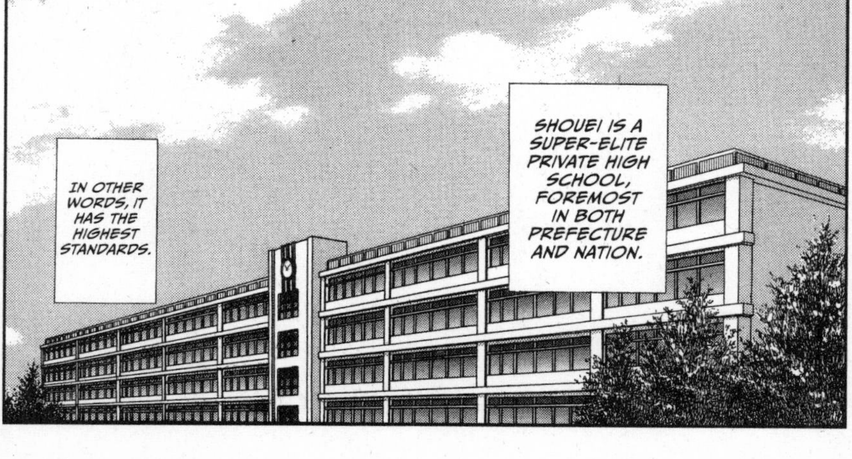
SHOUEI IS A SUPER-ELITE PRIVATE HIGH SCHOOL, FOREMOST IN BOTH PREFECTURE AND NATION.
IN OTHER WORDS, IT HAS THE HIGHEST STANDARDS.

3 Nature

This story takes place a fictional world, but is precisely because an imaginary world t it needs extra realis Check out the lovely fly serpents!

Tenkuu Seiryuu
("Heaven's Sacred Dragons")
(by Miyuki Yamaguchi, from *Melod*

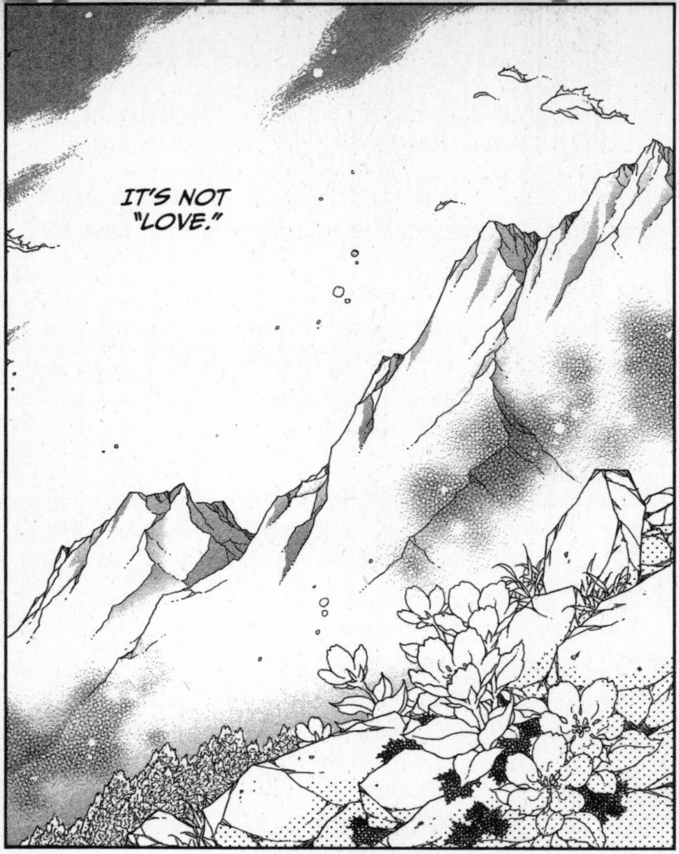
IT'S NOT "LOVE."

4 Cafe

It's a retro room! background is a p to the Taisho Era (1 1926).

Golden Days
(by Shigeru Takao,
from *Hana to Yume*)

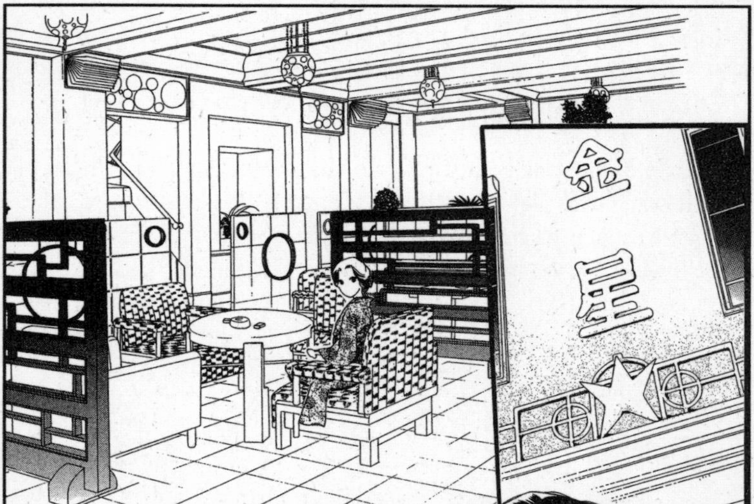
金星

Drawing Effects

Unlike movies and TV shows, manga doesn't have motion, lighting, or sound at its disposal. However, there are still ways to add a theatrical touch. The toolset used to create theatrical illusion is called "effects."

The prime example are effects lines. "Speed lines" express the movement of people and objects. "Focus lines" illustrate impact or intensity. "White bursts" or "beta flashes" draw the reader's eye or create an even greater impact (see the white bursts in black fields on page 38). (40)

In shojo manga, flowers, dots, and complex crosshatching are effects used in more showy scenes. Sometimes a whole background is made of effects. You'll probably never need to draw most of these opulent effects by hand, since they're available as tone, but it's still a good idea to learn how.

There are no laws regarding how to draw effects lines or effect backgrounds. It's an art that many artists have made their own. However, there's a knack for drawing them nicely, so you'll need to practice and master the skill. Someday you might even share a new technique you've found with your assistants!

Effect lines and crosshatching are very helpful for directing a reader's eye through the page. There's a lot of pressure though, because messing up on the effects means that you've ruined the beautiful drawing that's already there. Think carefully about what effect is appropriate for your panel, drawing on the expertise of professional manga artists to see how densely they draw the effects, and with what rules.

Our contests always receive a few submissions where the effects were drawn from vague memories, along the lines of, "I think they used this kind of effect for this kind of scene...?" The page ends up destroyed because the artist was careless. If you have ever gotten a critique that said, "Your manga is sloppy," pay more attention to how you use your effects.

Effects

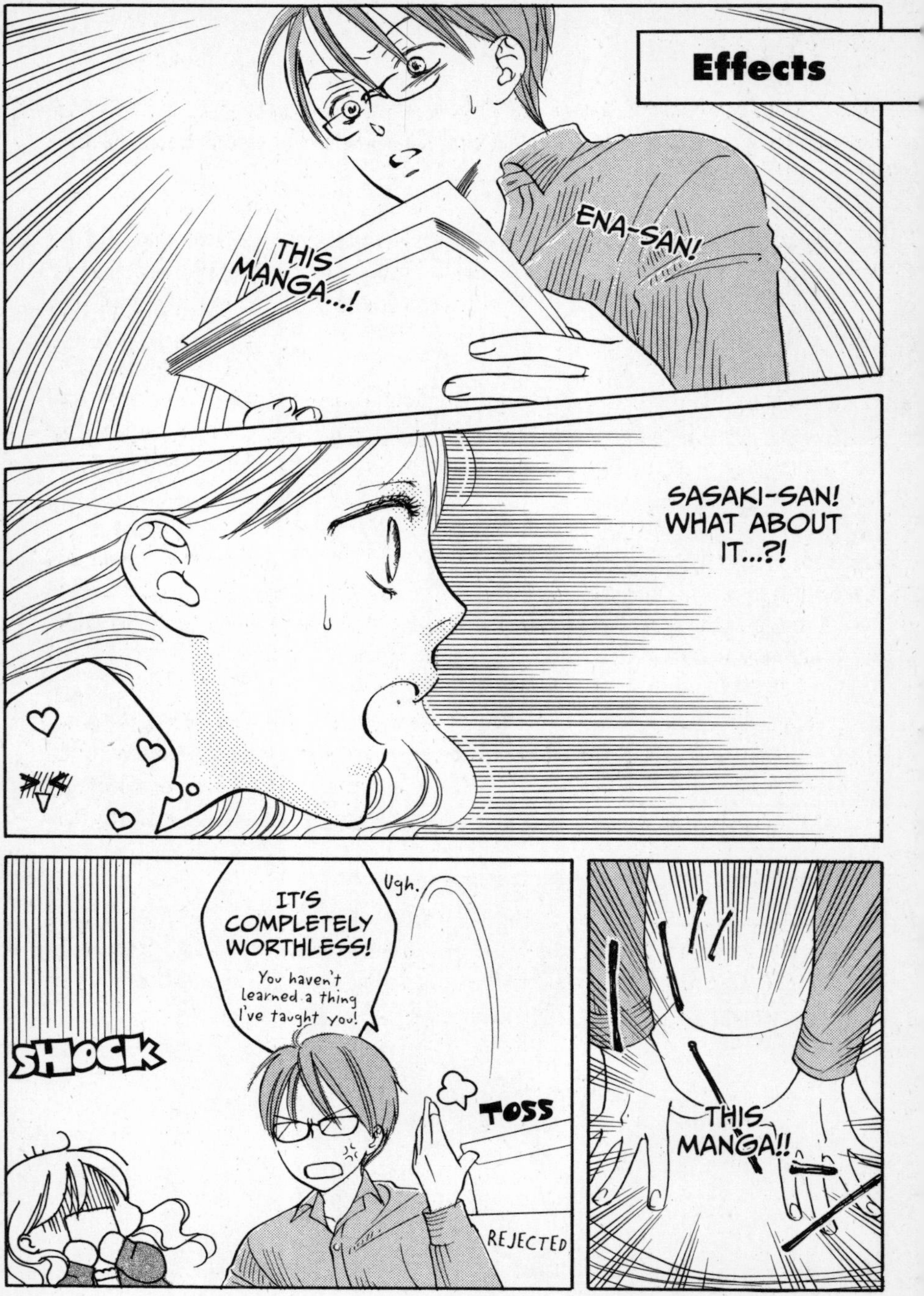
ENA-SAN!
THIS MANGA...!
SASAKI-SAN! WHAT ABOUT IT...?!
THIS MANGA!!
Ugh.
IT'S COMPLETELY WORTHLESS!
You haven't learned a thing I've taught you!
TOSS
SHOCK
REJECTED

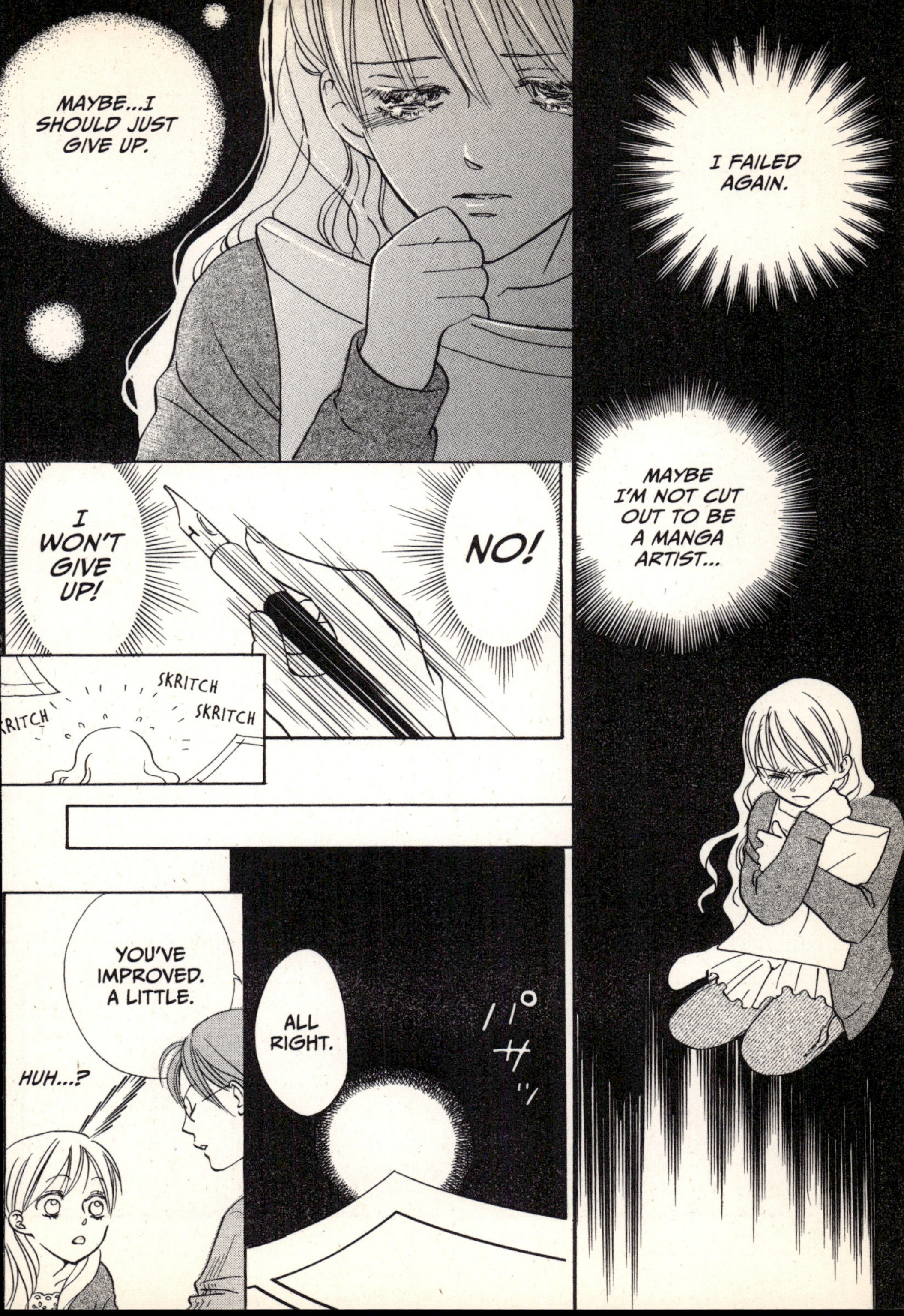
I FAILED AGAIN.
MAYBE I'M NOT CUT OUT TO BE A MANGA ARTIST...
MAYBE...I SHOULD JUST GIVE UP.
NO!
I WON'T GIVE UP!
SKRITCH
SKRITCH
SKRITCH
パサッ
ALL RIGHT.
YOU'VE IMPROVED. A LITTLE.
HUH...?

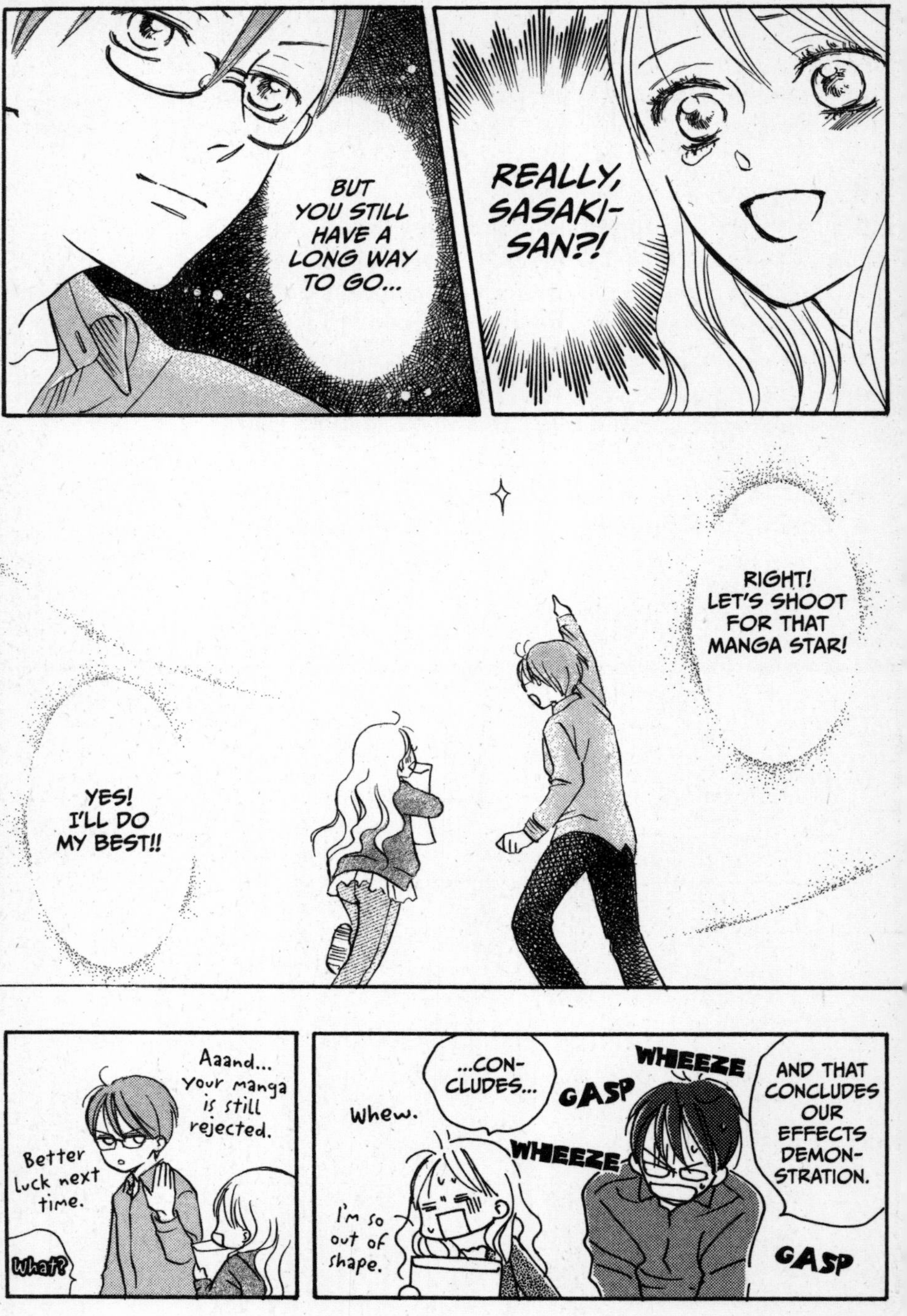
REALLY, SASAKI-SAN?!
BUT YOU STILL HAVE A LONG WAY TO GO...
RIGHT! LET'S SHOOT FOR THAT MANGA STAR!
YES! I'LL DO MY BEST!!
AND THAT CONCLUDES OUR EFFECTS DEMONSTRATION.
WHEEZE
GASP
...CON-CLUDES...
Whew.
WHEEZE
I'm so out of shape.
GASP
Aaand... Your manga is still rejected.
Better luck next time.
What?

Just like with effects lines and effect backgrounds, you can add theatrical touches with word balloons, sound effects, and asides. Careful, though! Here's a list of balloon and lettering "don'ts":

- Don't make the balloon too big or too small for the text.
- Don't create a jagged balloon for emphasis, but make it so small you end up cramming all the text in at a tiny size.
- Don't make your balloon shapes so unusual that the reader has to struggle to figure out who the tail is pointed toward/who's talking.
- Don't misspell your hand-drawn sound effects.
- Don't exaggerate your sound effects so much that they explode into the gutter or past the trim line and risk getting cut off at the printer, or so much that they're illegible.
- Don't let your sound effects get lost in the background.
- Don't write dialogue or thoughts that don't make sense.

You have to be careful!

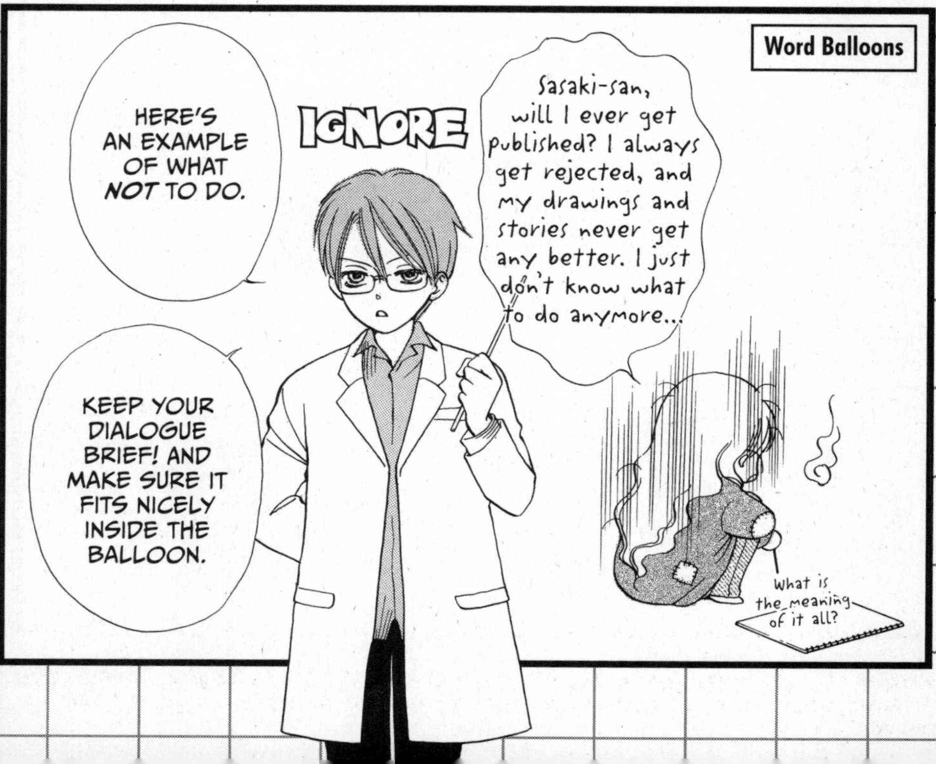
Word Balloons
Sasaki-san, will I ever get published? I always get rejected, and my drawings and stories never get any better. I just don't know what to do anymore...
IGNORE
HERE'S AN EXAMPLE OF WHAT *NOT* TO DO.
KEEP YOUR DIALOGUE BRIEF! AND MAKE SURE IT FITS NICELY INSIDE THE BALLOON.
What is the meaning of it all?

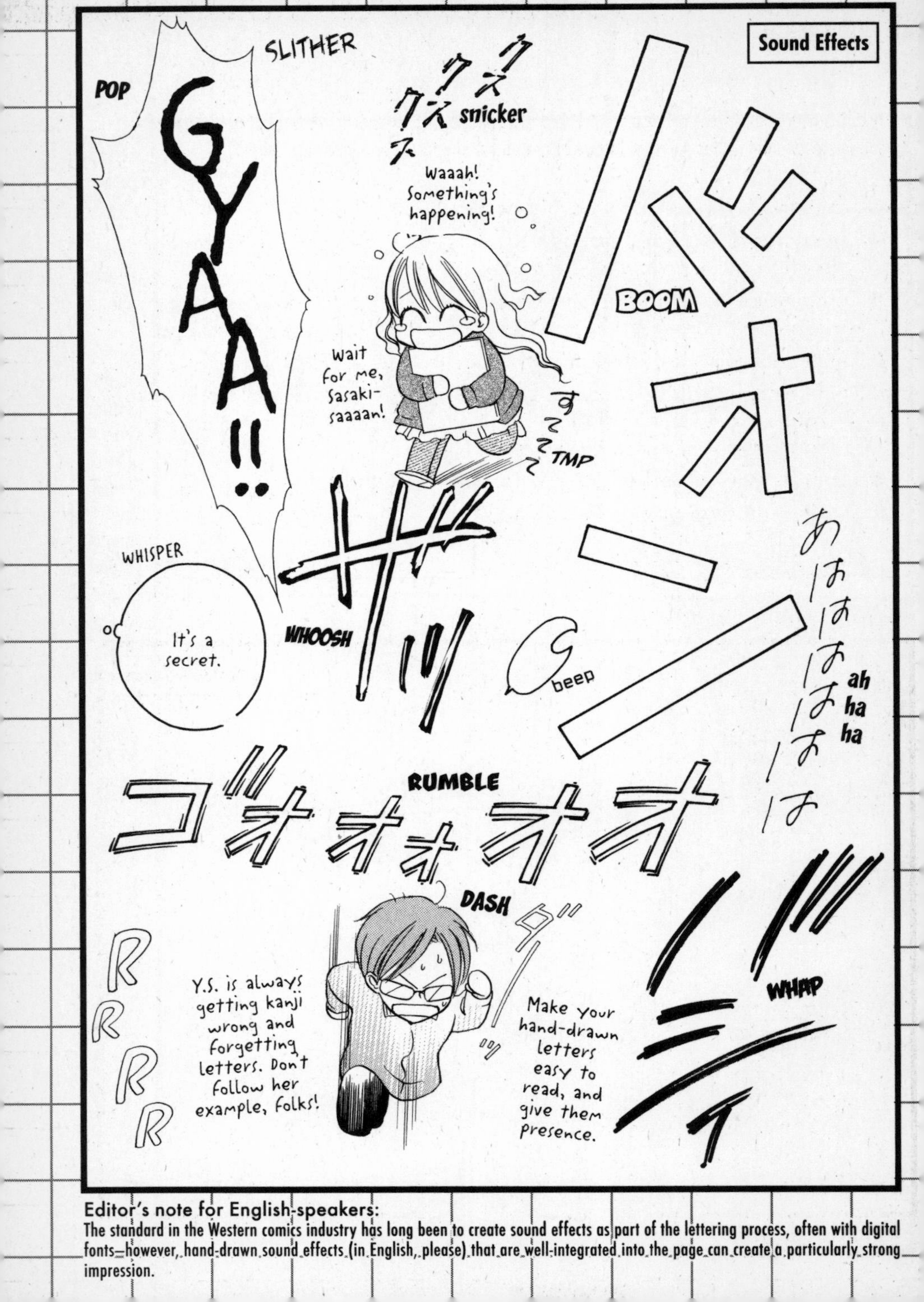
Sound Effects
BOOM
ah ha ha
snicker
SLITHER
POP
GYAA!!
Waaah! Something's happening!
Wait for me, Sasaki-saaaan!
TMP
WHISPER
It's a secret.
WHOOSH
beep
RUMBLE
WHAP
DASH
Make your hand-drawn letters easy to read, and give them presence.
Y.S. is always getting kanji wrong and forgetting letters. Don't follow her example, folks!
R R R R R

Editor's note for English-speakers:

The standard in the Western comics industry has long been to create sound effects as part of the lettering process, often with digital fonts—however, hand-drawn sound effects (in English, please) that are well-integrated into the page can create a particularly strong impression.

Not everyone is going to be good when they first get started!

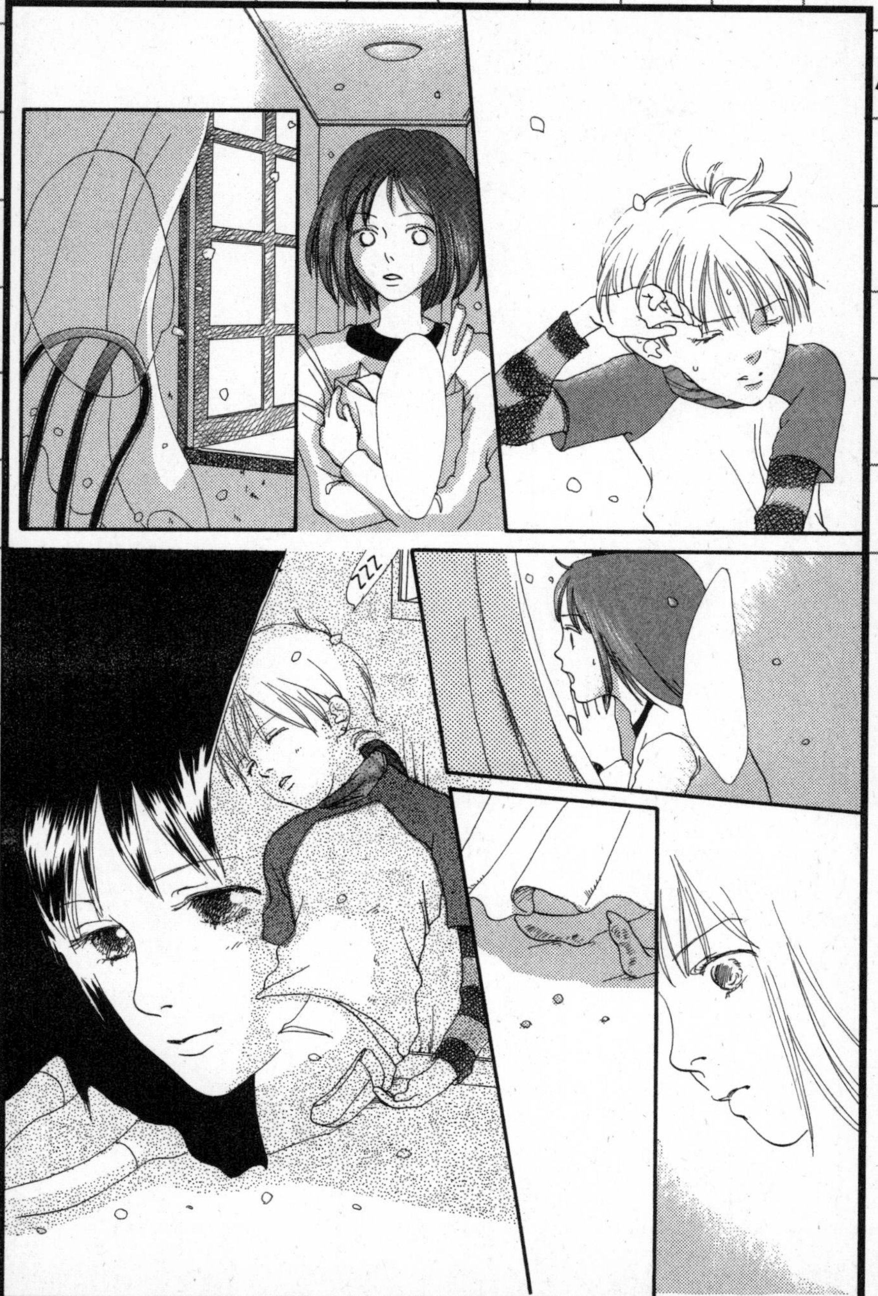
ZZZ

OLD WORK

(From a manga contest submission)

In this scene, there's a distinct lack of line variation. The character designs are questionable, and the character's expressions are stiff. Her finishing touches—tone-scraping and the like—are half-done.

THE MORE YOU DRAW, THE BETTER YOU GET!

Practice makes perfect. Just compare Yui Shin's old work with her newest page

NEW WORK

(*Ghost Only,* from Melody)

Check it out: An emotional presentation with rich facial expressions. Her linework is confident and alive. Her use of black areas and graded crosshatching is elegant.

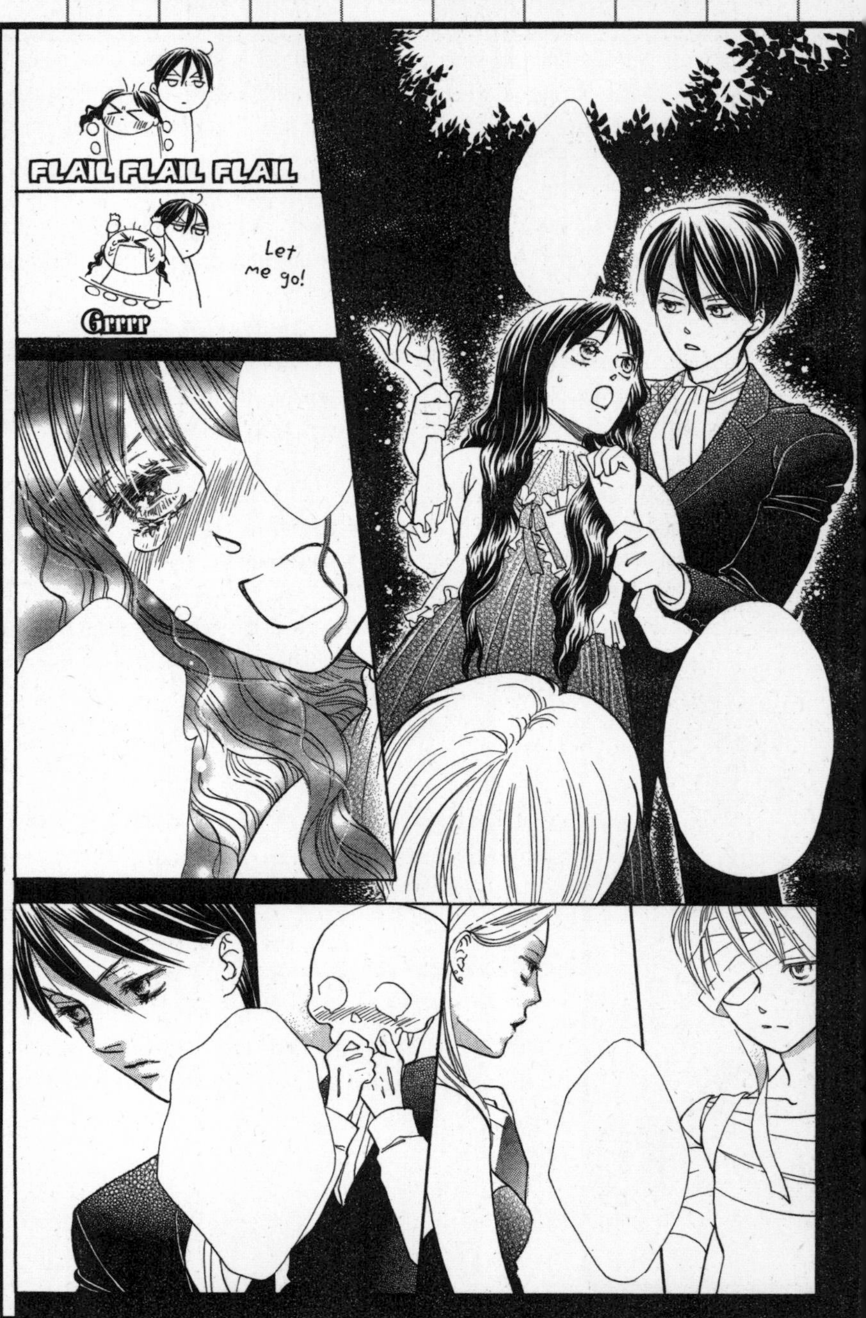
FLAIL FLAIL FLAIL
Let me go!
Grrrr

Brainstorming

In show business terms, submitting your manga to a contest is like a new actor going to an audition. Above all else, the judges are looking to discover "potential." We're not looking for perfection as much as we're looking for the sparkle of new talent found in your art, story, and style.

A manga contest is not a place where you are judged only on how good or bad your story is. Instead, think of it as a place where we discover your potential as an aspiring shojo manga artist, and as a place to expand that potential.

Each editorial department wants to see the talent and passion in your work. We will never write you off based on the quality of your first contest entry—we love to see serial submitters who improve with each new contest entry.

To anyone thinking, "I'll submit something someday, if I come up with a really good idea," first draw a manga at the level you're at now! Then get critique and use that feedback to help you with your next manga. It's a great way to use manga contests to your benefit.

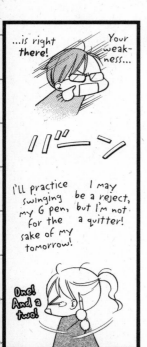

Your weak-ness...
...is right there!
I may be a reject, but I'm not a quitter!
I'll practice swinging my G pen, for the sake of my tomorrow!
One! And a two!

With that in mind, there are some things we don't want to see. The following are not suitable for submission to a Hakusensha (or any) manga contest:

- **Doujinshi/Fan Art.** We can't evaluate your potential based on your work with others' characters. Please send us something new!

- **Plagiarism.** We cannot print copies, tracings, or reproductions of manga, magazines, photo collections, or song lyrics without permission. Similarly, we cannot use works that are based on novels or essays.

Brainstorming cont'd.

We asked professionals how they come up with ideas, and we received a variety of answers. Some find inspiration in reading other manga, others by looking at magazines or photo collections, others by watching TV or listening to music, etc. Surprisingly, many artists reported inspiration striking while they were away from their desks. Some even said ideas came to them while they were falling asleep and staring into space, or while they were in the bath! It may be that it's easier to get flashes of inspiration when your brain is at rest.

And so we recommend keeping an idea notebook. If possible, get a notebook small enough that you can always carry it with you, and make a habit of noting the wisps of ideas that come to you. Whether you're out on the town or sitting in front of the TV, make a record of things you like, neat imagery, or bits of inspirational dialogue. You're bound to be able to combine some of the things in your notebook into something amazing. And while you're at it, if you always have a small digital camera with you when you go on walks, you can collect reference material, too. That's killing two birds with one stone! But don't get so caught up in collecting that you don't watch out for cars.

Furthermore, it is important to constantly be in touch with media other than manga—that means movies, novels, TV, magazines, and the internet. It is impossible to create a new manga if all you read is manga. Knowledge, information, and experience are ingredients for giving life to ideas. Be interested in life, and your manga will be interesting.

Another great idea is challenging yourself to think critically about the information you absorb. Ask yourself, "What if X was Y?" and keep walking down that mental road. Manga is a competition to see how wild your imagination can be. Think outside the box!

Once you've got an inkling of an idea, there's no one right way to go about turning that into a story. One of the most common questions we get from aspiring manga artists is, "Should I work on characters first? Or should I come up with a story first?" We've asked professional manga artists the same question a few times, but it seems there's no one way about it. It's all up to you.

Creating Characters

Once you've brainstormed a general concept and a few things you want to happen in your manga, it's time to create characters.

Sometimes, artists create a story simply around the idea, "I want to make a so-and-so character." As we stated earlier, the characters are the most important part of your manga. This is because no matter how excellent your story may be, if your characters have no charisma or appeal, the story will fail to be interesting almost every time. Especially in shojo manga, it's vital that the characters come off as appealing.

First, create your main character. Is your main character male? Or female? We understand that some other shojo manga magazines blindly follow the creed that "the main character must be a girl the same age as the readers," but Hakusensha's shojo manga magazines don't limit ourselves that way. Naturally we don't expect submissions to our manga contests to be that limited, either.

The core of your main character is their goal. What does the main character want to do? What do they want to obtain? A story is brought to life by the characters' goals and objectives. Even if there is nothing more to it than the main character having a goal (motivation) that they have to overcome an obstacle to achieve (a rival, conditions, etc.), it's still a story. On the other hand, sometimes stories start off with a character who has achieved their goals and just wants to live in peace, but they get mixed up in some situation that causes them to develop new goals.

Character creation literally means giving your characters "character." Looks, fashion, posture, manner of speech, habits, experience—what kind of characters do you want for your manga? In movie terms, you're not only casting the actors; you also need to choose their costumes and props, style their hair and makeup, direct their performances, and film them. Kind of exciting, huh?

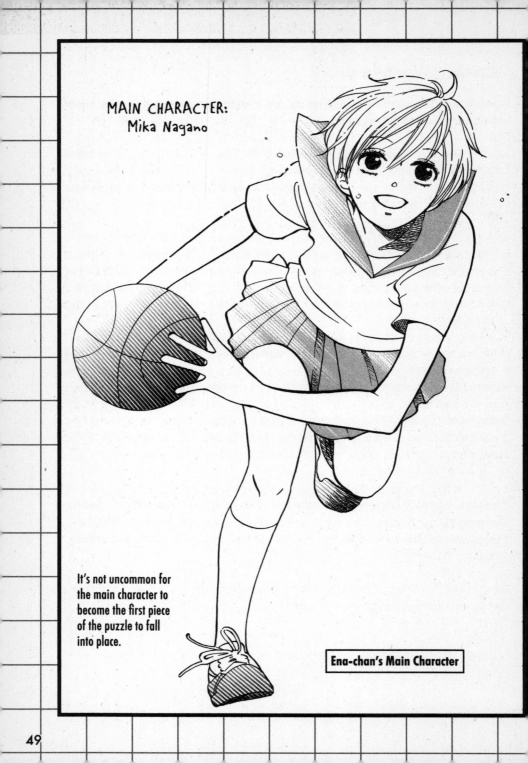

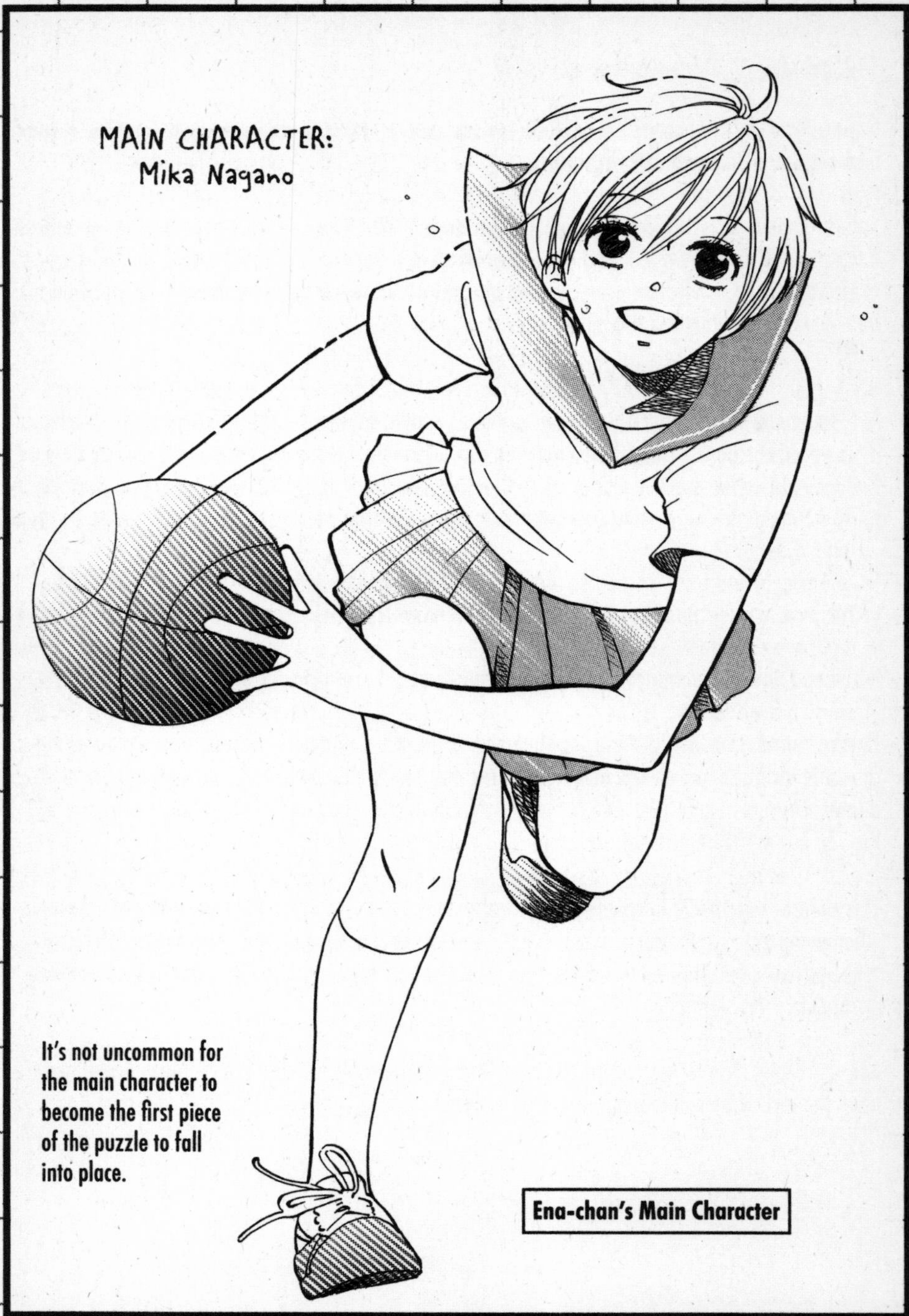
MAIN CHARACTER:
Mika Nagano
It's not uncommon for the main character to become the first piece of the puzzle to fall into place.
Ena-chan's Main Character

Creating Characters cont'd.

Once you've decided on the main character(s), then create side characters such as the love interest, the antagonist, friends, etc. Give these characters looks and behavior appropriate to their roles in the story. What will they look like, and how will they talk? Does that fit the role they're supposed to fill in the story? Or will they be too atypical? Use your best judgment, and a dash of creativity. Still, the important thing is to build up the main character. There are exceptions, such as ensemble pieces. Manga contests have page limits, though, so you won't be able to have too many characters.

Hook your readers right off the bat with your main character's appeal. Average looks, personality, and behavior won't leave a deep enough impression on the judges. We receive plenty of submissions where the supporting cast members are the most memorable characters, and they eat up the main character, so to speak. We end up wanting to suggest to the artist that they just make the supporting characters into the main characters.

Sometimes the main character is so non-distinct that it makes the plot difficult to follow. Design your characters so that we can tell who they are, even from behind (see page 23).

When you have a general concept for your characters, make a character sheet.

On the character sheet, draw a rough sketch of all the characters, including the supporting cast, and include some details about them. It's like a mini bio page. Write down the characters' names, characteristics, and any personality traits that pop up in the story. It's also good to include a few different facial expressions.

This sheet will help you keep your details consistent when you get to the storyboard stage and when you write your dialogue. It also helps out other people who are reading your storyboards. When artists have their own editor, they often share the character sheets with their editor during story meetings.

Above all else, name your character something memorable. If characters have nicknames, keep the nickname use to a minimum so as not to confuse your readers.

Manga Story 101

When you're creating manga, remember that it is a visual medium. The climax of your story should also be the most impressive moment in the art. Occasionally, we see submissions that begin with conversation, and end with conversation. Because the entire story is made up of dialogue, the pictures become just illustrations of a conversation.

In Osamu Tezuka's day, manga went through a radical evolution wherein it adopted cinematic techniques. Tezuka discovered that depending on how an image is presented in a panel, the readers experience the moment differently. Ever since, cinematic paneling has been the norm, with manga-specific improvements and the discovery of new techniques added.

If you want to create a manga story, you need to turn the story in your head into pictures. Everything depends on how effectively you fit the given set of characters, story, and dialogue into a series of panels.

We recommend that you constantly watch movies for research. You can learn an awful lot from how scenes are framed by a camera. Of course, novels and plays are helpful too, but nothing beats movies, which, like manga, are created shot by shot (or panel by panel). We even recommend researching technical directors—the prime example being Steven Speilberg.

Because you have a limited number of pages when submitting work to a manga contest, you can't draw the kind of long, complex story that needs a graphic novel to fit it all in. Complicated settings, subplots, or a series of big plot twists are a no go.

In any case, the judges evaluate your submissions based on the ideas contained within, how those ideas are cooked up into a story, and how appealing you've made the characters. We like to see that you've been researching and thinking hard.

Outlines

Once you've solidified your ideas and characters, it's time to write up an outline. By outline, we mean a summary of all the scenes of your story. It's a battle plan for your entire manga.

With a good outline, you'll always have something to reference during the storyboard phase. It will help you avoid problems such as forgetting to include important events and dialogue, or going way over the page count.

There are no rules for how to construct an outline. It's not a script per se, so you don't need to write down every detail as if it were a TV show or novel. In fact, you'll make a lot of corrections before the project is done, so it's counterproductive to fixate on little details.

After you've got an outline for the overall manga (scenes, how the events connect, foreshadowing, placement of important dialogue and the climax), make notations for page breakdowns. In every story there's an introduction, development, a twist, and the conclusion. Many people misinterpret this; it does not mean that the story should be divided into four even sections. All you need to do is to make sure you have a beginning to the story, a build-up, a climax, and an ending.

Script-writing courses and the like often instruct, "When you're planning out a story, write all the scenes down on index cards." The idea is that you can re-arrange the scenes written on the index cards by shuffling the cards around. You can borrow this technique for manga--it works just the same.

Because movie and TV scriptwriters collaborate with directors, actors, stylists and more, there are other people who give life to and tweak the visual elements. Their most important job is rearranging and rewriting scenes, and creating dialogue. You can see how the index card method would be useful for scriptwriters, because it's an organizational tool for rewriting.

Outlines cont'd.

Manga, however, is created by an individual. It's not uncommon to come up with your dialogue later, during the storyboarding process. So, once again, don't focus on details too early in the process the way a scriptwriter might, but still learn from their method of blocking out scenes with index cards. Overall, your outline should be intelligible and thorough enough that an editor can read it at a story meeting.

Okay, let's get back to writing this outline. First, write down the scenes you want to draw. A scene is one unit consisting of a place, a set amount of time, and what the characters say and do in that amount of time. You go on to the next scene when the place or time changes, or when the characters' actions are finished. If you're having trouble imagining what constitutes a scene, ponder what comes to mind when you think of "action scene" or "love scene."

There's no one right way to write an outline. Use whatever works best for you. Of course you'll want to note the important dialogue, and it would also be good to sketch out scenes you definitely want to draw on a separate sheet of paper. That sketching process is called drawing an "image board" in the movies, by the way.

It doesn't matter if your outline is bare; just line up your scenes from beginning to end. And it can be a guess-timate, but remember to assign page numbers.

Once you've got a finished outline, review it. Imagine your finished manga. Does it look like you can fit it all into the assigned number of pages? Your introduction isn't too long, is it? Is the climax thrilling? It doesn't end too abruptly, does it? If you're dissatisfied with anything, now's the time to delete what you don't need and add what you do need. If you need more pages for your climax, then delete material from elsewhere so you don't mess up the page count.

The beginning of your manga is vitally important, especially if you're submitting it to a manga contest. Don't make your readers wait to meet the main character, and don't wait too long to get to the action. Grab your reader right away with a clever hook, and don't let them go.

TITLE TBD, 16 PAGES, SCHOOL DRAMA

Main characters:

- ● Female Mika Nagano (15) —— Genuine and blunt. Messes up a game and loses her enthusiasm.

  Call each other by last name, no "-san".

- ● male Hayami (15) —————— Mika's classmate. Bookish. Close enough friends to joke around with Mika. Likes photography.

PAGE

Outline

Reflected → in a camera lens

② Big game. The last game of her third year in middle school. They're down 54-52, with a chance for a come-from-behind victory. Mika misses the three-point shot and they lose.

① While everyone around her is busy taking high school entrance exams, Mika, who figured she'd be accepted to any school she wanted because of her basketball skills, spends every day staring blankly into space.

① One day in the hall, she bumps into a boy in her grade, Hayami. They have a minor quarrel. Mika helps him pick up all the photos he dropped.

Hayami has a goal and → that's really cool.

② Beautiful photos of landscapes. She is jealous that Hayami has a passion. As he says, "I have prettier pictures," she leaves.

① The next day, her former teammates say mean things to Mika. Mika runs out into the hall, and Hayami follows.

① Mika is covering her face with her hands. Hayami thinks she is crying and peels her arms away, but her face is blank. With the one line, "Stop trying to hold it all in!!" from Hayami...

① Mika starts crying. Hayami drags Mika to the gym. (What is he thinking?)

① In the gym. Hayami shoots. He makes a basket, but when it lands...

Hayami had discovered Mika's worth.

① He gets an intense pain in his leg. She says, "Are you okay?!" and runs up to him. Their faces are very close (b-dmp b-dmp). Hayami confesses that he hurt his leg playing basketball and gave up on the sport.

Mika discovers her worth through Hayami.

① Hayami says, "I can't fly. Fly in my place." (Like he's comparing Nagano's playing to flying or something.)

② Mika shoots. (Serious eyes.) (Hayami takes a bunch of pictures to give off the effect of slow motion. Will it go in?)

① On the way home, Mika pulls out a picture of herself that she found among Hayami's photos earlier and asks, "Hey, is this the picture that's prettier than those landscapes?" Hayami: "!!" (His feelings are revealed.)

Ena-chan has finished her outline. Now she's got a base for constructing her manga!

ENA-CHAN'S OUTLINE

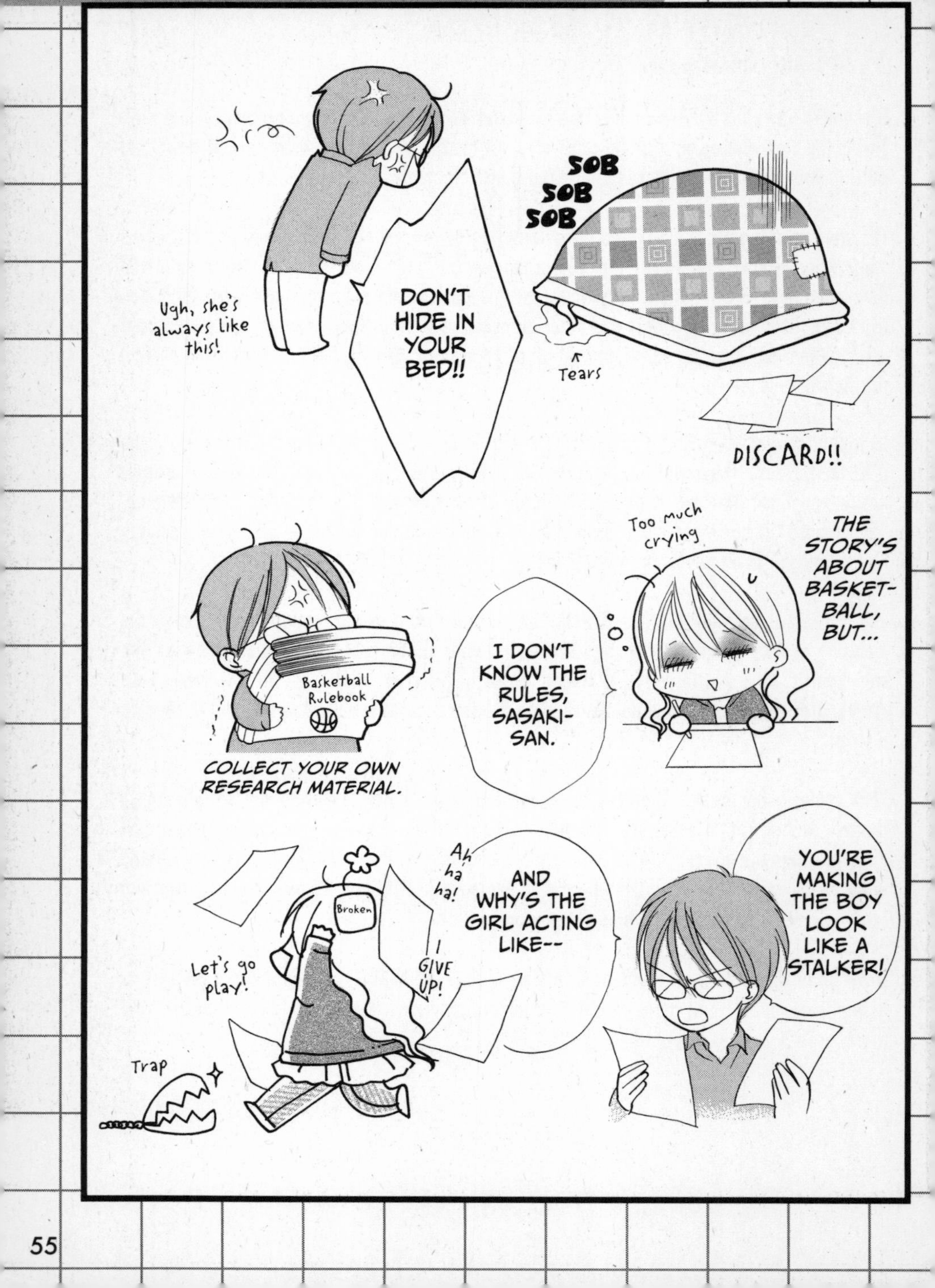
SOB
SOB
SOB
DON'T HIDE IN YOUR BED!!
Tears
Ugh, she's always like this!
DISCARD!!
THE STORY'S ABOUT BASKET-BALL, BUT...
Too much crying
I DON'T KNOW THE RULES, SASAKI-SAN.
Basketball Rulebook
COLLECT YOUR OWN RESEARCH MATERIAL.
YOU'RE MAKING THE BOY LOOK LIKE A STALKER!
AND WHY'S THE GIRL ACTING LIKE--
Ah ha ha!
Broken
I GIVE UP!
Let's go play!
Trap

What are Storyboards?

It's time to turn your finished outline into storyboards. Storyboards are your manga's blueprint. This is the part where you actually construct your manga by placing panels on each page and putting your characters in those panels. You'll also create dialogue at this stage.

The storyboarding process is where the overall flow of your manga is finalized. This is the first stage where you can really say that you're making a manga. How you pace your manga will determine how entertaining it is, so revise at this stage until you're completely satisfied. You can even show your storyboards to other people too, so that their opinions can shape your work. When you have an editor, almost all of your story meetings will be conducted around the storyboards (see page 78).

In Japan, a rough sketch of a whole story is known as a "name" ("neemu"). However, in the U.S., the term is "thumbnail" or "storyboard." "Thumbnail" comes from the world of graphic design and illustration, where extremely rough, small sketches are made during brainstorming. "Storyboard" is borrowed from filmmaking, where storyboarding is the process of deciding how many shots will be needed for a scene.

The difference between the classic definition of storyboard and a manga storyboard is the inclusion of text. Sometimes, manga artists and their editors will call the dialogue itself the storyboards. As a matter of fact, "name" originally meant "dialogue." In any case, since storyboards contain all the dialogue, reading the storyboards is almost equivalent to reading a script.

That aside, a beginner mistake is to focus heavily on dialogue during the storyboarding process. Manga isn't a novel, it's a visual experience. If you arrange your images around the dialogue, then the images turn into illustrations of dialogue. That's boring. In fact, your manga ought to be so visually interesting that even someone just flipping through your manga, not reading any of the text, would find it engaging.

Draw all of the scenes you divided up in your outline. Remember to create visual interest by giving large panels and more space to important moments. Revise, revise and revise some more, even if you get sick of it!

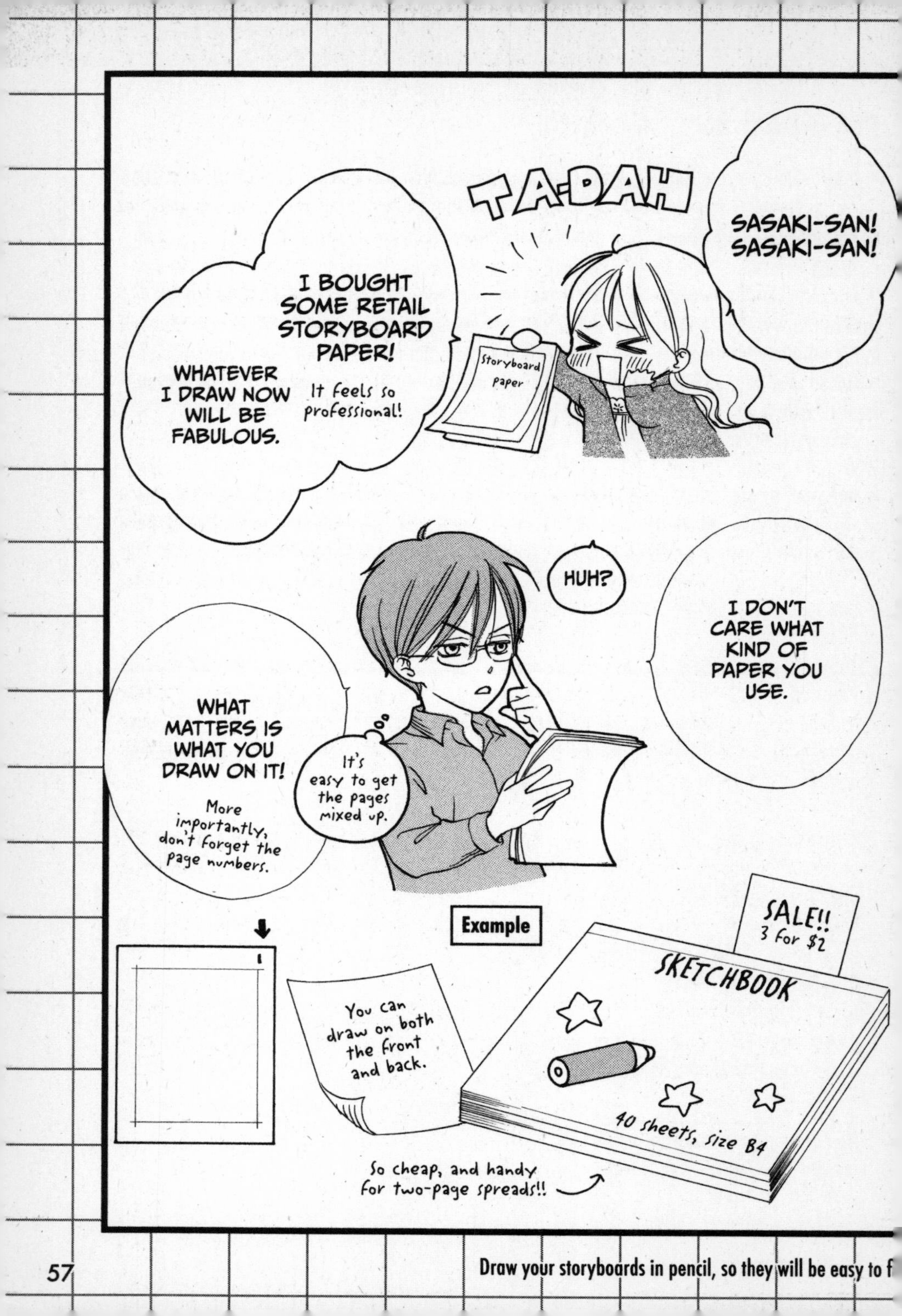
SASAKI-SAN! SASAKI-SAN!
TA-DAH
Storyboard paper
I BOUGHT SOME RETAIL STORYBOARD PAPER!
It feels so professional!
WHATEVER I DRAW NOW WILL BE FABULOUS.
HUH?
I DON'T CARE WHAT KIND OF PAPER YOU USE.
It's easy to get the pages mixed up.
WHAT MATTERS IS WHAT YOU DRAW ON IT!
More importantly, don't forget the page numbers.
SALE!! 3 for $2
SKETCHBOOK
40 sheets, size B4
So cheap, and handy for two-page spreads!!
Example
1
You can draw on both the front and back.

Draw your storyboards in pencil, so they will be easy to f

Panel Layout

Placing panels on your page is called "laying out" panels.

As you know, there's a correct reading order to manga panels and pages. Basically, you read from top to bottom, right to left in Japan, left to right in the West. Poor panel layout means that no one can follow your story. Sometimes there's a reason for panel layout to be complex, such as the "overlap" paneling technique, which expresses events happening at the same time, but if you put your panels in a difficult-to-understand order for no reason, the readers will be confused. Avoid doing anything that throws your readers out of the reading experience, even for a second.

With shojo manga in particular, panel layout is often complex and impressionistic. It takes the cooperation of panel layout, words balloons and character thoughts to weave the complete world of your story. No matter how much thought you've put into building your world and the mood, it won't mean anything if you don't convey it to your readers, so be careful.

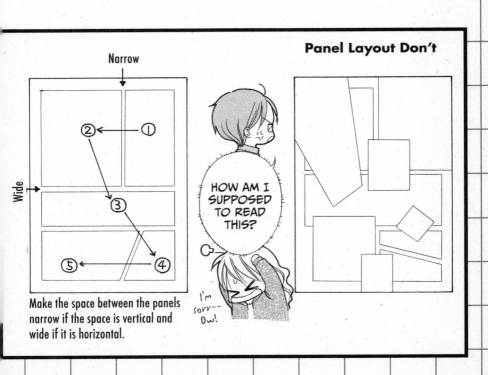

Panel Layout Don't

Narrow
Wide
①
②
③
④
⑤

Make the space between the panels narrow if the space is vertical and wide if it is horizontal.

HOW AM I SUPPOSED TO READ THIS?
I'm sorr-- Ow!

Eye-Grabbing Page Turns

You've got to turn the page to read what comes next in manga. Everyone knows that, right? But did you know that you can use that bottom left corner of the left page to your advantage to build up the reader's anticipation?

You can use a page turn to indicate a time shift and "start over" on the new page, but a page turn is most effective when it's used to surprise the reader. It's great for springing unexpected developments, and for scenes and dialogue that you want to emphasize and give a strong impression. If you can hook the readers at the bottom of the page and make them ask "What next?!" as they turn the page, then you've succeeded.

This is one tool you don't want to leave out of your manga toolbox!

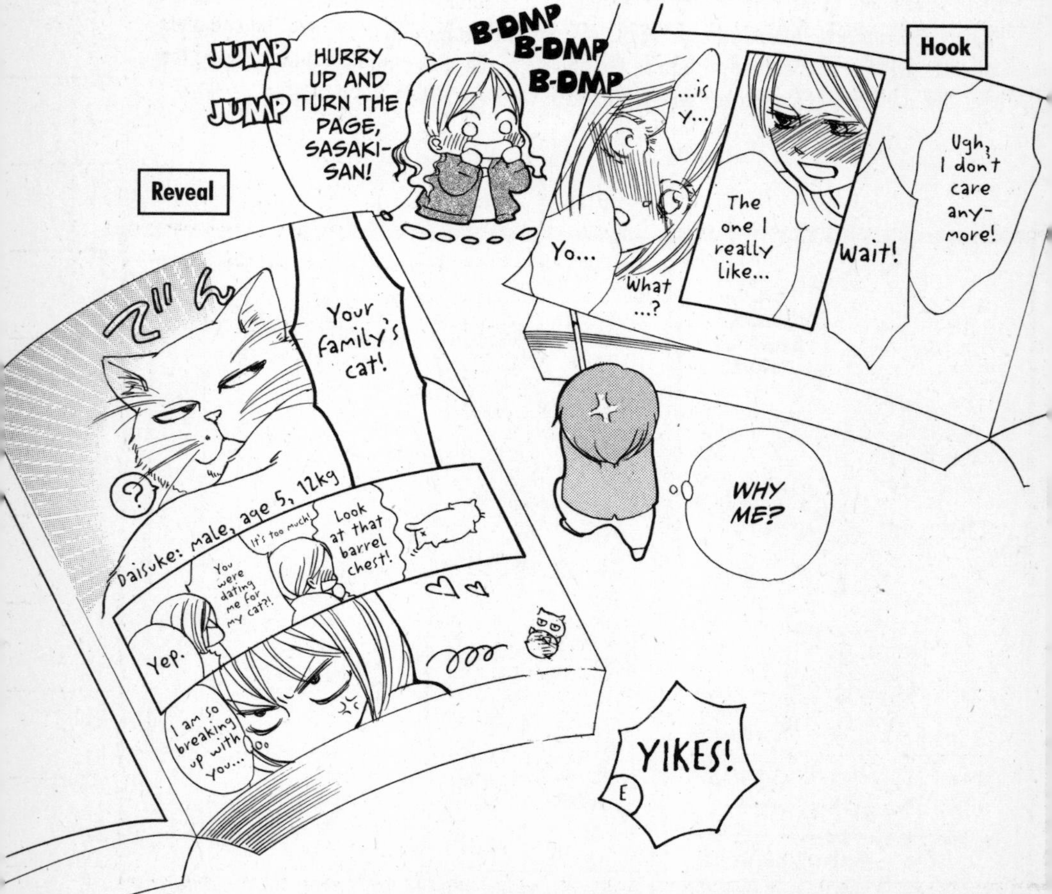
Hook
...is Y...
Ugh, I don't care any-more!
Wait!
The one I really like...
Yo...
What ...?
B-DMP
B-DMP
B-DMP
HURRY UP AND TURN THE PAGE, SASAKI-SAN!
JUMP
JUMP
Reveal
Your family's cat!
Daisuke: male, age 5, 12kg
Look at that barrel chest!
It's too much!
You were dating me for my cat?!
Yep.
I am so breaking up with you...
WHY ME?
YIKES!

Panel Rhythm

Each page needs a rhythm. If all the panels are the same size, and the characters just sit there talking, that's no fun to read (warning—this tends to happen when you compose your scenes around dialogue). Also, people have a hard time reading manga where the art is cropped a lot, so lots of close-ups will seem dull to your readers. The important thing is to use variation in your paneling so that your readers' eyes flow over the page in a directed manner.

First, think about all that has to fit onto the page. Choose which moment you want to be most important. Which panel do you want to have the biggest impact? Which panel do you want your readers to remember most? Do whatever you can to make that panel stand out.

There's all kinds of ways to go about highlighting a panel: you can make the panel itself bigger, you can give the interior of the panel a unique composition, you can make the word balloon unique, you can alter or remove the panel's borders, you can bleed the image off the page, etc. A little bit of research into existing works will give you a lot of ideas.

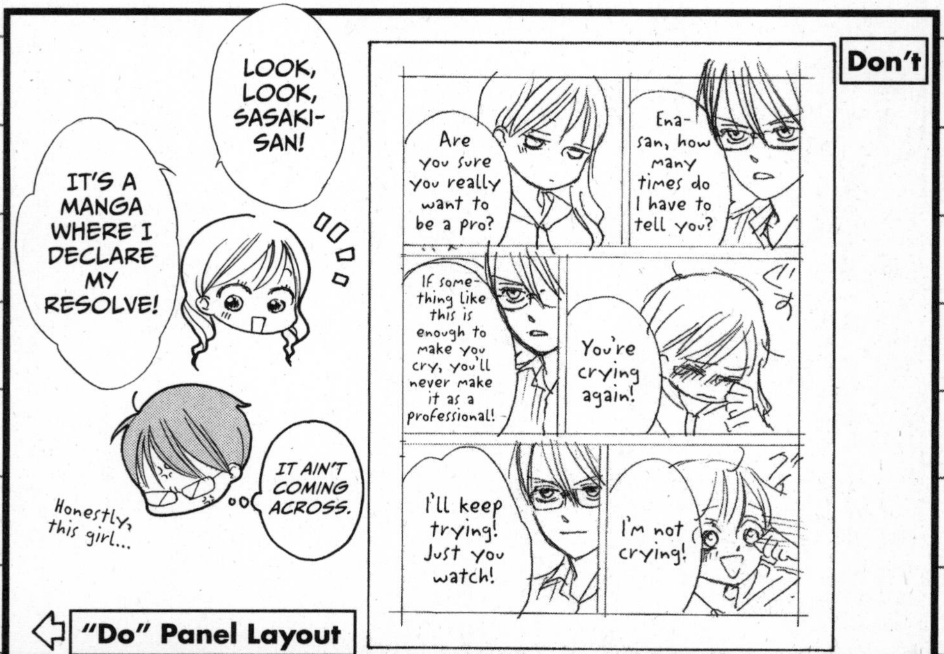
Don't
Ena-san, how many times do I have to tell you?
Are you sure you really want to be a pro?
You're crying again!
If something like this is enough to make you cry, you'll never make it as a professional!
I'm not crying!
I'll keep trying! Just you watch!
LOOK, LOOK, SASAKI-SAN!
IT'S A MANGA WHERE I DECLARE MY RESOLVE!
IT AIN'T COMING ACROSS.
Honestly, this girl...
"Do" Panel Layout

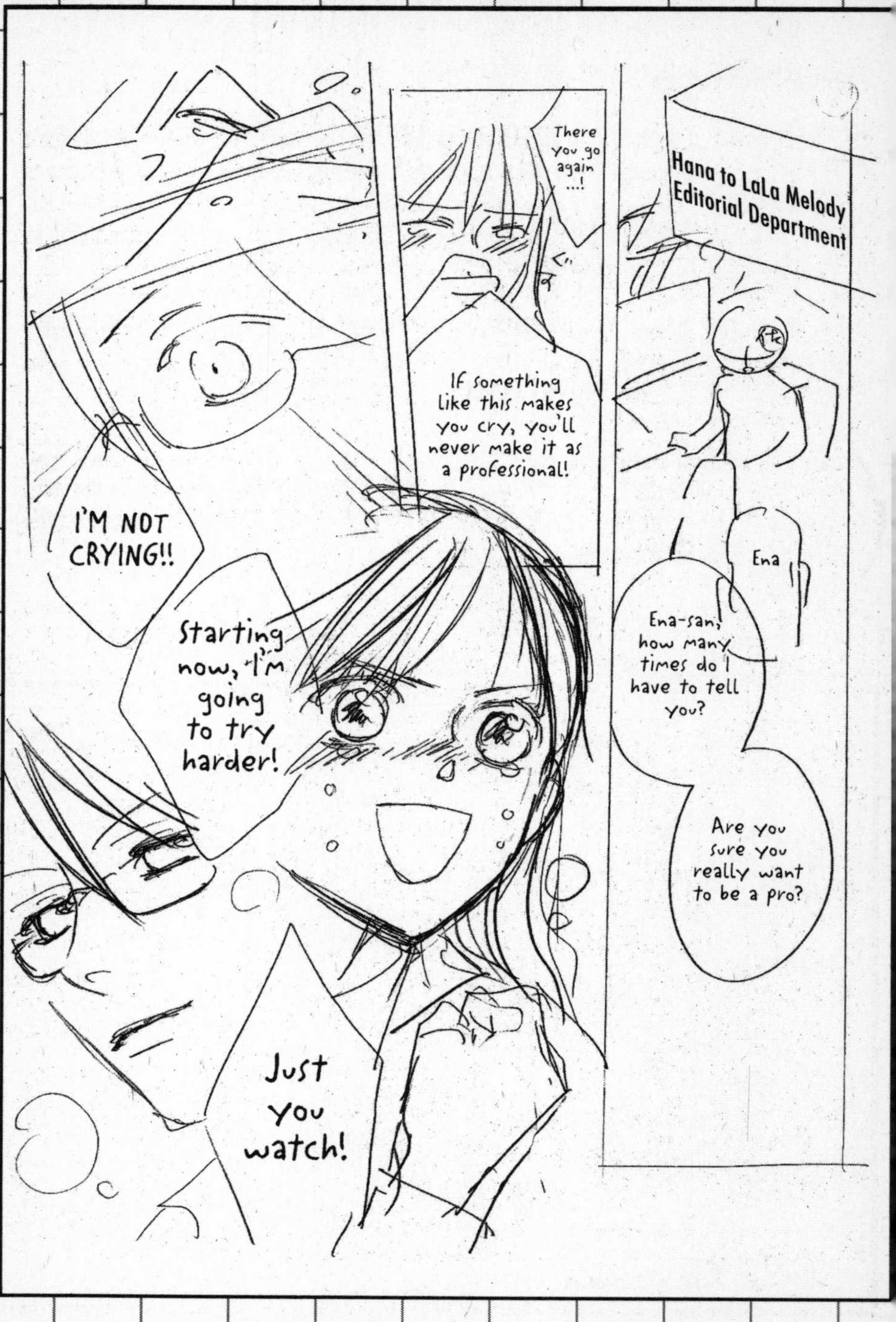
Hana to LaLa Melody Editorial Department
Ena
Ena-san, how many times do I have to tell you?
Are you sure you really want to be a pro?
There you go again ....!
If something like this makes you cry, you'll never make it as a professional!
I'M NOT CRYING!!
Starting now, I'm going to try harder!
Just you watch!

Composing a Two-Page Spread

Now that you know how to effectively compose one page, let's look at how to compose two-page spreads.

When you're reading manga, you see two pages at the same time. When they relate to each other, it's called a "spread," and there are plenty of times when you'll be able to draw a scene across both pages. A good two-page spread draws the readers' eyes across both pages. Both pages should seem to leap up at once when the reader opens the book to that spot. Even when art won't be spread across both pages, there should be a decent flow between the two. If you divide one sheet of paper evenly into two on your storyboard paper, you'll be able to compose the pages of the spread together.

As you might imagine, it is extremely important to know which page is the right page, and which is the left page. Always make sure to write page numbers on your pages. As you revise, update the page numbers.

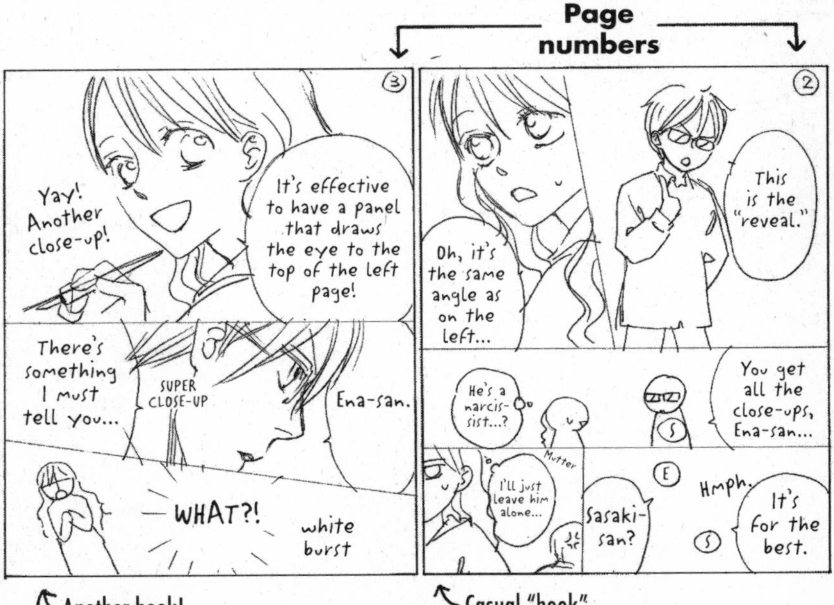
Page numbers
2
This is the "reveal."
Oh, it's the same angle as on the left...
You get all the close-ups, Ena-san...
S
He's a narcis-sist...?
Hmph.
It's for the best.
S
E
Sasaki-san?
Mutter
I'll just leave him alone...
3
It's effective to have a panel that draws the eye to the top of the left page!
Yay! Another close-up!
Ena-san.
SUPER CLOSE-UP
There's something I must tell you...
white burst
WHAT?!
Casual "hook"
Another hook!

Fruits Basket (by Natsuki Takaya, from *Hana to Yume*)

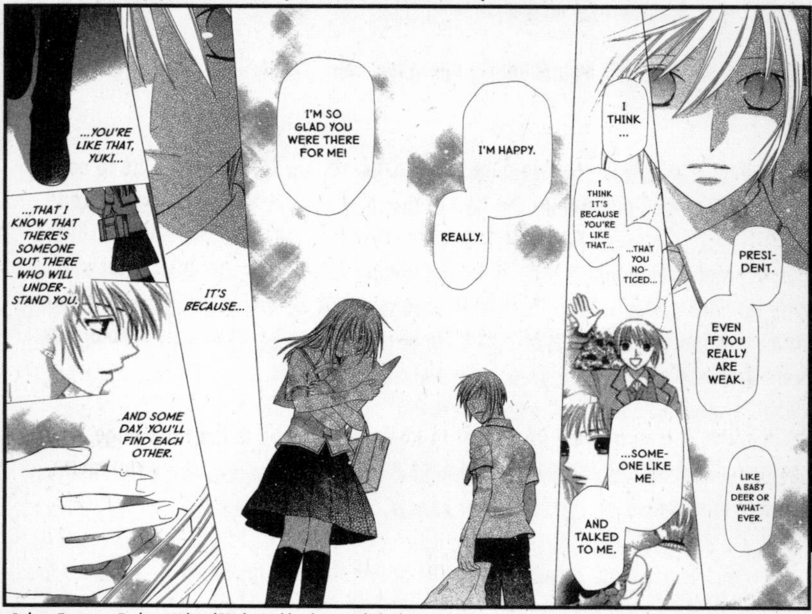
I THINK ...
PRESIDENT.
I THINK IT'S BECAUSE YOU'RE LIKE THAT...
...THAT YOU NOTICED...
EVEN IF YOU REALLY ARE WEAK.
LIKE A BABY DEER OR WHATEVER.
...SOMEONE LIKE ME.
AND TALKED TO ME.
I'M HAPPY.
REALLY.
I'M SO GLAD YOU WERE THERE FOR ME!
IT'S BECAUSE...
...YOU'RE LIKE THAT, YUKI...
...THAT I KNOW THAT THERE'S SOMEONE OUT THERE WHO WILL UNDERSTAND YOU.
AND SOME DAY, YOU'LL FIND EACH OTHER.

The modulation between current events and flashback is particularly captivating.

Boku o Tsutsumu Tsuki no Hikari ("Embraced by the Moonlight") (by Saki Hiwatari, from *Bessatsu Hana to Yume*)

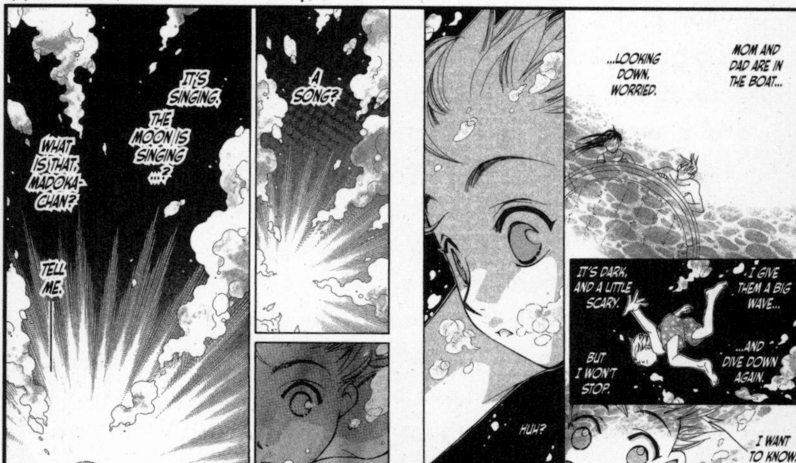
MOM AND DAD ARE IN THE BOAT...
...LOOKING DOWN, WORRIED.
I GIVE THEM A BIG WAVE...
...AND DIVE DOWN AGAIN.
IT'S DARK, AND A LITTLE SCARY.
BUT I WON'T STOP.
I WANT TO KNOW.
MADOKA-CHAN TOLD ME.
HUH?
I HEAR SOMETHING.
MEMORIES MELT INTO THE OCEAN.
A SONG?
WHAT IS THAT?
IT'S SINGING.
THE MOON IS SINGING ...?
WHAT IS THAT, MADOKA-CHAN?
TELL ME.

The readers' eyes are drawn from right to left, mimicking the character's descent into the ocean.

Composition Inside Panels

How you position the images inside your panels will make or break how your work is perceived.

This positioning of characters, backgrounds and other things inside a panel is called "composition." Composition determines the flow of the readers' eyes through each panel.

No matter how great your panel layout, if all the images inside the panels are close-ups of people facing forward and a little to the left, your manga will be extremely flat and difficult to read. When you look at the work of professional manga artists, you will notice that the characters are drawn in a variety of sizes, from a variety of camera angles, and cropped in a variety of ways. There's no such thing as a manga that's just a series of beautiful close-ups.

There is significance to the composition of each and every panel. Get familiar with a number of different ways to compose the inside of your panels.

Each panel contains one "shot." Depending on the scope of things included in the shot, the panel will be classified as wide shot, mid-distance shot, body shot, or close-up:

● A long, or wide shot portrays actions or environments from a distance. It's a good shot for conveying the time, place, season, etc. Long shots are often used as "establishing shots"—that is, for openings or scene changes.
● A medium shot is from a middle distance. It's at a slightly narrower scope than a long shot, and shows where the characters are in relation to each other, and what they are doing.
● A full body shot shows a character's whole body. It is used to portray the character's full image, their clothes, and mood.
● A close-up shot zooms in on a thing or a character's face. It is used to highlight a character's expression or the presence of an important object. With people, a shot from the chest up is called a bust (up) shot, and from the waist up is called a waist shot.

By employing a variety of shots, you can successfully illustrate a scene and express characters' emotions. A great use of shots grabs the readers' attention.

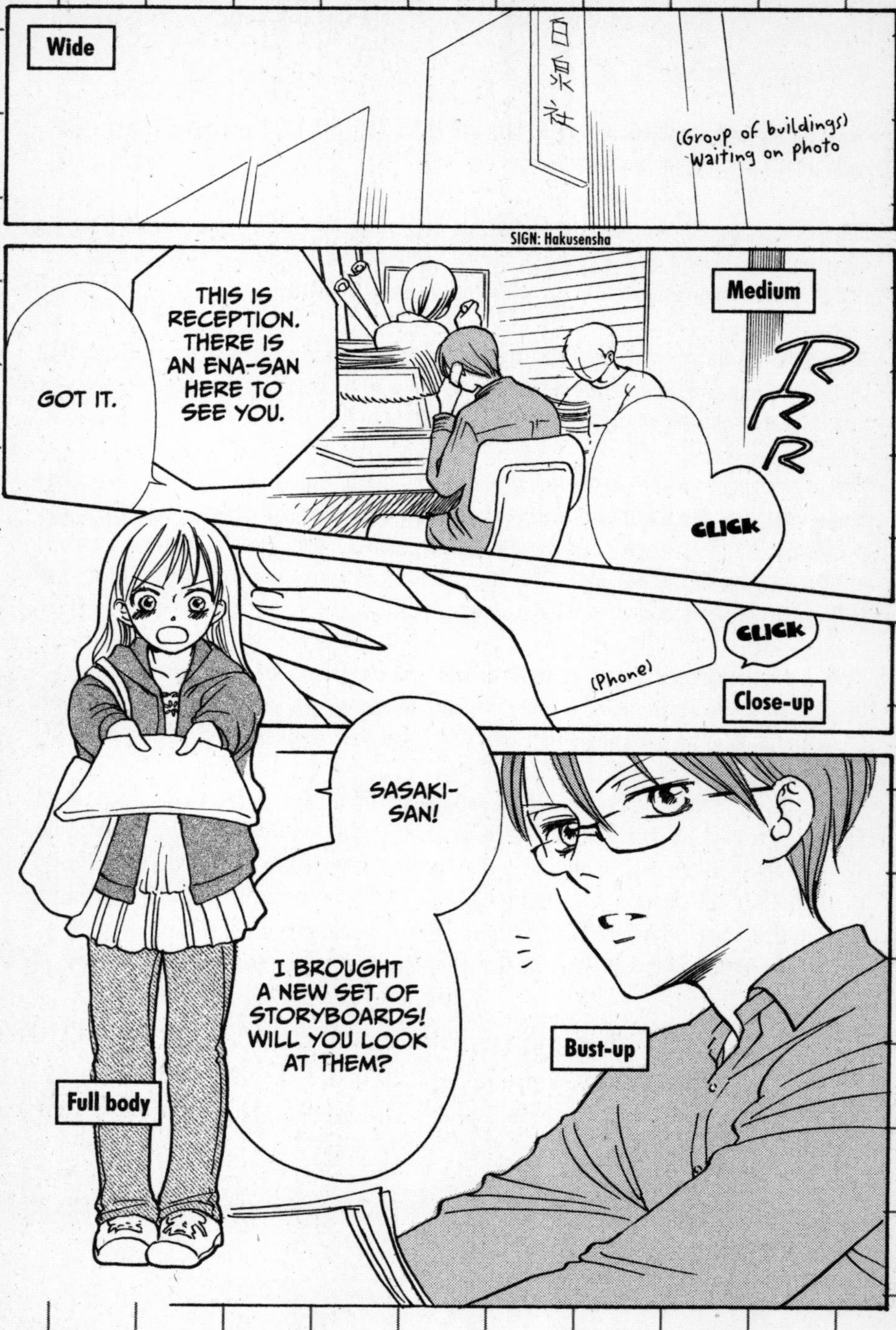

Wide
白泉社
(Group of buildings) waiting on photo
SIGN: Hakusensha
Medium
RRR
CLICK
THIS IS RECEPTION. THERE IS AN ENA-SAN HERE TO SEE YOU.
GOT IT.
CLICK
Close-up
(Phone)
Bust-up
SASAKI-SAN!
I BROUGHT A NEW SET OF STORYBOARDS! WILL YOU LOOK AT THEM?
Full body

Point of View

Next, we will talk about point of view, also called "camera angle." The exact same scene can vary greatly depending on where you put your camera.

Imagine a scene with two characters talking to each other. If you draw one of them from the other character's point of view, you can show the other character's reaction immediately. This is a great technique for getting across a character's true emotions.

If you put the camera somewhere that captures both of them from the side, you can draw the characters from a third party position. This makes your readers feel they are following the events from a calm, nonpartisan vantage point.

Now, try moving your camera angles up and down. A point of view even with the horizon line conveys stability, but it can be dull. Move your camera up and look down on the action. This is called a "bird's-eye view." Because the higher camera angle allows us to see the ground or floor, we can clearly see where the characters are in relation to each other. It's a good technique for when you want to include backgrounds.

Next, move your camera down to the floor and look up. This is called a "worm's-eye view." Because the angle of the shot is so dramatic, focused towards the sky or the ceiling, it's also a bit exhilarating. It's a good angle for expressing heightened emotion.

Various points of view and camera angle techniques are used in filmmaking as well. Akira Kurosawa, famous for such films as *The Seven Samurai*, directed dynamic staging with bird's-eye view far shots that vividly captured depth. Because he was able to show the setting in an expansive way, the character close-ups pop out even more in comparison. On the other hand, Yasujiro Ozu, famous for such films as *Tokyo Story*, reproduced mundane 1950s life through the use of a variety of low angles, with the camera fixed in a low position creating a sense of intimacy.

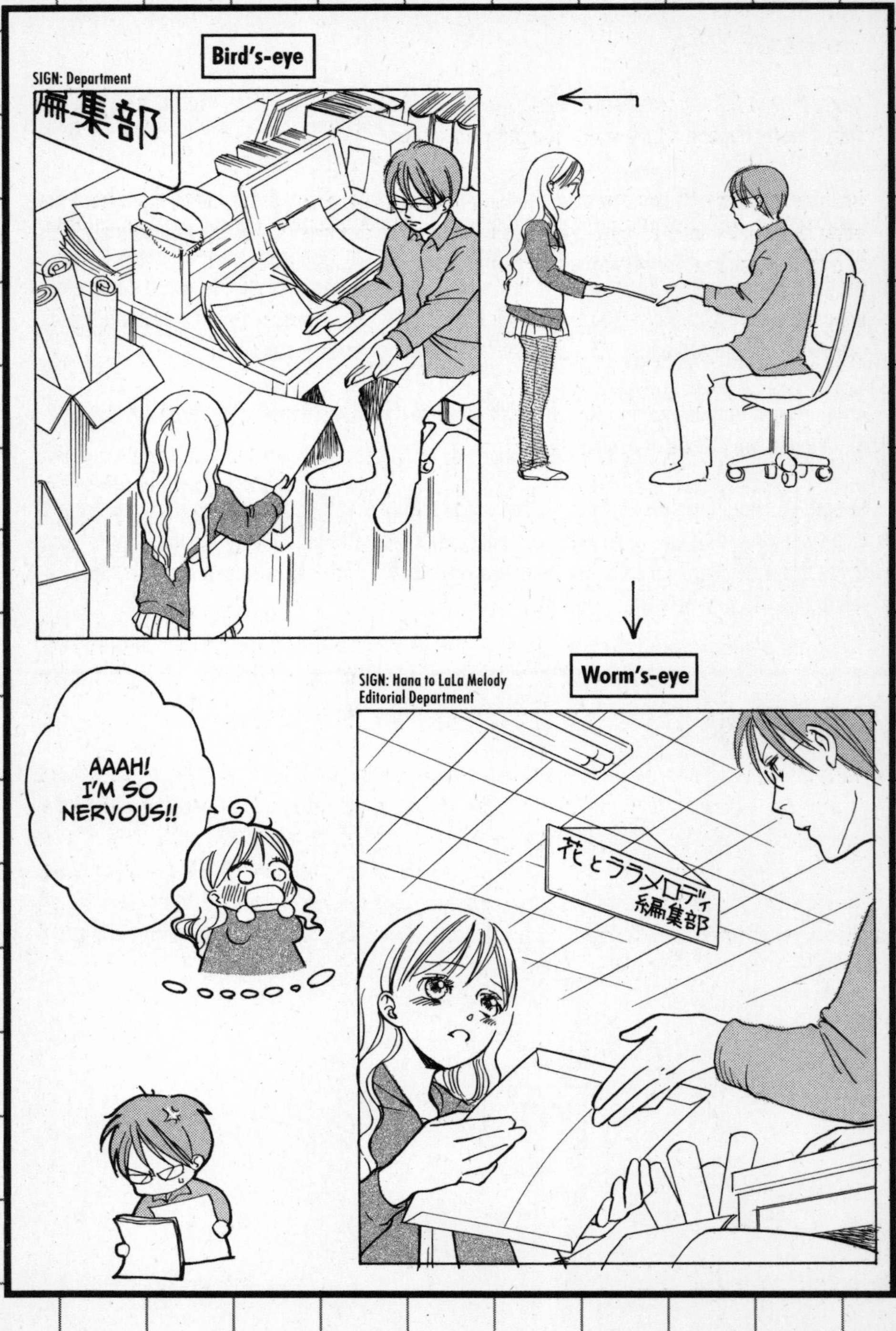
Bird's-eye
SIGN: Department
Worm's-eye
SIGN: Hana to LaLa Melody Editorial Department
花とララメロディ
編集部
AAAH! I'M SO NERVOUS!!

You don't even need dialogue to convey a character's emotions if your use of camera angles is strong enough.

For example, by placing a character at a diagonal within the panel, the composition becomes unstable, allowing you to express the character's anxiety, nervousness, or fear. When drawing the inside of a square room from a bird's-eye view, you can change the mood completely depending on if you place the room at an angle or not. In general, diagonals create unstable compositions and can express a character's anxiety...no words required!

Another tried-and-true composition trick (this time to create loneliness) is placing your character all alone in the middle of a wide shot.

Imagine a lone figure on a school rooftop under a blue sky. If you draw that character from a bird's-eye view, as if you're up in the air in a crane or on a helicopter, they'll appear lonely. But if you draw the character from a worm's-eye view, looking up at the character and sky beyond, the image will overflow with a sense of freedom.

Diagonal

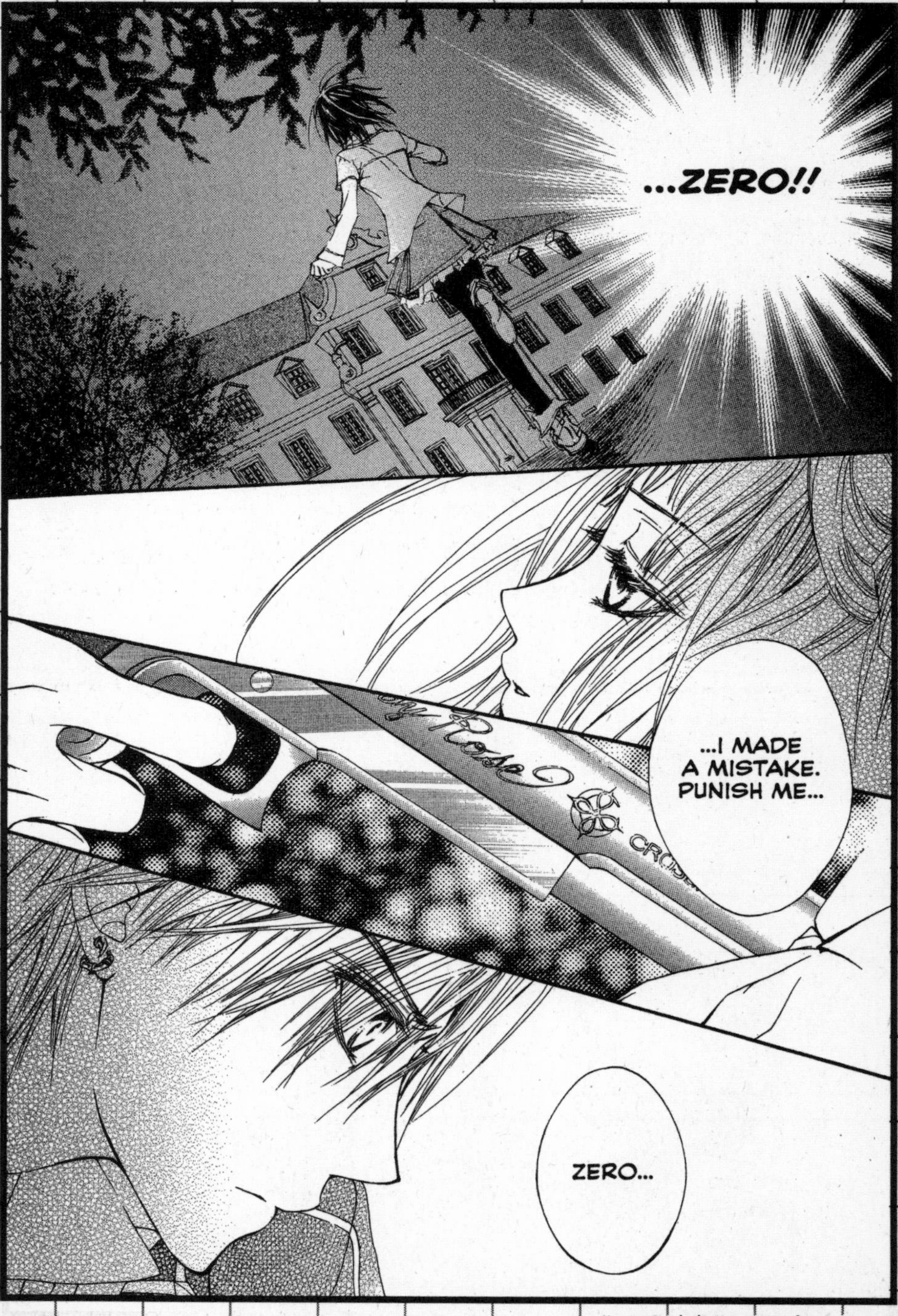
...ZERO!!
...I MADE A MISTAKE. PUNISH ME...
ZERO...

A lot of the tension in this scene is created by cutting between diagonal shots.

Vampire Knight (by Matsuri Hino, from *LaLa*)

Moving the Camera

Let's look at and compare cases where the camera moves from panel-to-panel, and cases where it doesn't.

When a scene isn't especially intense, and you want it to have a calm mood, you can deliberately keep the camera angle and vantage point steady. But when you want to illustrate scenes with a sense of action, moving the camera will help you pack more of a punch.

Fixing the camera is great for expressing a change or movement of things in the same scene, or expressing the passage of time. If we had to describe the fixed camera angle in one word, it would be "calm."

The more you move your camera around, the more intense the scene becomes. It will help you emphasize speed and emotions. However, manipulate the panel dimensions and orientations to follow suit otherwise you'll stymie your readers. Also, be careful not to move the camera around so much that your readers get dizzy.

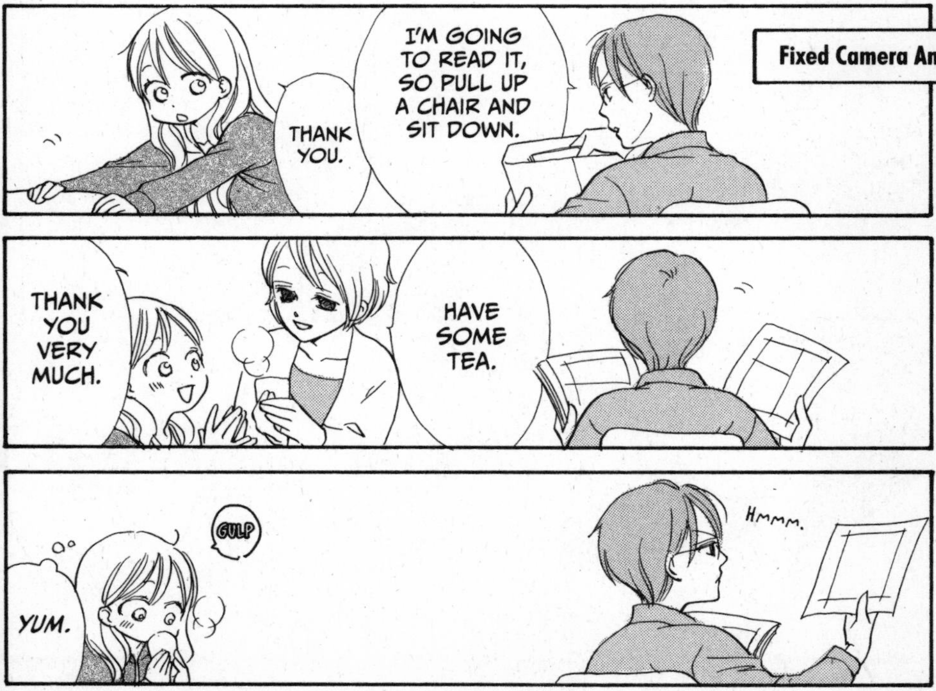
I'M GOING TO READ IT, SO PULL UP A CHAIR AND SIT DOWN.
THANK YOU.
HAVE SOME TEA.
THANK YOU VERY MUCH.
HMMM.
GULP
YUM.

Fixed Camera Angle

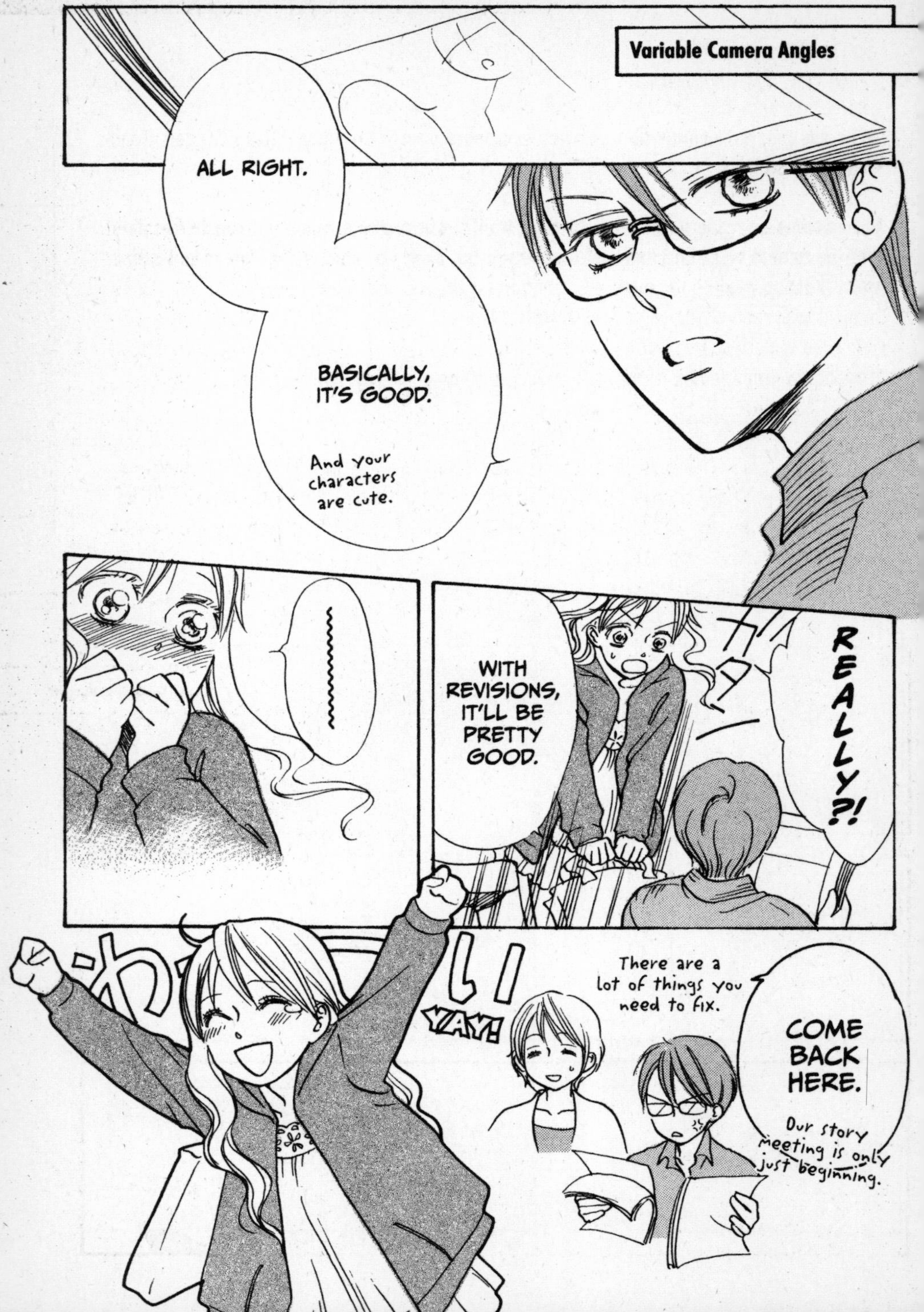
Variable Camera Angles
ALL RIGHT.
BASICALLY, IT'S GOOD.
And your characters are cute.
REALLY?!
WITH REVISIONS, IT'LL BE PRETTY GOOD.
COME BACK HERE.
Our story meeting is only just beginning.
There are a lot of things you need to fix.
YAY!

Cutaway

Alternating back and forth between shots of the same scene is called a "cutaway." It's a technique that amps up tension and creates a sense of urgency. It may also be called a "cut-back" or "reverse shot."

For example, imagine a scene in which shots of people crossing a rickety bridge are spliced with shots of the people anxiously watching them. Pretty dramatic, huh? A use of cutaway shots that you might be familiar with is that of a chase scene—shots of a person running are intercut with shots of the people chasing after them.

Once again, avoid reader confusion by using cutaway paneling in moderation.

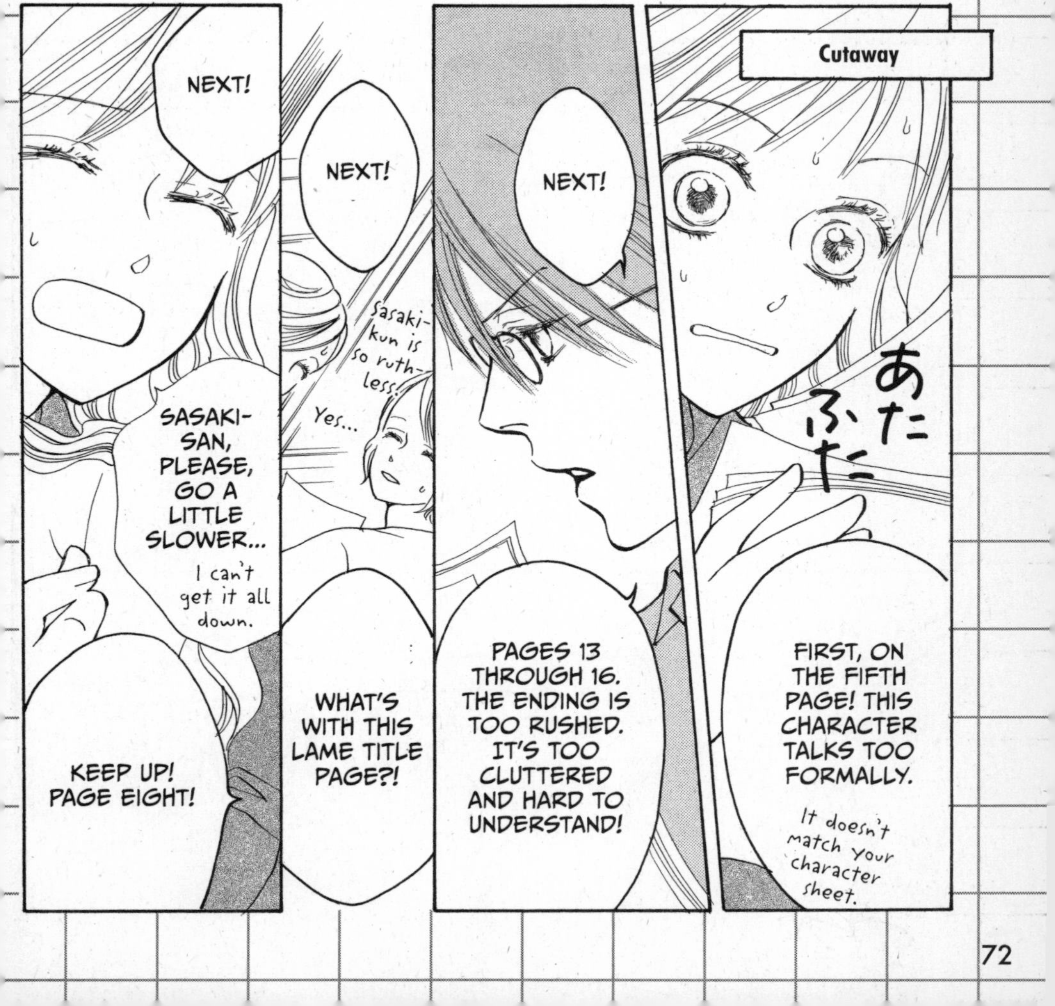
Cutaway
あたふた
FIRST, ON THE FIFTH PAGE! THIS CHARACTER TALKS TOO FORMALLY.
It doesn't match your character sheet.
NEXT!
PAGES 13 THROUGH 16. THE ENDING IS TOO RUSHED. IT'S TOO CLUTTERED AND HARD TO UNDERSTAND!
NEXT!
Sasaki-kun is so ruthless.
Yes...
WHAT'S WITH THIS LAME TITLE PAGE?!
NEXT!
SASAKI-SAN, PLEASE, GO A LITTLE SLOWER...
I can't get it all down.
KEEP UP! PAGE EIGHT!

Overlap

When two pictures interplay over each other in one big panel, it's called an "overlap." This kind of panel is used to show two things that are happening at the same time, or two things that happen in rapid succession.

For example, one way to use this technique is to draw a body shot of two people embracing, and overlap it with a close-up on the faces of one or both of them. You can use this to show what the characters are doing and how they feel at the same time, or to show things that are hard to see.

If you overlap two shots of the same size, the picture will get very strange. Variation in shot distance between the two overlapping panels is essential.

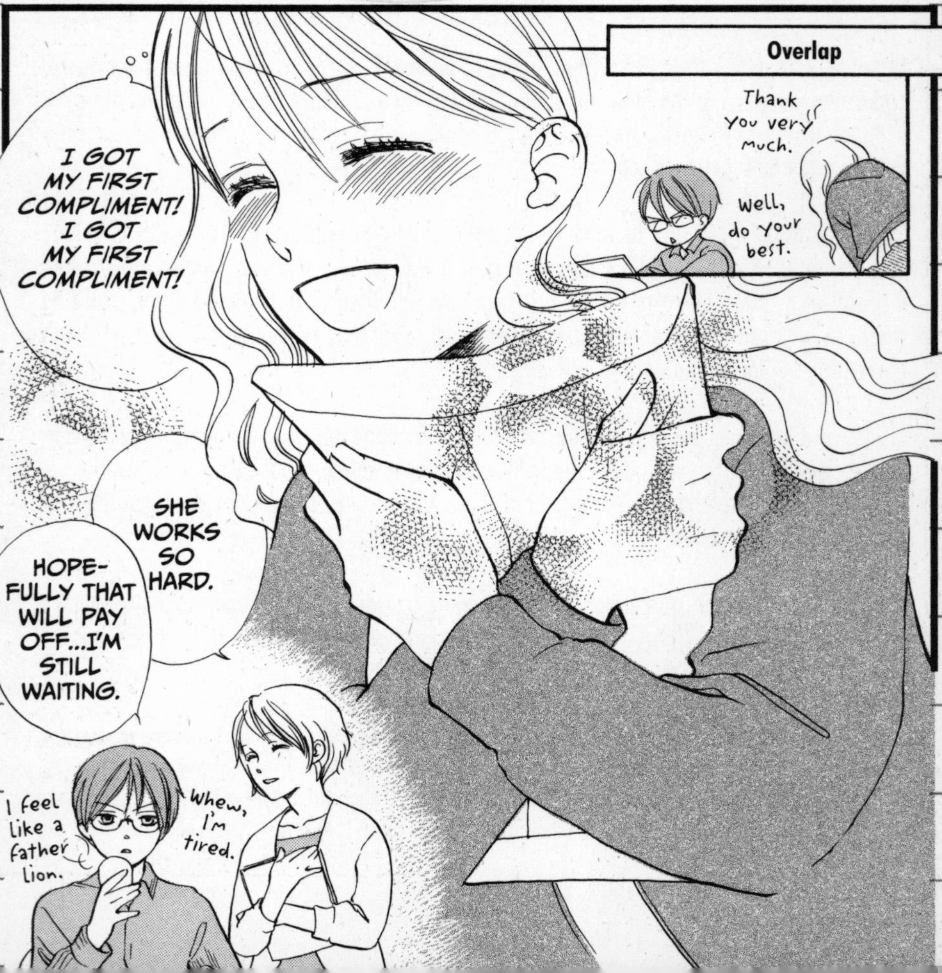

Overlap
Thank you very much.
Well, do your best.
I GOT MY FIRST COMPLIMENT! I GOT MY FIRST COMPLIMENT!
SHE WORKS SO HARD.
HOPE-FULLY THAT WILL PAY OFF...I'M STILL WAITING.
Whew, I'm tired.
I feel like a father lion.

Dialogue

Dialogue is generally created in the storyboard stage. Some artists begin their storyboards only after an intense scripting process, but keep in mind that storyboards are meant to be revised. The dialogue will often change based on your panel layout and the images it accompanies. The position, size, content, and line breaks inside word balloons, etc. will change based on your revisions.

Just like the order of panels on a page, the flow of time within a panel moves from top to bottom, right to left. Be careful when showing multiple people conversing inside one panel. There are times when you just won't be able to fit all your word balloons into the panel in an orderly fashion. Whatever you do, avoid work-arounds that confuse the readers, even the tiniest bit.

Lettering manga is a little like writing a line of poetry. Plan for your line breaks to come at opportune moments in the sentence. If you're breaking a sentence across two balloons, try to keep the text close to the image it's related to. Manga is best when the pictures and text enter the eye and are understood together.

Make it a habit of writing in ruby (furigana) for hard-to-read kanji, kanji with a unique reading, or kanji with multiple readings. It is also kind to your readers to include ruby when a character's name shows up for the first time. We will discuss this in detail at the penciling stage, but you must leave space between the lines, space that your furigana will need. Don't try to cram too much into a small balloon.

Inside word balloons, the regular rules of punctuation don't apply. That means no paragraph indents, and minimize punctuation marks like commas or colons/semi-colons. Additionally, we generally do not use text of varying sizes or fonts in the same balloon (obviously not the case for sound effects or asides).

Make sure your readers and editor can differentiate between thoughts and spoken words. It's common to mark the difference by using different fonts or italics and the style of balloon.

Editor's note for English-speakers:
Some of the notes above (and the ones later on lettering) are very specifically for Japanese text, so it may not make much sense unless you're familiar with the Japanese written language. However, the notes on punctuation and fonts are definitely transferable, and we've added some additional information in the later section to make it more useful to English-speakers.

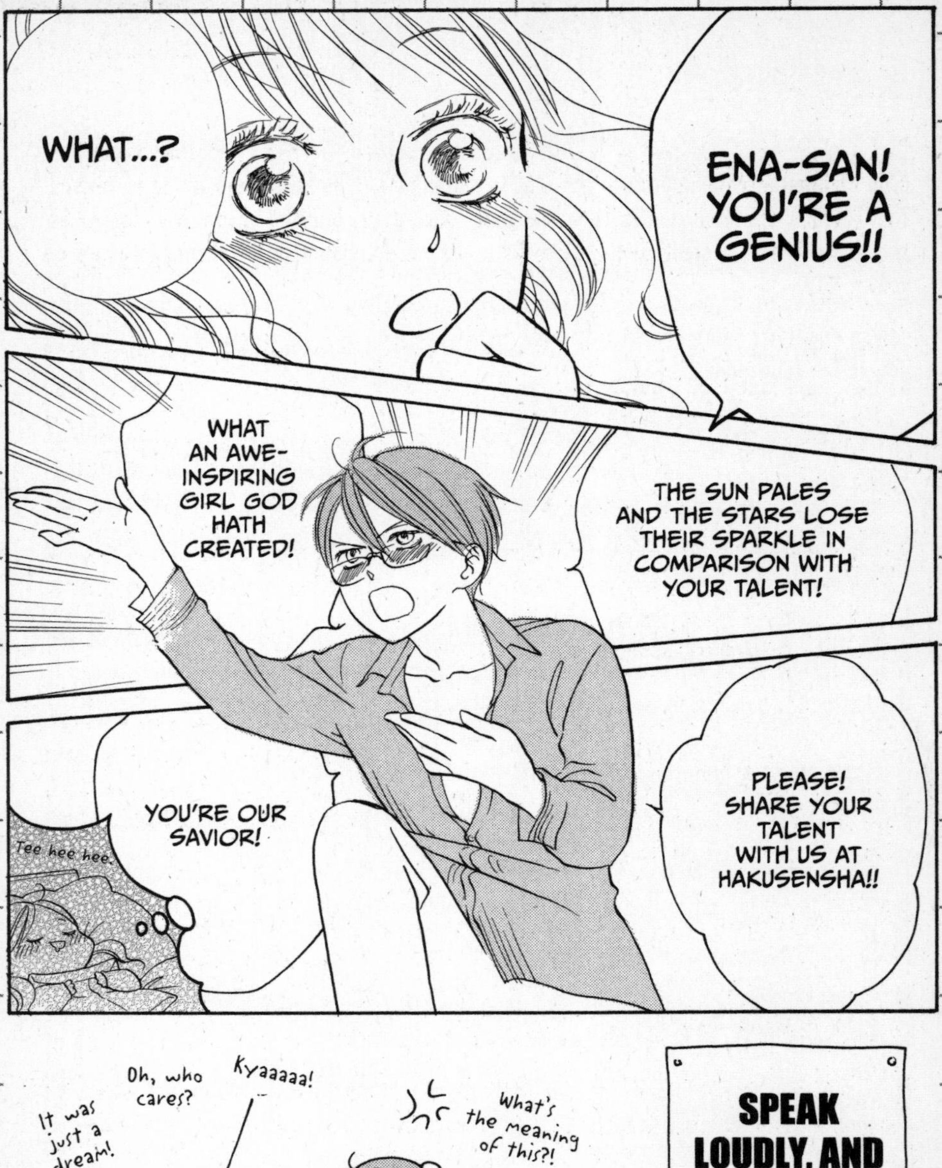

ENA-SAN! YOU'RE A GENIUS!!
WHAT...?
THE SUN PALES AND THE STARS LOSE THEIR SPARKLE IN COMPARISON WITH YOUR TALENT!
WHAT AN AWE-INSPIRING GIRL GOD HATH CREATED!
PLEASE! SHARE YOUR TALENT WITH US AT HAKUSENSHA!!
YOU'RE OUR SAVIOR!
Tee hee hee.
SPEAK LOUDLY, AND REGRET NOTHING
What's the meaning of this?!
Kyaaaaa!
Oh, who cares?
It was just a dream!

Scene Changes

As your story progresses, you will need to change scenes, show the passage of time, or flash back to the past. Fortunately, there's already a set of techniques in existence for signaling each of those events.

Beginners may make the mistake of being inconsistent or incorrect in their implementation of these techniques. Remember, as the artist, you already know what's happening in your story, so you might not notice problems yourself. When checking over your storyboards, try putting yourself in your readers' shoes.

When changing scenes, symbolize the shift in setting by starting out the new scene with an establishing shot. As already described, an establishing shot is generally a long shot. Alternately, if your story takes place in a school, another technique you can use is an establishing shot that's a close-up of a placard or sign, like "Art Room"—something that indicates where the characters are. (ouran: Third music room)

Some ways to express the passage of time include placing a small panel between scenes, or fading out the scene with panels that slowly get smaller and smaller. But when it comes to illustrating the new time or season, you'll still need an establishing shot.

It is possible to express these things with narration, but as they say, a picture is worth a thousand words.

Flashback scenes are the ones that require the most care. If a whole page is a flashback, use extremes to set the past off from the present, such as making the area outside the panels black.

If a flashback occurs in the middle of a page, set the flashback panels off by making their borders super thick, or by double-bordering them with thick or narrow lines. Do as much as you can to show that the clothing and scenery are different. You might even want to change the shape of the word balloons.

If your flashback panel should happen to overlap a panel taking place in the present, fade out the image that's taking place in the past. You will probably also want to fade out any text that takes place in the past, too. The whole flashback image will look as if it is shrouded in fog. Use this fade-out technique, or some of the other mentioned techniques, to make the time shift clear to the readers.

Flashback Scenes

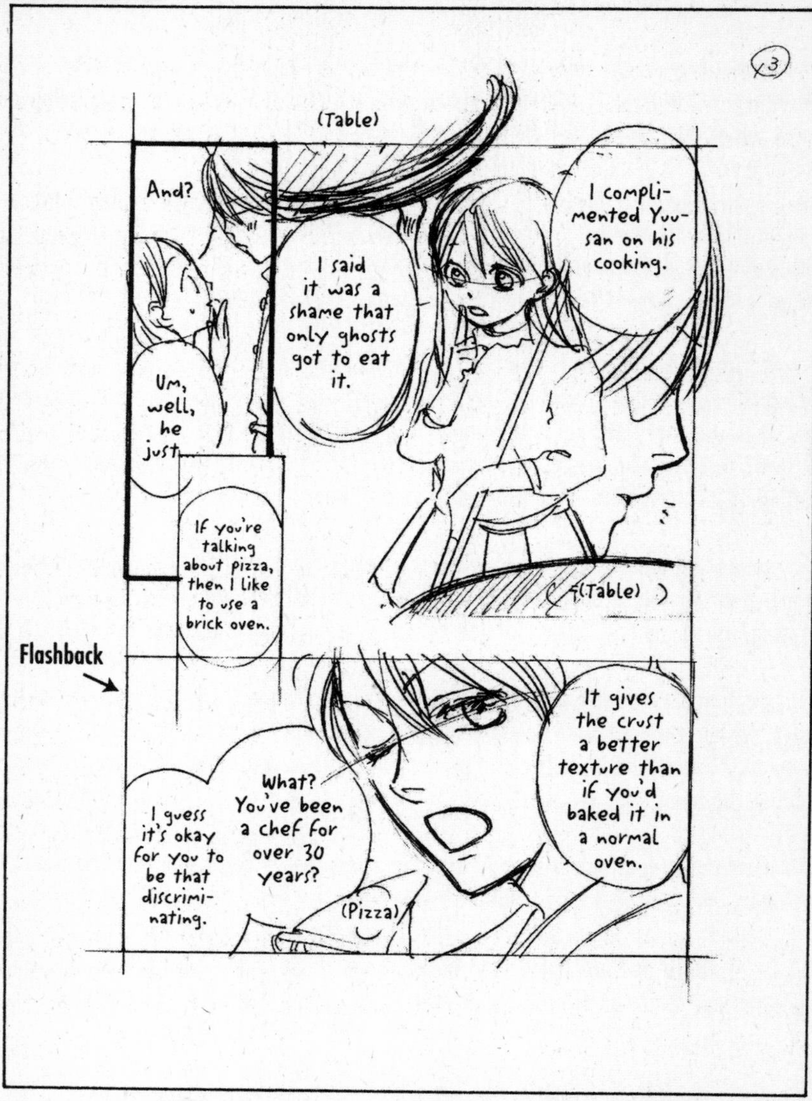
3
(Table)
I compli-mented Yuu-san on his cooking.
I said it was a shame that only ghosts got to eat it.
And?
Um, well, he just...
If you're talking about pizza, then I like to use a brick oven.
(Table)
Flashback
It gives the crust a better texture than if you'd baked it in a normal oven.
What? You've been a chef for over 30 years?
I guess it's okay for you to be that discrimi-nating.
(Pizza)

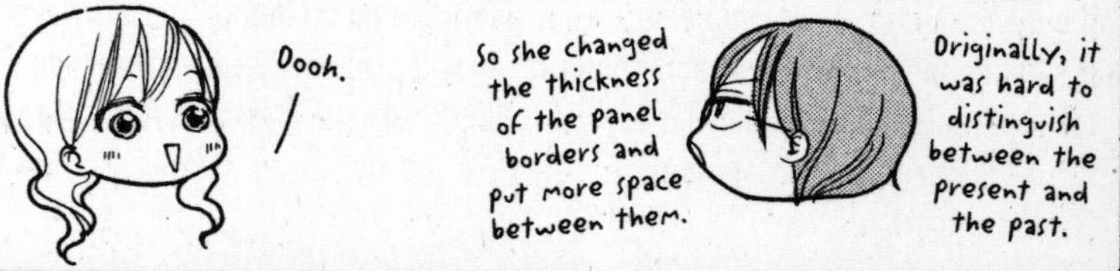
Originally, it was hard to distinguish between the present and the past.
So she changed the thickness of the panel borders and put more space between them.
Oooh.

Revising Your Storyboards

Now that you've done all your storyboards, you're just beginning. Sure, you'd love to start drawing for real as soon as possible, but revisions are an essential part of the storyboarding process. You'll want to read over them yourself, of course, and if possible, get someone else to read them and give you their opinions.

We all have blinders about our own work. It's not unusual to create a manga that makes perfect sense to you, but leaves your friends with questions. Be your own editor first, but also listen to what your friends have to say, and most importantly, revise according to their comments.

The best trick for being able to approach your work with cool, calm judgment is to put some time between finishing and reading. Read your storyboards as if you're someone who doesn't know where the story will go. Is there anything that is difficult to understand? Is it slow or awkward? Can you empathize with the characters? Is the climax exciting? And more than anything, is it entertaining? That is the most important question.

When you ask for others' opinions, make sure you ask them whether or not they understood it rather than whether or not they liked it. Even if they tell you something was only "sort of confusing," go ahead and revise that part so that it becomes perfectly clear to your readers.

Perhaps even more crucially, don't let the criticism discourage you. Confront your flaws! If you discover obvious compositional flaws or inadequacies in your events or characters, redraw your storyboards. The difference between a professional manga artist and an aspiring one is how hard they can be on their own work.

If the flaws are widespread, you may have to redraw every page. You may even feel that you're making your pages worse. But the key to improvement is always to keep drawing!

Don't be afraid to pat yourself on the back, either. If you did a good job on this or that, congratulations! Every bit of praise is welcome while you're revising your storyboards.

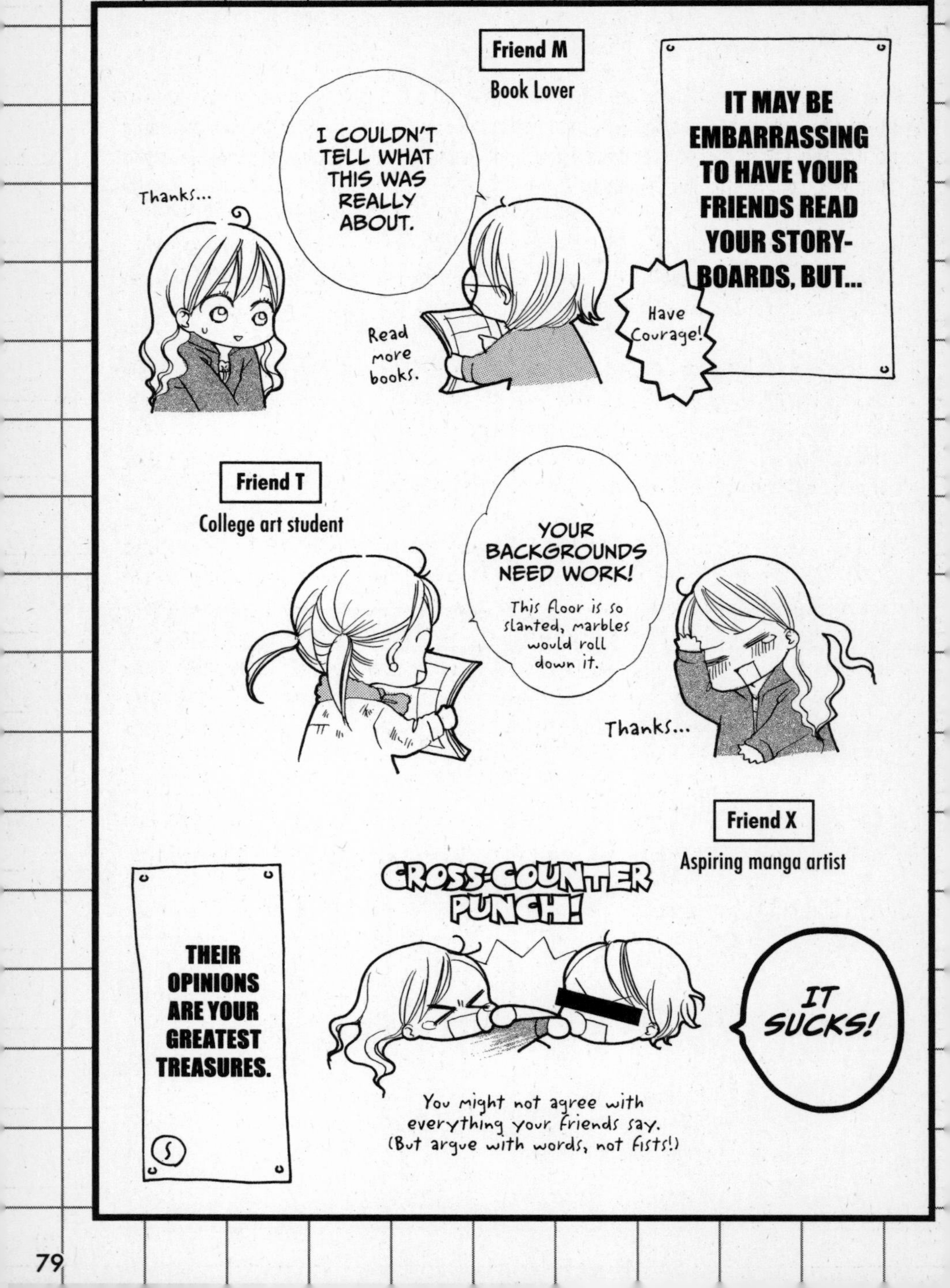

IT MAY BE EMBARRASSING TO HAVE YOUR FRIENDS READ YOUR STORY-BOARDS, BUT...
Friend M
Book Lover
Have Courage!
I COULDN'T TELL WHAT THIS WAS REALLY ABOUT.
Read more books.
Thanks...
Friend T
College art student
Thanks...
YOUR BACKGROUNDS NEED WORK!
This floor is so slanted, marbles would roll down it.
Friend X
Aspiring manga artist
IT SUCKS!
CROSS-COUNTER PUNCH!
You might not agree with everything your friends say. (But argue with words, not fists!)
THEIR OPINIONS ARE YOUR GREATEST TREASURES.

2
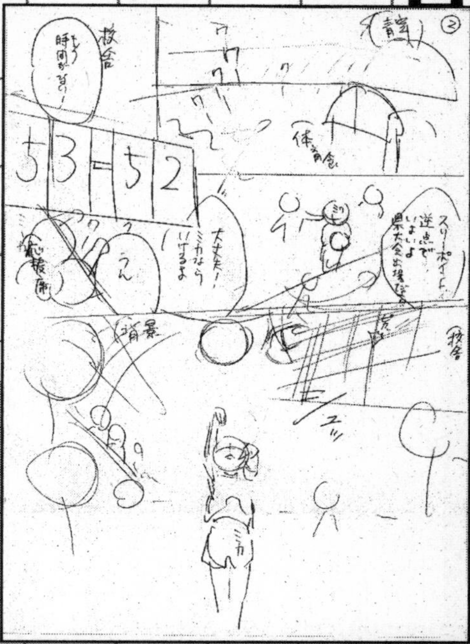
青空
校舎
もう時間がない!
53-52
体育館
スリーポイント逆点でいいよ 県大会出場だ!
大丈夫! ミカならいけるよ
うん
応援席
背景
校舎
シュッ
ミカ

3
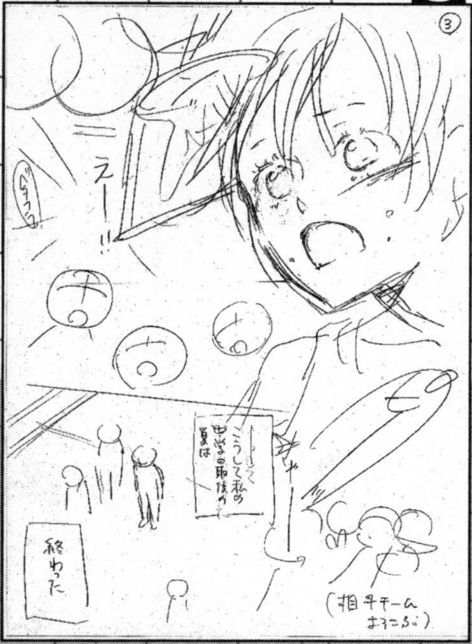
ズー!!
こうして私の中学最後の夏は
終わった
(相手チーム)

4
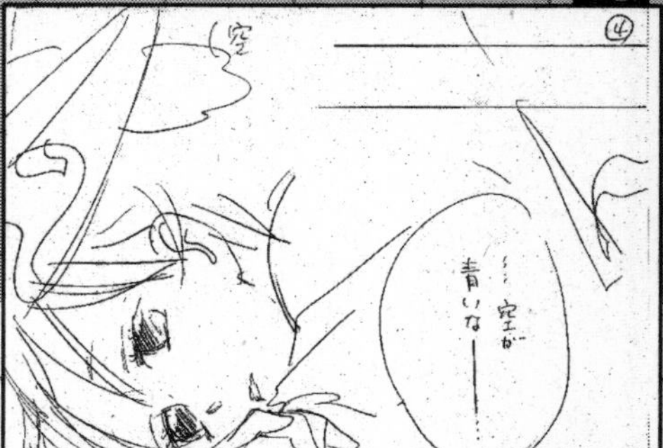
空
……空が青いな――…
(皆 受験勉強中)
空って何で青いんだっけ
ミカ
先生
「長野! お前バスケで高校推薦とれるかもしれないぞ!」
「え…」
「高校でもお前の活躍を期待してるからな!」
「…はい」
回想
バスケのやりかたなんて忘れちゃったよ――…

5
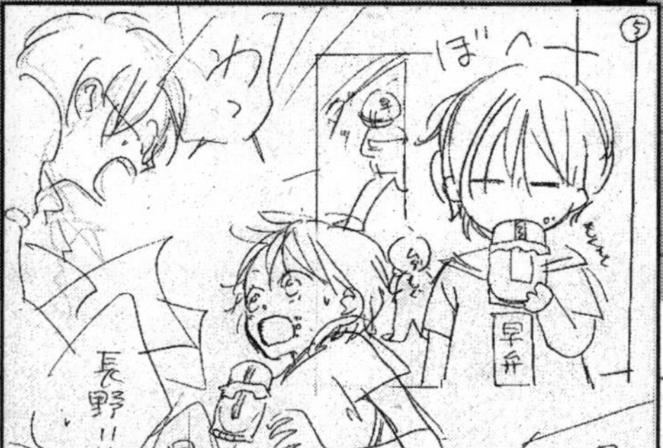
ぼへー
早弁
長野!!
女子が廊下で早弁なんかしてんなよー
飛び出てくるアンタがわるいんでしょー

6

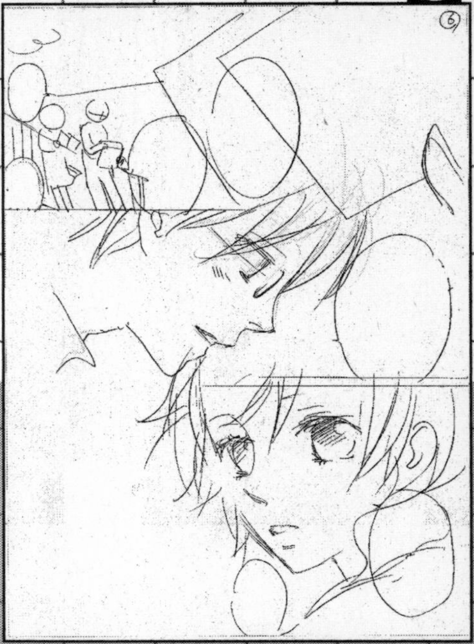

7

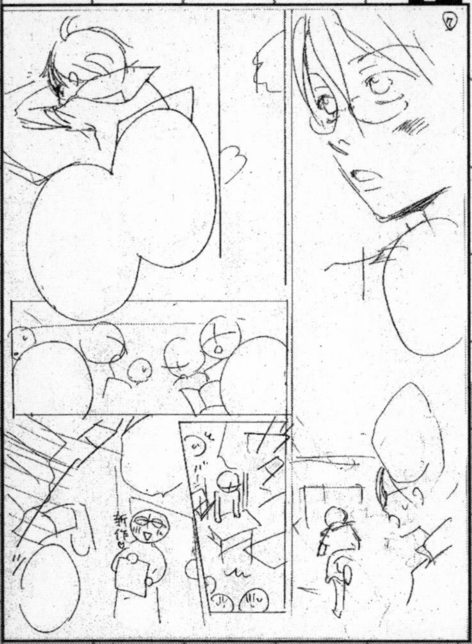

8

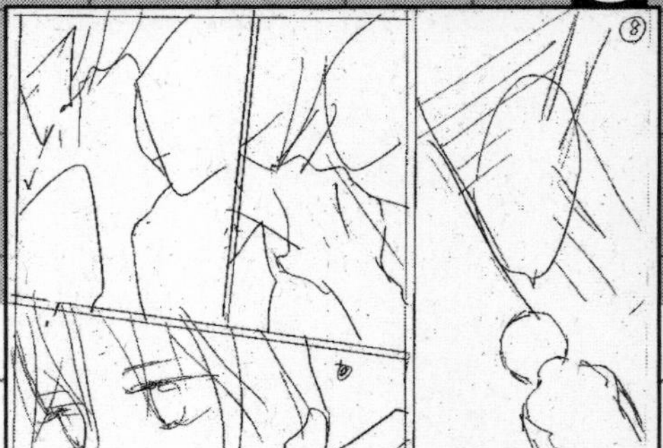

9

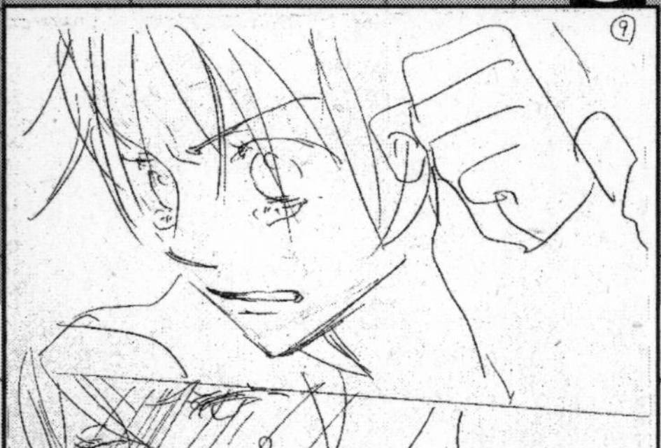

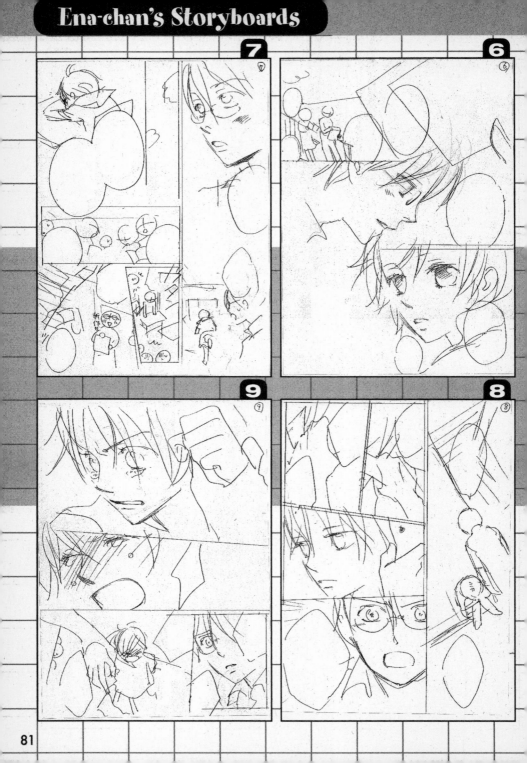

10

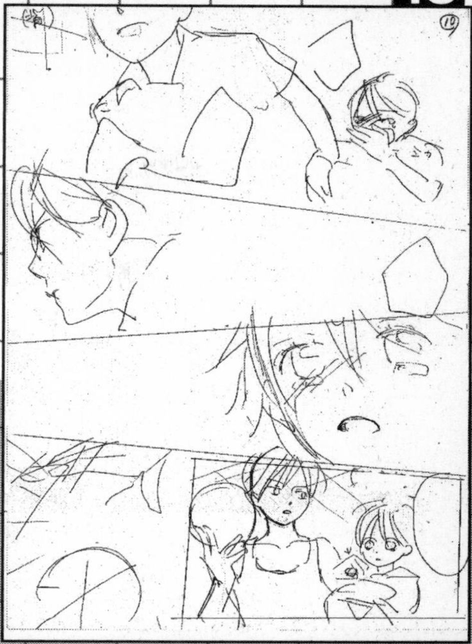

11

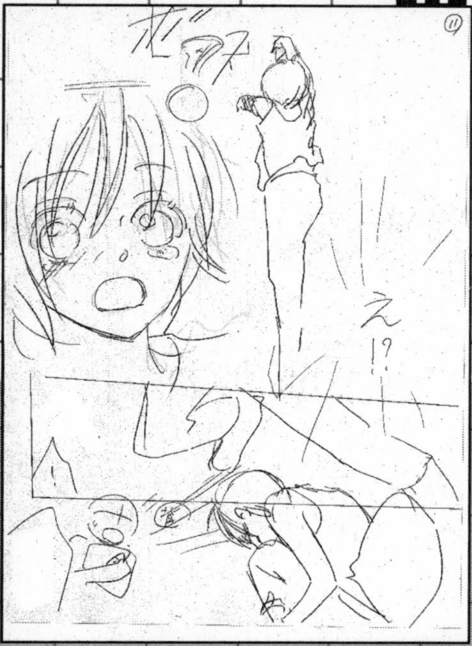
え
!?

12

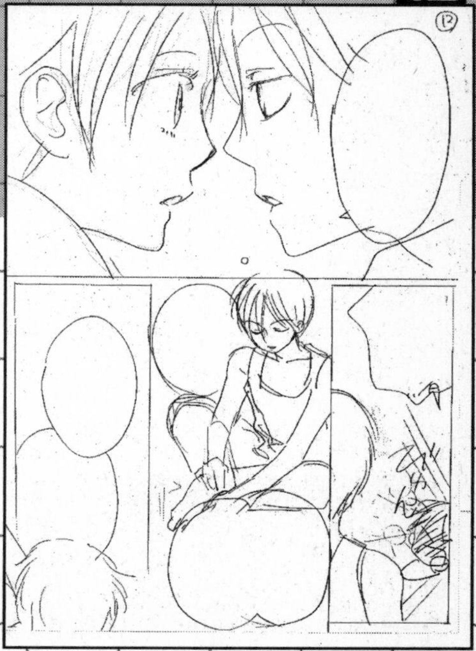

13

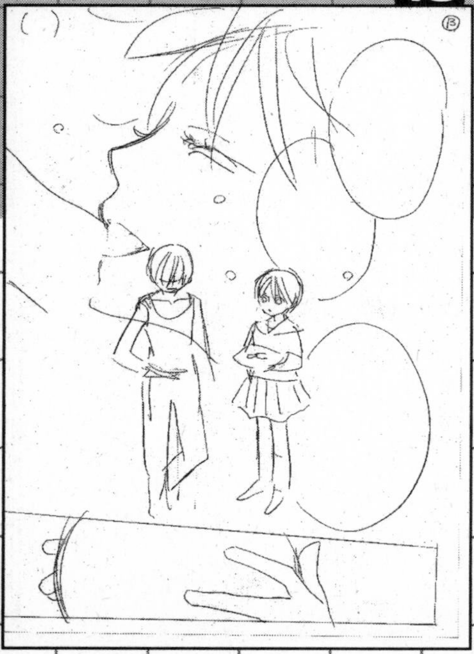

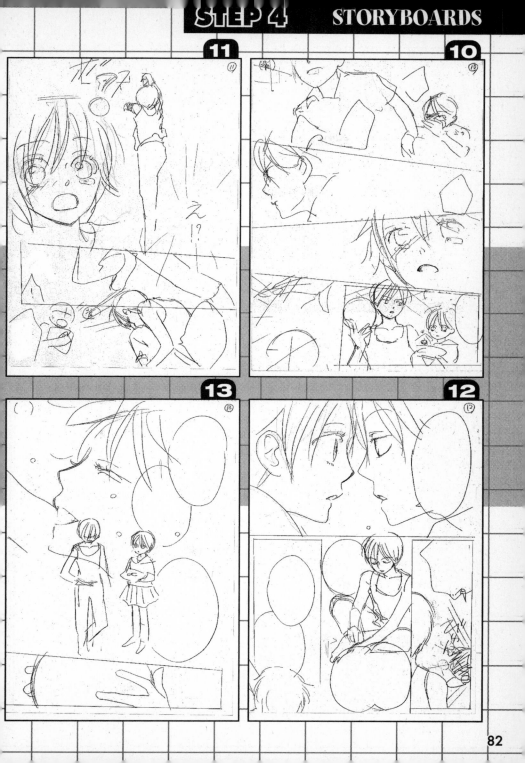

Ena-chan's Storyboards

14

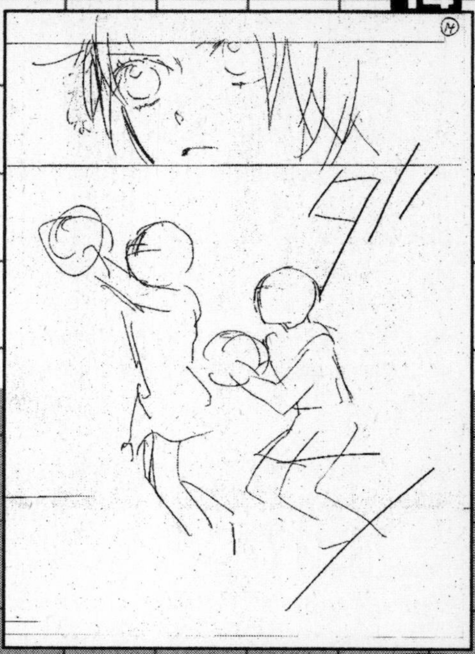

15

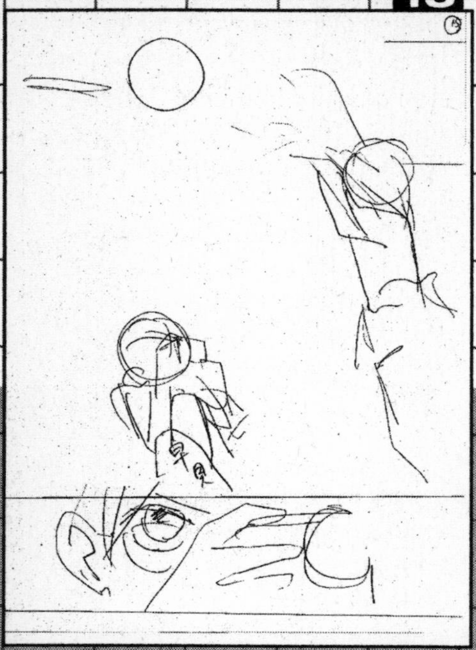

16

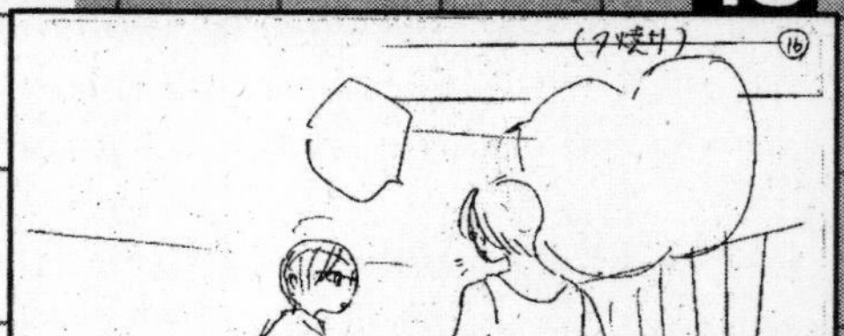

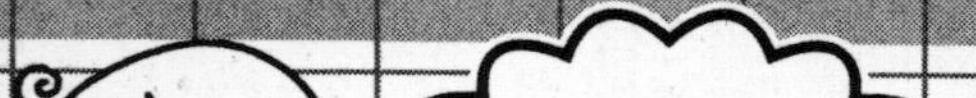
I FINALLY FINISHED THE STORYBOARDS FOR MY MANGA! I WANNA GET TO INKING RIGHT NOW!
WHAT ARE YOU TALKING ABOUT?! FIRST YOU BETTER REVIEW AND REVISE YOUR STORYBOARDS UNTIL THEY WORK!

Compare these with the finished manga starting on page 131 to see how much she revised her storyboards!

Character Designs

Okay, now that you've finished your storyboards, it's time to begin on the pencils. This is the first time you'll be doing refined drawings. Everything that you've conceptualized and mapped out up to this point will now take its final shape. So, you'll need to finalize your designs, too.

Look over your storyboards and identify what kinds of hair, clothes and objects you'll need to draw frequently. Before you start penciling, you want to have a lot of practice drawing these key elements. The amount of effort you invest in the characters, setting and objects will make the difference between your work coming off as amateurish or looking professional. We see too many manga that come off half-hearted because the artist drew her pencils all out of her head. ✦ *life drawing is a must* ✓

Also, something very important to keep in mind is that if you reference photos for select objects, those parts can come off as strangely realistic, and they might not match your art style. Tweak those items to the same extent that you tweak your characters, and your work will become cohesive. Remember, manga art is the result of stylization. It can look strange when the people are simplified considerably, but their bicycle, dog, or cat looks realistic.

Look at professional manga to see what's been omitted and what's been exaggerated in the designs of clothing and objects. The good news is that once you've hit upon a pattern of stylizations, your future assistants will have a clear idea of how to translate new objects and characters into your style. The more that you don't have to think about each time, the better!

Don't forget that expressions are a part of your characters. While you're practicing hair, clothing and objects, also practice the expressions that you know your character will wear. Don't try to take a shortcut and go straight into the real thing without practice!

Character Design

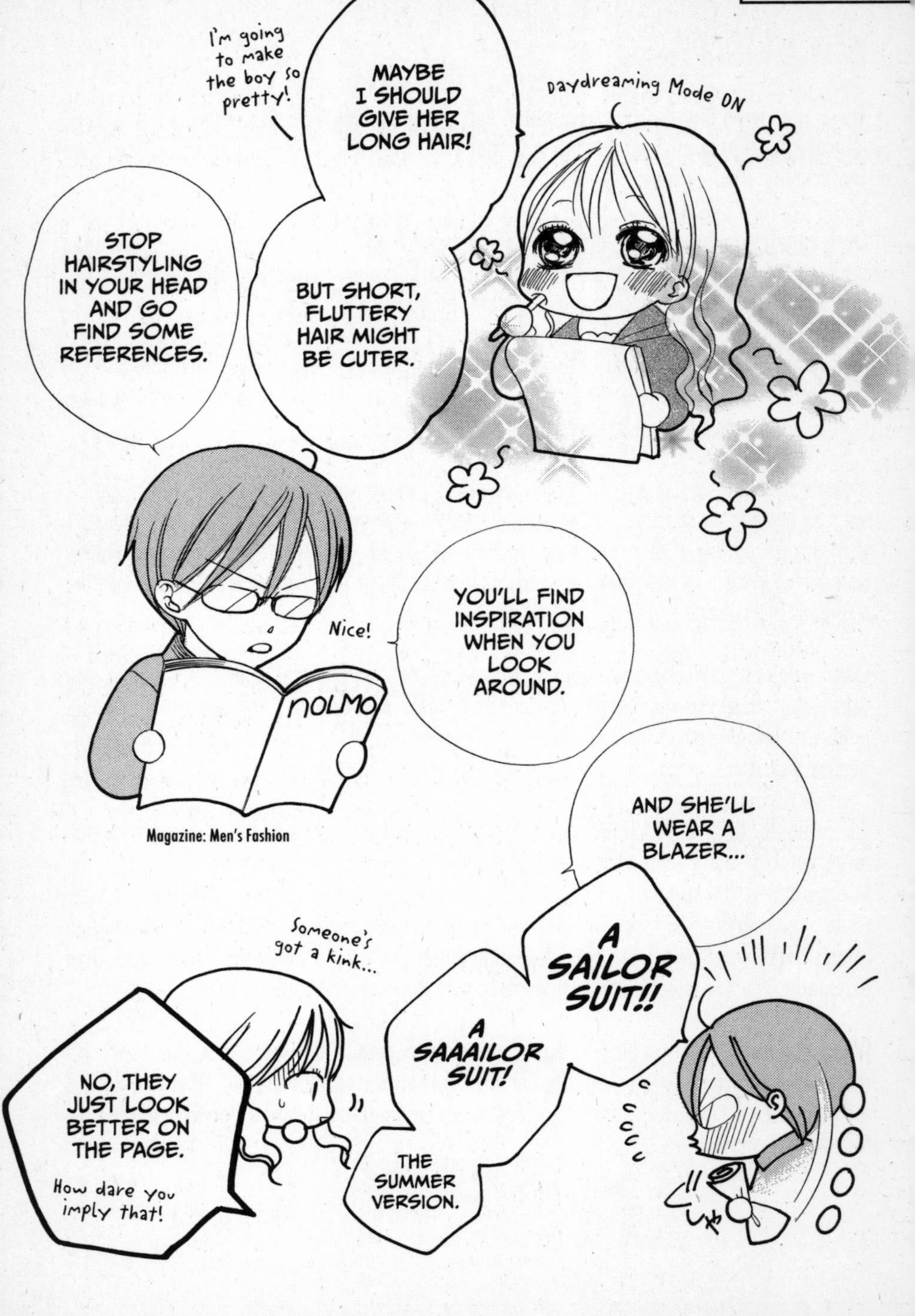
Daydreaming Mode ON
MAYBE I SHOULD GIVE HER LONG HAIR!
I'm going to make the boy so pretty!
BUT SHORT, FLUTTERY HAIR MIGHT BE CUTER.
STOP HAIRSTYLING IN YOUR HEAD AND GO FIND SOME REFERENCES.
YOU'LL FIND INSPIRATION WHEN YOU LOOK AROUND.
Nice!
NOLMO
Magazine: Men's Fashion
AND SHE'LL WEAR A BLAZER...
A SAILOR SUIT!!
A SAAAILOR SUIT!
THE SUMMER VERSION.
Someone's got a kink...
NO, THEY JUST LOOK BETTER ON THE PAGE.
How dare you imply that!

Background Designs

There is no need to draw a background in every single panel. Actually, having a background in every panel only ends up making your manga so busy that it's hard to read and therefore confusing to your readers.

Look over your storyboards and make the final call about which panels will really need backgrounds. Knowing which panels will need backgrounds before you start penciling will prevent you from wasting effort drawing stuff you don't need.

As a general rule, it's enough to draw one background per scene change, and only enough background during a scene to clarify what the main character is doing. About one or two panels with backgrounds per page is good.

Make a habit of basing your backgrounds off of pictures you took yourself. You might be tired of hearing us say this, but copying straight out of magazines or off of other people's photos is plagiarism. If there's no way around it, then add your own original arrangements to an existing picture by changing the angle or leaving things out. Tracing scenes from existing manga is inexcusable. *use own refrences/photos/stetches*

When you're composing your panels, remember that perspective applies to people, too (remember those skeleton frame drawings you did?). The characters and background should adhere to the same perspective and fit together realistically. If the characters' and backgrounds' perspectives don't match, the drawing will look unnatural and awkward.

For example, to give your readers the impression that a hand is reaching out toward the foreground, you'll be drawing that hand with exaggerated or forced perspective. If the background in that scene doesn't share the same exaggerated perspective, then the character could appear to float and they will look unnatural. You can work around this issue by using an effects background, but if you have determined that you need an accurate background, then exaggerate the background perspective along with the character's hand.

When composing and handling backgrounds, make decisions that serve your characters. No matter how extraordinary your background is, if it buries your characters, then it will have the opposite effect of what you're going for. Always manipulate the background to make your characters stand out.

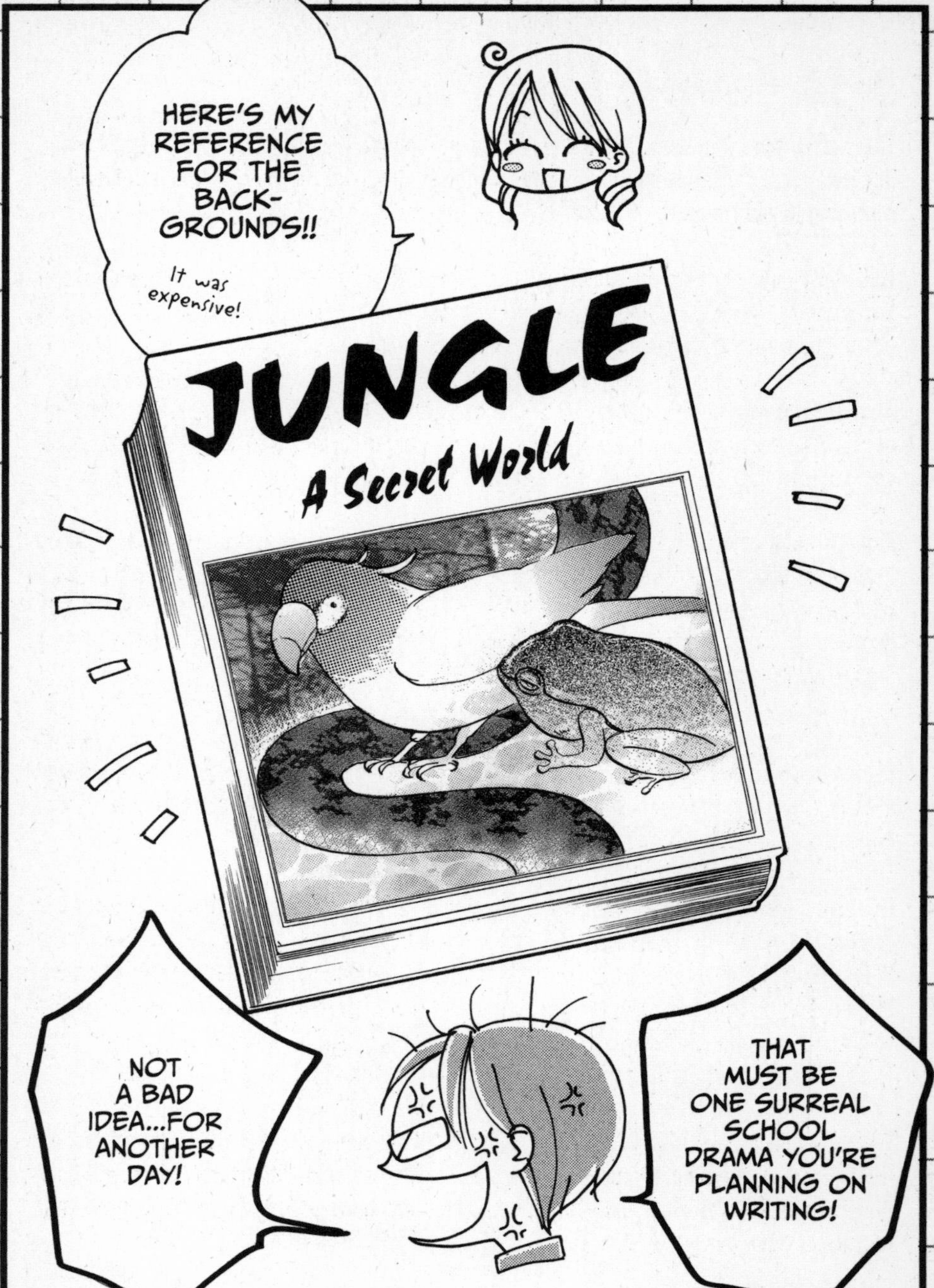
HERE'S MY REFERENCE FOR THE BACK-GROUNDS!!
It was expensive!
JUNGLE
A Secret World
THAT MUST BE ONE SURREAL SCHOOL DRAMA YOU'RE PLANNING ON WRITING!
NOT A BAD IDEA...FOR ANOTHER DAY!

Character Designs

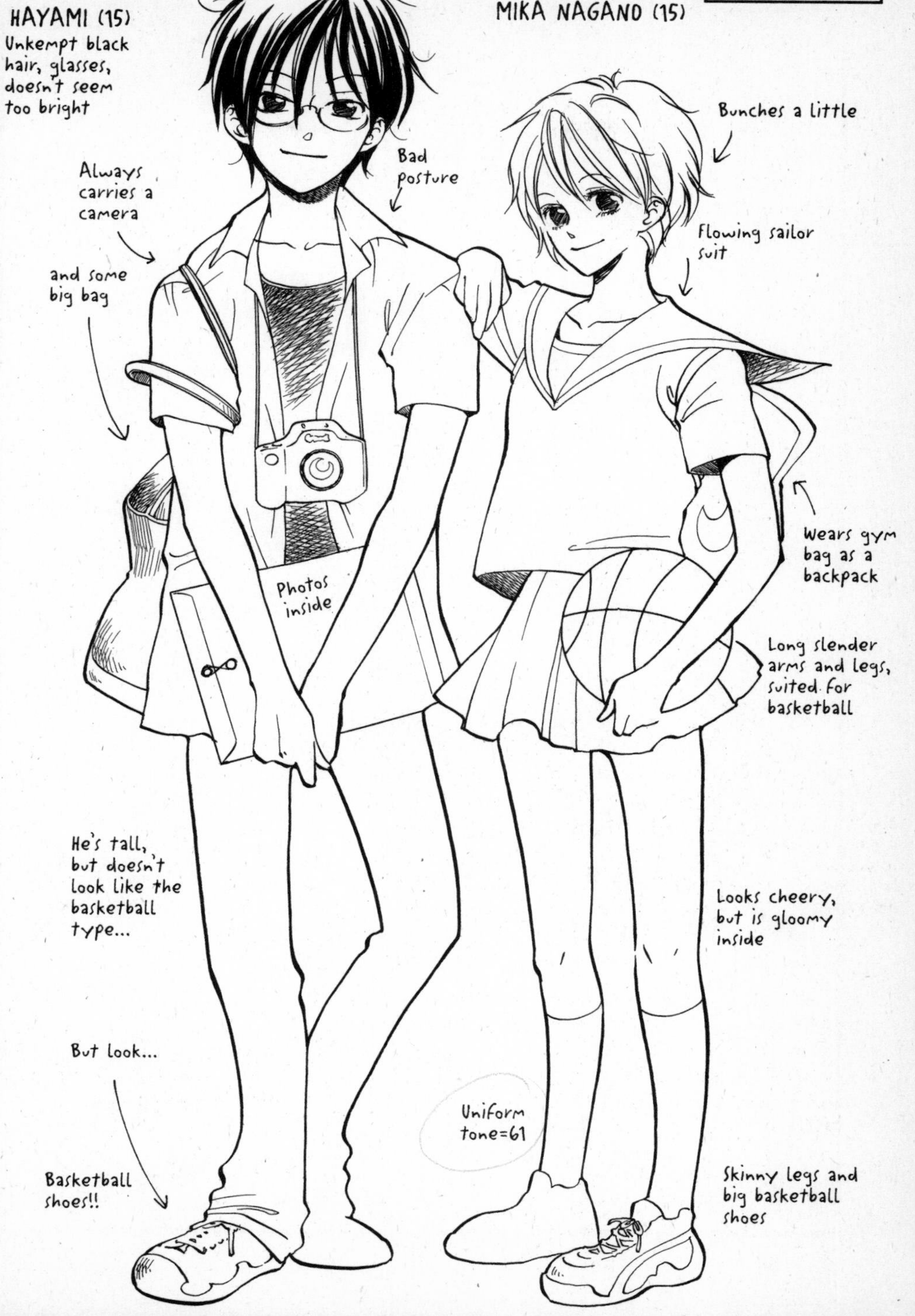
HAYAMI (15)
Unkempt black hair, glasses, doesn't seem too bright
Always carries a camera
and some big bag
Bad posture
Photos inside
He's tall, but doesn't look like the basketball type...
But look...
Basketball shoes!!
MIKA NAGANO (15)
Bunches a little
Flowing sailor suit
Wears gym bag as a backpack
Long slender arms and legs, suited for basketball
Looks cheery, but is gloomy inside
Uniform tone=61
Skinny legs and big basketball shoes

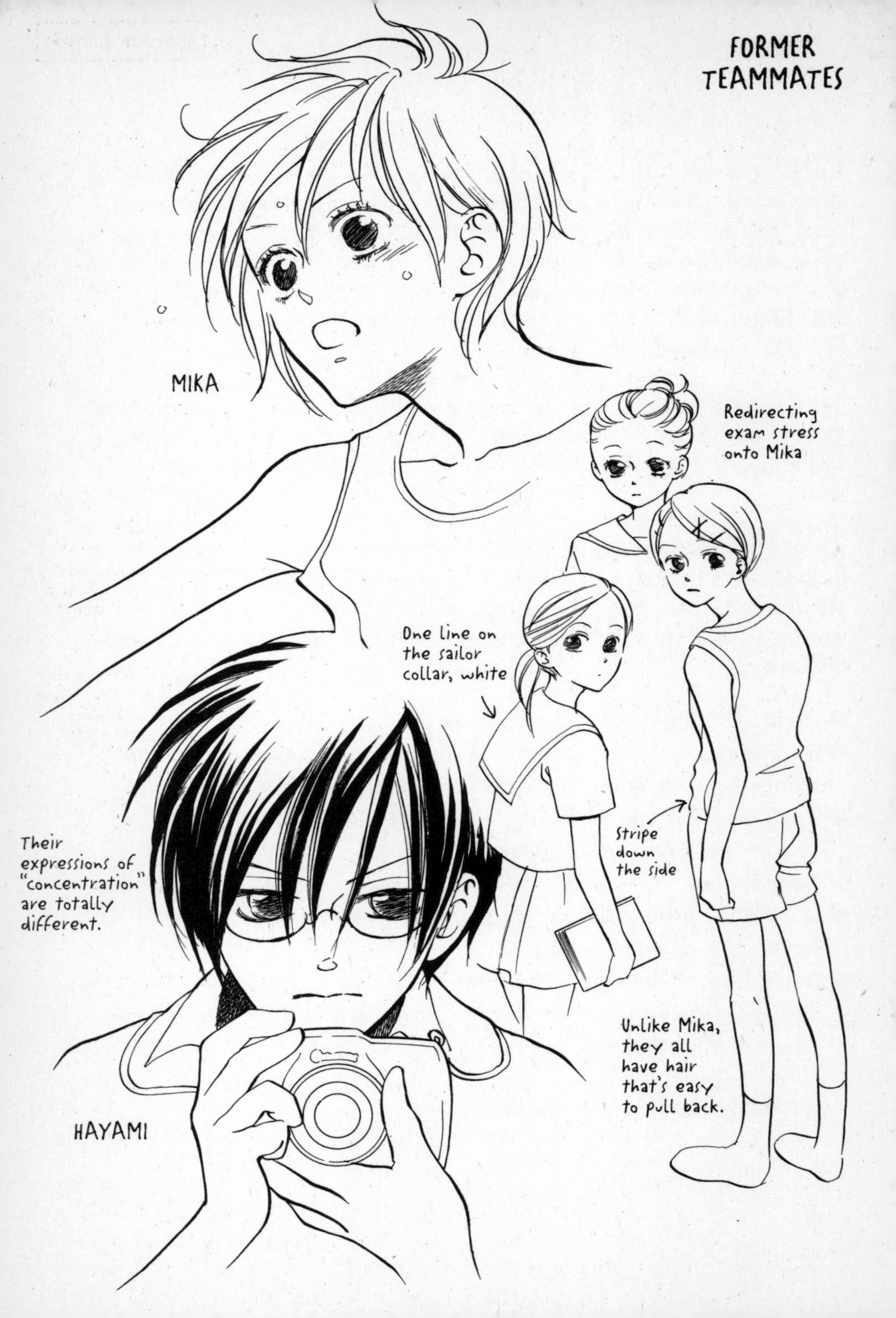
FORMER TEAMMATES
MIKA
Redirecting exam stress onto Mika
One line on the sailor collar, white
Stripe down the side
Their expressions of "concentration" are totally different.
Unlike Mika, they all have hair that's easy to pull back.
HAYAMI

Gutters and Trim

Finally, it's time to get out the manga paper! You figured out your story and paneling in the storyboard stage. Now, with a pencil, you'll draw out your manga in detail. This process is called "penciling." We went over this on page six, but it will be helpful for beginners to use size B4 manga paper made for manga contest submissions. For those of you who are particular about paper quality and want to make your own manga paper, draw a basic grid-line box that's 180mm tall and 270mm wide to mark the safe zone (see left). Anything beyond these lines risks being trimmed off at the printer.

On the outside of these lines, draw new lines, one 30mm above and below, and 30mm toward the front edge (the side the book opens on). Draw another line 20mm toward the gutter (the book binding). These are the "trim edges." Anything beyond these lines will be cut off at the printer.

It may be a surprise to some aspiring manga artists to hear that at least 24mm of your size B4 page is cut off at the printer. The reason we recommend drawing a "safe zone" box at 180x270mm is because there may be misalignments at the printer that cause more or less of any given page to be trimmed off. In addition to all of that, here's a list of measurement do's and don'ts:

● Do fit all of the text in your balloons inside the safe zone.
● Do fit important pictures like faces and hand-written text you don't want cut off no more than 20mm outside the safe zone.
● Don't risk it around the gutter. Never put text there, and remember that images deep in the gutter will disappear once the book is bound.
● Don't draw panel borders that align with the trim edges or in misleading or weird positions.
● Don't draw all the way to the edge of the paper. This is because if you cover the edges of the paper in ink, there's a chance you'll get your hands or the paper dirty.

Always make sure to follow those rules while penciling.

Drawing a Left-Facing Page

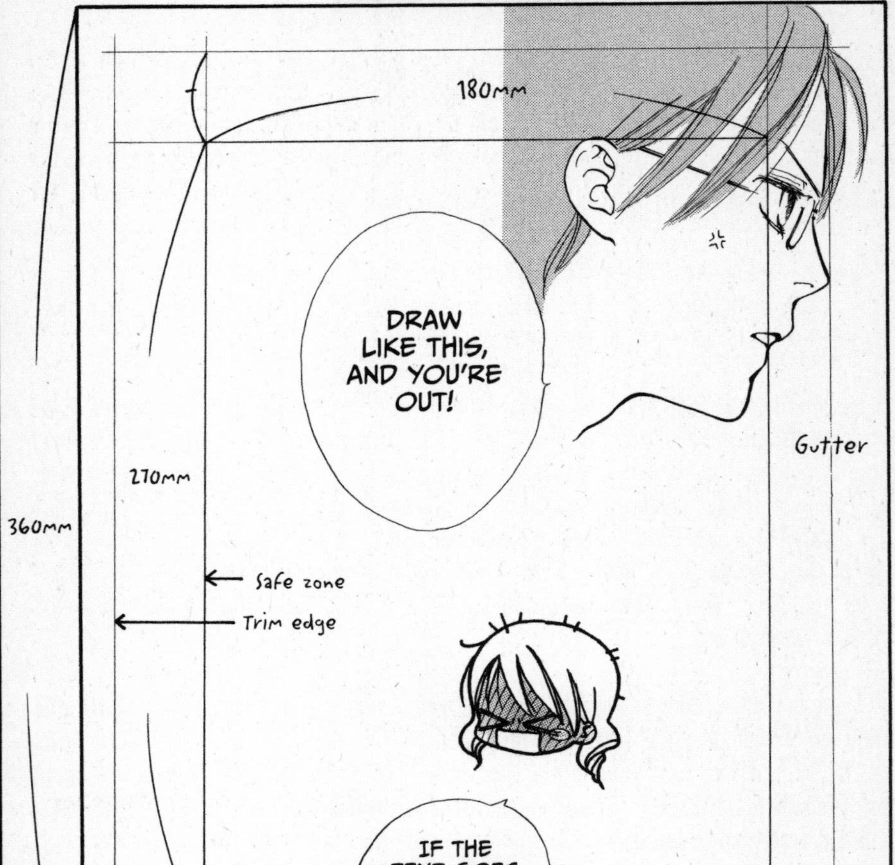
180mm
DRAW LIKE THIS, AND YOU'RE OUT!
Gutter
270mm
360mm
Safe zone
Trim edge
IF THE TEXT GOES OUTSIDE THE SAFE ZONE, IT'LL BE CUT OFF AND THE READERS WON'T BE ABLE TO READ IT!
30mm
20mm
270mm

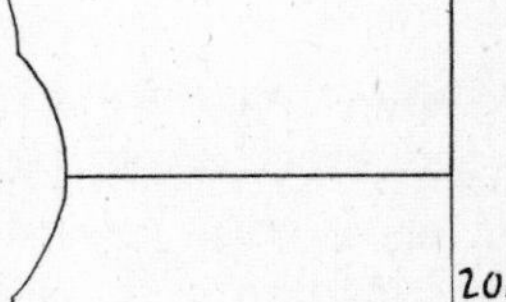
RESULTS

For a template for a right-facing page, flip this image (the gutter will be on the left).

Lettering and Balloon Sizes

There is a set basic font size for text that goes in word balloons. Font size is measured in points.

In Hana to Yume and Bessatsu Hana to Yume, we use 20 point font size. In LaLa and Melody, the basic size is 18 point, and we use those sizes for anything other than yelling.

Draw your word balloons so that that font size will fit inside them as nicely as possible. Don't forget to allot ruby (furigana) space. Not all manga publishers use ruby, but Hakusensha does. You will need to leave space between your lines for that.

Please refer to the diagram on the left for font size and line spacing. Larger bookstores and art stores also carry a tool called a "phototype scale." It's a grid tool that shows what size each character is at each point size. Also, you will need one unit of space each for the small character tsu (つ), in things like bikkuri (びっくり), and the small ya, yu, yo (や, ゆ, よ) in things like shou ga nai (しょうがない). They're smaller characters, but they get the same space as the regular ones. Furthermore, when a balloon has two or more lines of text, they will both start at the same level. When drawing your balloon, keep in mind that a rectangular grid of text should fit easily inside it.

For manga artists working in English, the same type of spacing rules apply—think of the area inside the balloon as a grid to fill up with words. Keep a margin of space around that grid. For English font size, most manga are lettered in 7 point. Look at how manga is lettered professionally to get a sense of how to balance the size of text in a balloon. You don't want it to look too crowded or dense!

Keep the following in mind for your manga contest submissions. When text falls on top of a character or background (outside of a balloon), the editorial department will place a white or black outline (called "stroke") around the affected letters before the manga is printed. If the text is floating in a field of black, we'll make the text legible by inverting it to white. (P.63)

In those cases, put tracing paper over the finished page and write the text on it. Tracing paper tears easily, so cut it a little big, and fix it securely to your paper with tape so that it doesn't get torn off. You'll eventually have to erase any text you write on your pencil page, so writing your text on tracing paper now means you won't forget it later.

☆ use tracing paper
  for text

18 point

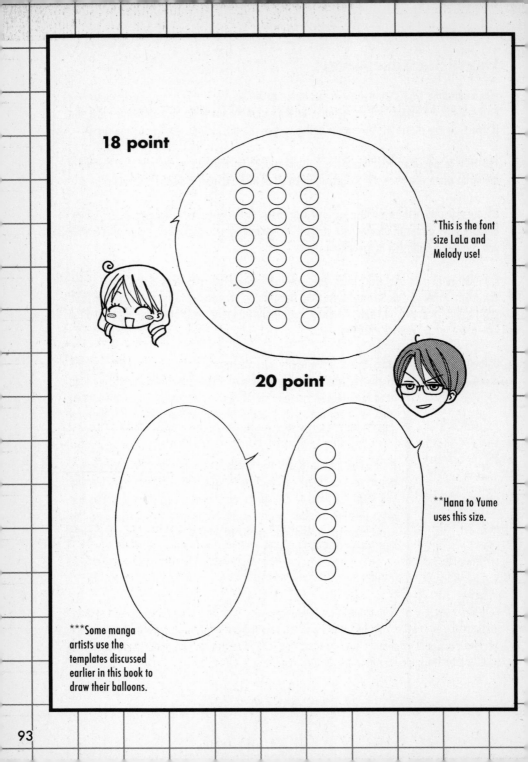

*This is the font size LaLa and Melody use!

20 point

**Hana to Yume uses this size.

***Some manga artists use the templates discussed earlier in this book to draw their balloons.

Visualizing Your Manga

When penciling, you should draw in this order: panel borders → balloons → characters → backgrounds → effects. It's not going to be the end of the world if you violate this order, but if you draw the characters before the balloons, you risk the balloons ending up too small.

The trick to penciling is to keep the finished manga in mind as you draw. You created a blueprint when you were storyboarding--take all of that and give it a solid concrete shape.

Of course you need to have a firm grasp of your character designs and background compositions, but also have a specific idea of your stage direction and effects, and pencil them in. This way, you can avoid confusion in the inking stage.

If you leave in a lot of sketchy lines, then you risk inking the wrong ones in the inking stage. You might think you've inked the drawing beautifully, but when you take your eraser to it, you see you've drawn all kinds of wonky lines. In particular, when drawing buildings and the like, use a ruler. Even for windows.

Unless they are very experienced, we're pretty sure there aren't many people who can ink a drawing with just a rough idea of where everything goes. You don't need to draw every single line of your effects, but if you place at least some of them precisely, you can prevent accidents such as the focal point shifting while you're drawing.

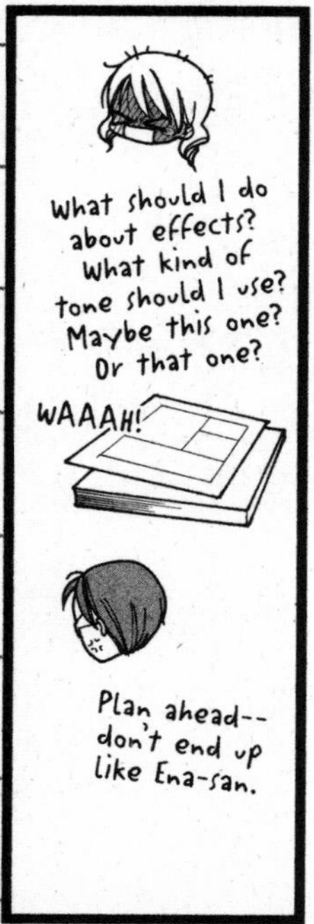
What should I do about effects? What kind of tone should I use? Maybe this one? Or that one?
WAAAH!
Plan ahead--don't end up like Ena-san.

It's a good idea to write instructions for the finishing touches on your paper, such as "black fill" and "tone here," in accordance with the way you want the finished manga to look. Professional manga artists put notes like this on their pencils as instructions to their assistants. This saves everyone a lot of confusion, without the artist needing to explain each panel to their assistants.

THE MARGINS OF MANGA ARE FOR NOTES!!

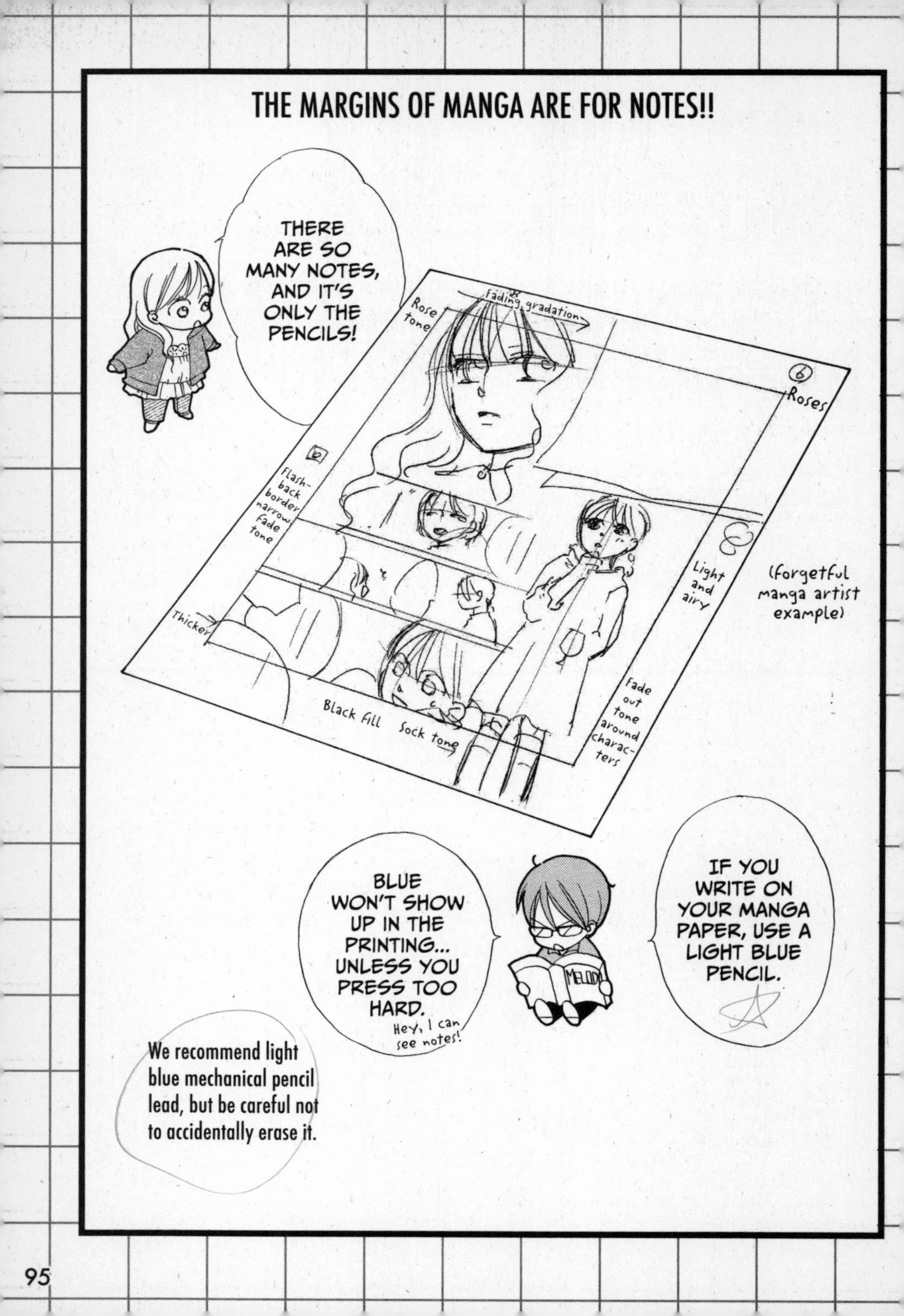
THERE ARE SO MANY NOTES, AND IT'S ONLY THE PENCILS!
Fading gradation
Rose tone
Roses
Flash-back border narrow. Fade tone
Light and airy
(forgetful manga artist example)
Thicker
Black Fill
Sock tone
Fade out tone around characters
IF YOU WRITE ON YOUR MANGA PAPER, USE A LIGHT BLUE PENCIL.
BLUE WON'T SHOW UP IN THE PRINTING... UNLESS YOU PRESS TOO HARD.
Hey, I can see notes!
MELODY
We recommend light blue mechanical pencil lead, but be careful not to accidentally erase it.

How to Draw a Two-Page Spread

In the past, when magazines were bound with twine, the gutter was completely obscured by the binding process. But now Hakusensha manga magazines are all "perfect bound," meaning the spine is bound with glue. Because of that, we can see much more of the gutter.

Before, artists would often cut off the gutter parts, connect the right and left pages of their manga, and draw on it like that, but that made the center of the magazine conspicuously blank. How much of the art in the gutter get published varies slightly depending on the dimensions of the magazine, but if you draw about 12mm into the gutter side of your paper, it should be safe.

Please use the diagram below for reference. It's fine to cut off or fold the parts that you won't need. As a general rule, don't put faces or any important art into the center.

Draw for about 12mm

MAKE SENSE?

Long cat is not long.

A Two-Page Spread at the Printer

Ghost Only (by Yui Shin, from *Melody*)

- **The top two pages are pencils.** (Important lines have been inked.)
- **The bottom pages are as they appear in the magazine.** (Completed and as bound into a book.)

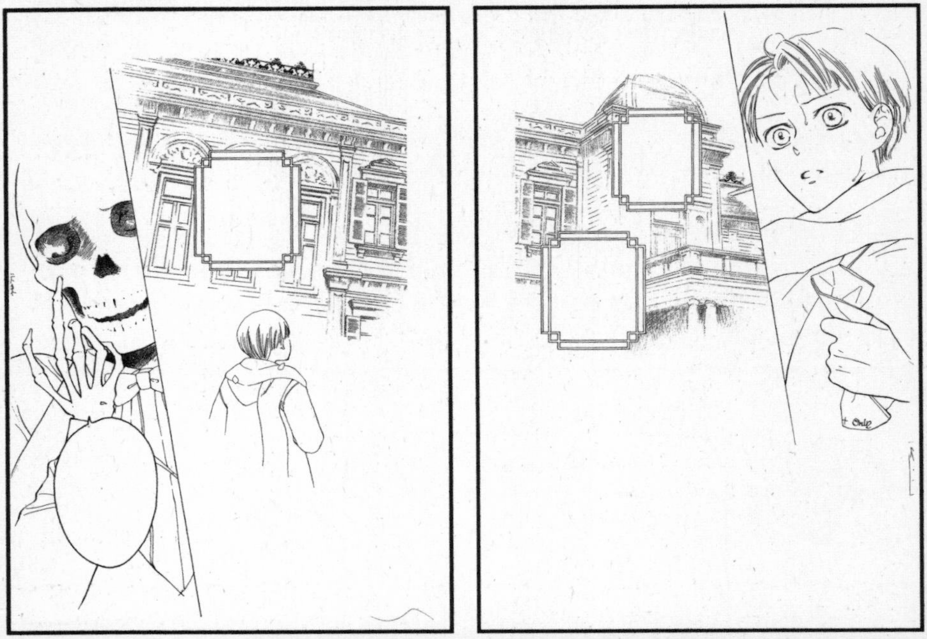

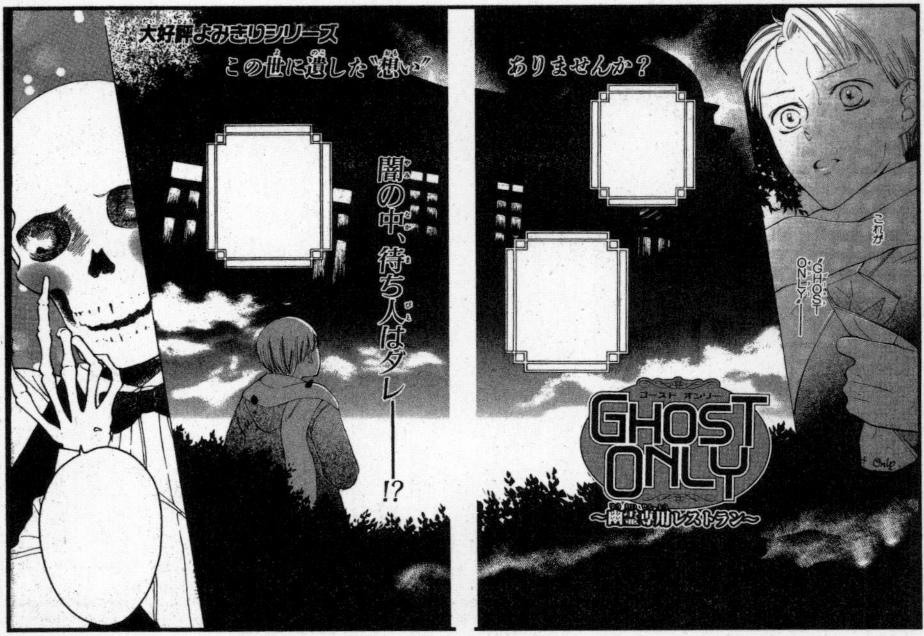
大好評よみきりシリーズ
この世に遺した〝想い〟
ありませんか？
闇の中、待ち人はダレ——!?
これが
〝GHOST ONLY〟——
ゴースト オンリー
GHOST ONLY
〜幽霊専用レストラン〜

Portions of the margins have been cropped at the trim edge at the printer.

Title Pages and Titles

In Japan, the first page of the manga—the title page—is called a tobira ("door"). It's the gateway to your manga. When we ask for a 16-page manga contest submission, the title page is one of those pages.

The editorial department will create a logo for you, so either write your title on the back of your title page paper, or put tracing paper on your paper and write the title on that in pencil.

We don't think this happens in 16-page submissions, but in cases when the title page is on page two or later, it is our rule to write the title and artist's name in small print on the first page. This is so that the readers know that a new manga is beginning, and it's not a continuation of a previous manga.

Don't →
● There's a face in the gutter.
● There's no space for the title.
● The theme is unclear.

← Do

The battle begins at the title page!

Ooh.

Title Pages and Titles cont'd.

The title page is like a poster advertising your work. Make it a fantastic piece of art. Great title pages also tell the reader what to expect in the story. If your title page catches the judges' eyes and makes them interested, then you've won.

There are no rules for titles, but think "easy to remember" and "catchy." Leave an impression on the judges. Professional manga artists sometimes come up with a great title first, and then write a story around it.

HOW TITLE PAGES ARE PRINTED:

Gakuen Alice (by Tachibana Higuchi, from *Hana to Yume*)

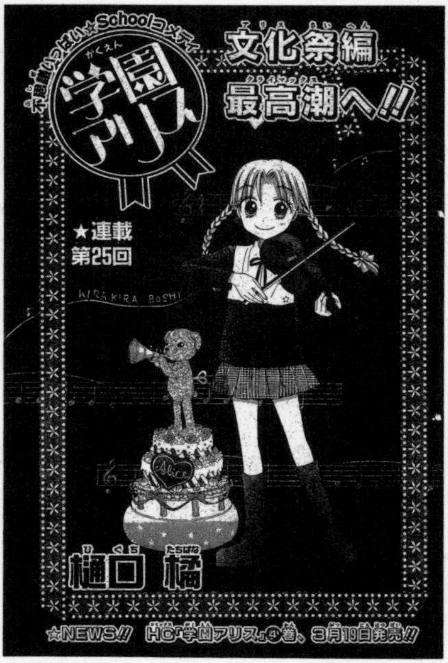
不思議いっぱい☆Schoolコメディ
学園アリス
文化祭編
最高潮へ!!
★連載
第25回
KIRA KIRA BOSHI
樋口 橘
☆NEWS!! HC「学園アリス」④巻、3月19日発売!!

Printed Title Page

The title and supplemental text is laid out in a way that doesn't cover up the characters or main parts of the picture.

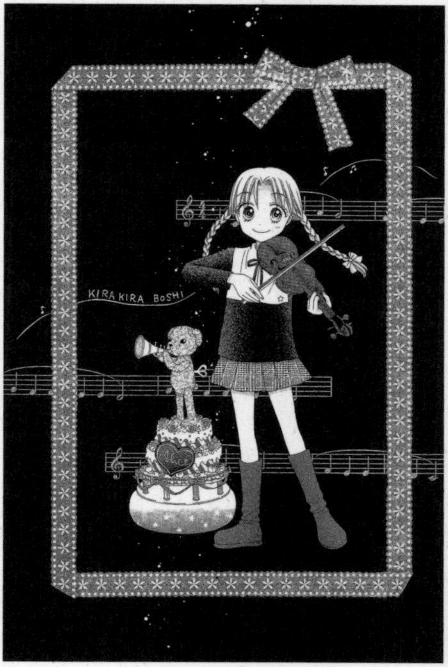
KIRA KIRA BOSHI

Title Page Art

Leave room in advance for the title, artist name, and tagline.

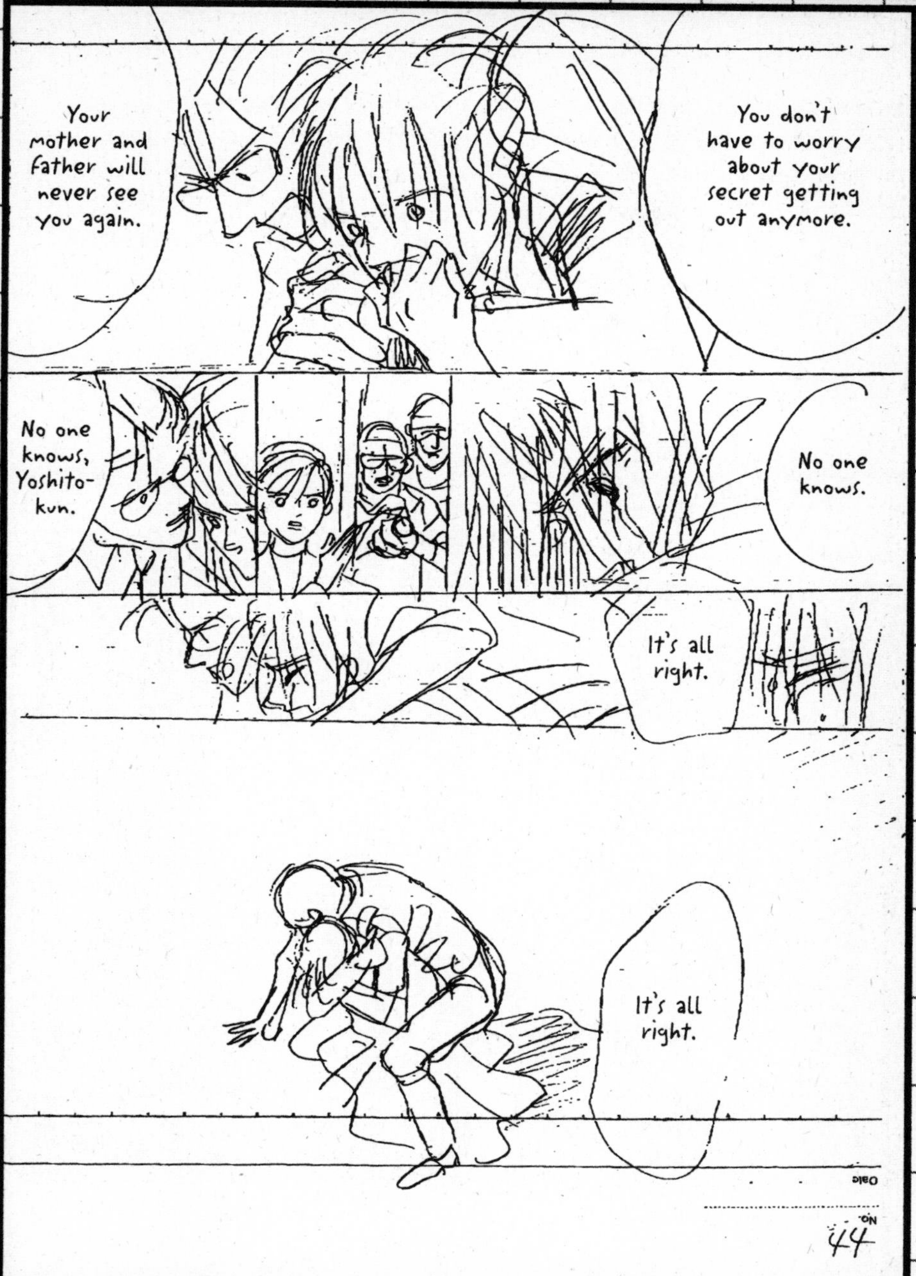
You don't have to worry about your secret getting out anymore.
Your mother and father will never see you again.
No one knows.
No one knows, Yoshito-kun.
It's all right.
It's all right.
44

On the right is a storyboard, drawn on size B5 paper. On the left is the pencil, drawn on size B4 manga paper. Nothing changed much from the storyboard to pencil. And just as we'd expect from Reiko Shimizu, the storyboard is a compelling and beautiful piece of art in its own right.

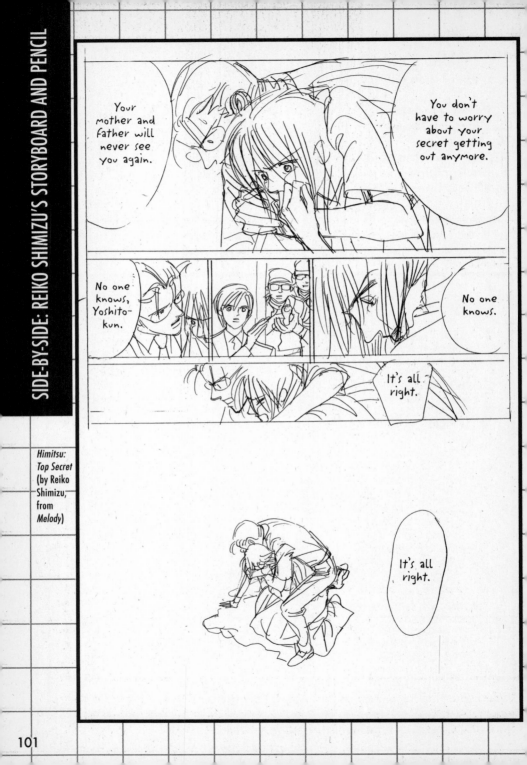

Himitsu: Top Secret (by Reiko Shimizu, from *Melody*)

Inking Order

Here's the order in which you should ink:

1. Panel borders
2. Word balloons
3. Characters
4. Hand-written text
5. Backgrounds
6. Effects lines

After you've inked everything, it's time to move on to finishing touches. You don't have to follow the order exactly, and it's okay if you work panel-by-panel. There are also cases where it's better to fill in spot blacks on the characters first, in order to see how they balance with the background.

MY FINGERS HURT... MY HAND HURTS... I CAN'T DRAW ANOTHER LINE, SASAKI-SAAAAN...
TAKE A HINT FROM THE PROS AND TRY OUT ONE OF THE TRICKS SHOWN TO THE BOTTOM RIGHT.
INDIFFERENCE
There's a giant callus on your finger from drawing.
SOME ARTISTS GET WORN OUT ANYWAY, SO THEY START BY INKING THE MOST IMPORTANT PAGES FIRST.
I guess it's too much to expect you to be a master yet.
Cover the part where your finger grips the pen with rubber, or wrap tissue or cloth around it with tape.

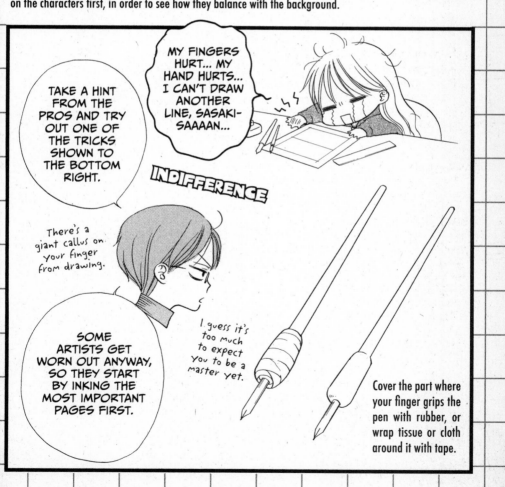

Pen Strokes

We think that those of you who have tried out your pen nibs already will know this, but the lines you can draw vary greatly based on the type of pen nib you use and how you apply pressure to the pen.

In manga, you have to emphasize your characters over backgrounds and effects, so use your pen strokes to make the characters pop.

Outline people's faces with thicker lines, and use thinner lines to ink the details of their faces, such as the eyes, wrinkles on clothes, and hair. To create thin lines, use a maru pen or fine felt-tip pen. The contrast between thick and thin is all it takes to give your image a three-dimensional feel.

For objects and architectural backgrounds, it's standard to draw thick lines for the outline and thin lines for the inside. Also, you can express depth and dimension by using thick lines for things in the foreground and thin lines for things further away.

3-D

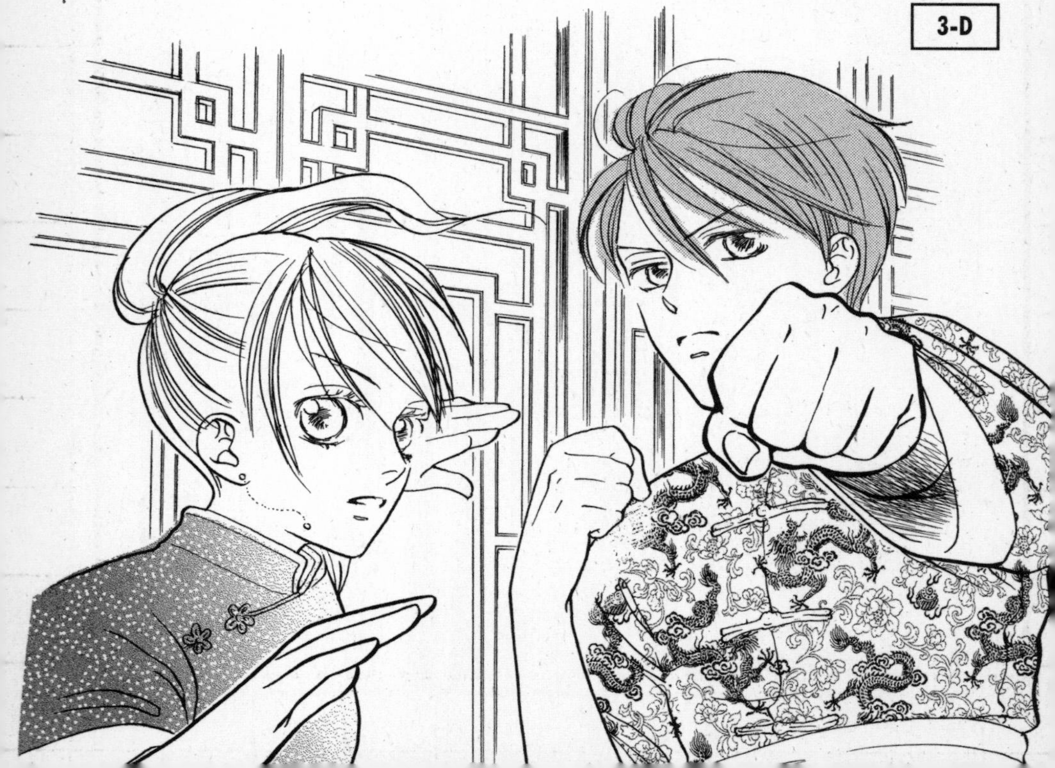

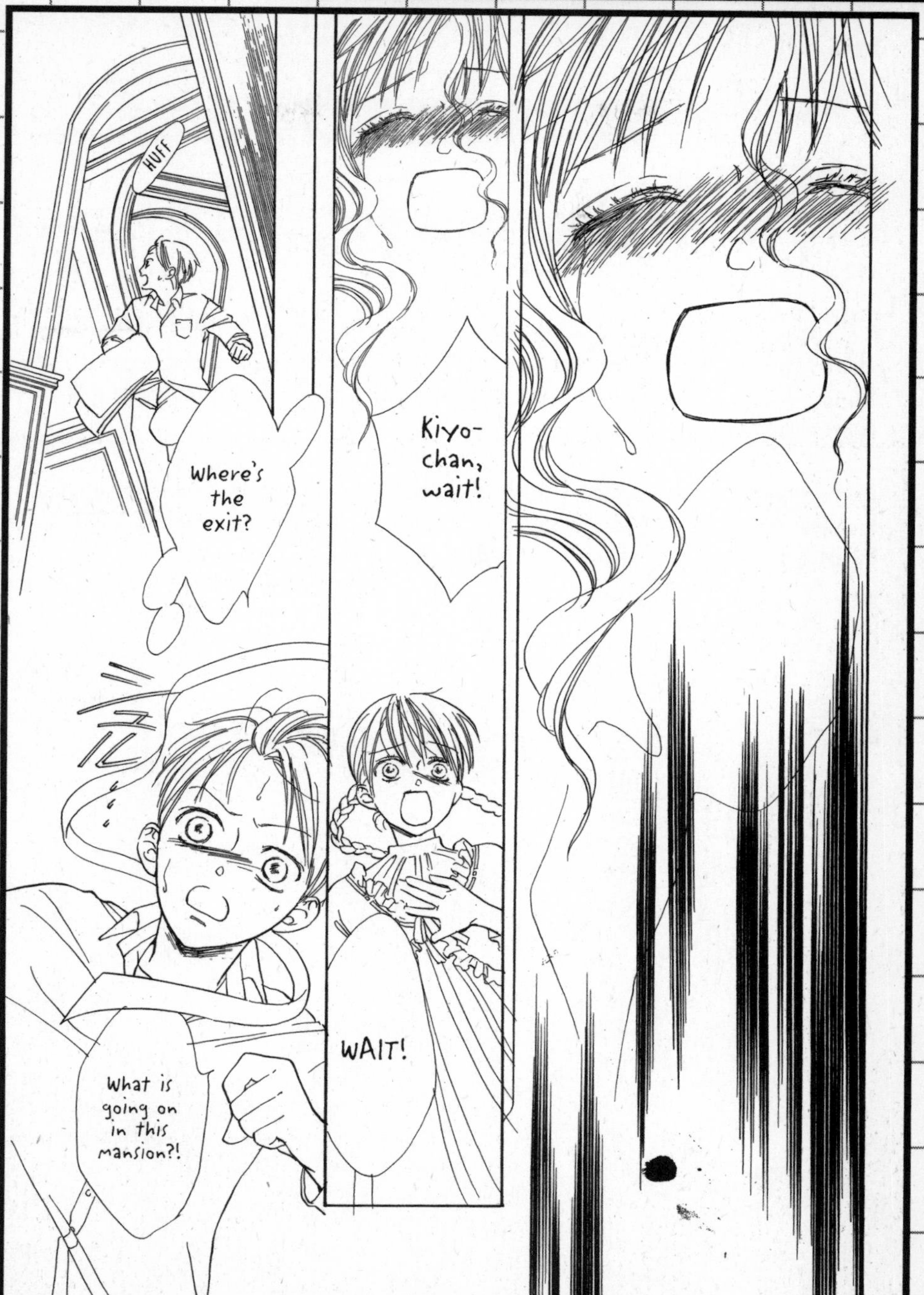
Kiyo-chan, wait!
WAIT!
HUFF
Where's the exit?
What is going on in this mansion?!

An inked page. The finishing touches—black areas, white highlights, and tone—will be added later.

Ghost Only (by Yui Shin, from *Melody*)

Background Treatments

When it comes to backgrounds, it doesn't matter whether you're illustrating natural scenery or a man-made landscape. Ink things that are up close clearly, and fade out things that are far away.

For example, just by inking a nearby building with bold lines and inking faraway mountains, buildings, or forests with thin lines, you've created a background with a sense of depth.

Well-placed shadows can really make your foreground pop. Use rich blacks, crosshatching, and tone to create a three-dimensional look.

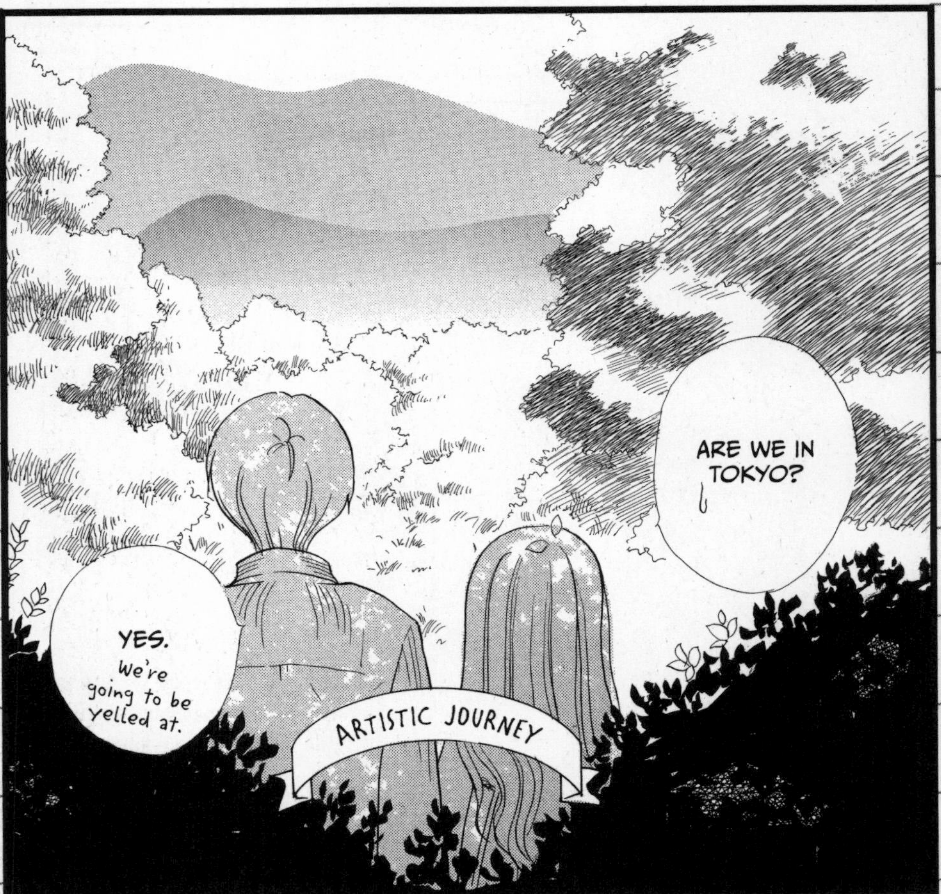
ARE WE IN TOKYO?
YES. We're going to be yelled at.
ARTISTIC JOURNEY

Adding Effects

We introduced effects lines and effects backgrounds on page 36. Have you practiced them?

If you don't practice beforehand, there's the distinct possibility that you'll ruin the page you've worked so hard to create. Make sure to practice the necessary effects lines on a different sheet of manga paper before you try them on the real thing.

The trick to effects lines is to keep the amount of ink on your pen steady, and to draw the whole effect at once. Learn what you need to do to ink focus lines and speed lines at a good pace.

We will show you a few other tricks for drawing effects lines. It's great reference, we promise!

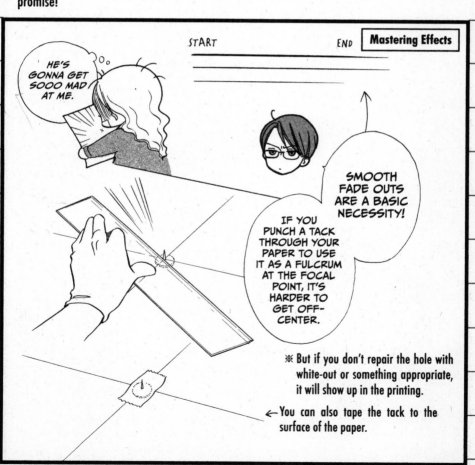

Mastering Effects
START
END
SMOOTH FADE OUTS ARE A BASIC NECESSITY!
IF YOU PUNCH A TACK THROUGH YOUR PAPER TO USE IT AS A FULCRUM AT THE FOCAL POINT, IT'S HARDER TO GET OFF-CENTER.
HE'S GONNA GET SOOO MAD AT ME.
※ But if you don't repair the hole with white-out or something appropriate, it will show up in the printing.
← You can also tape the tack to the surface of the paper.

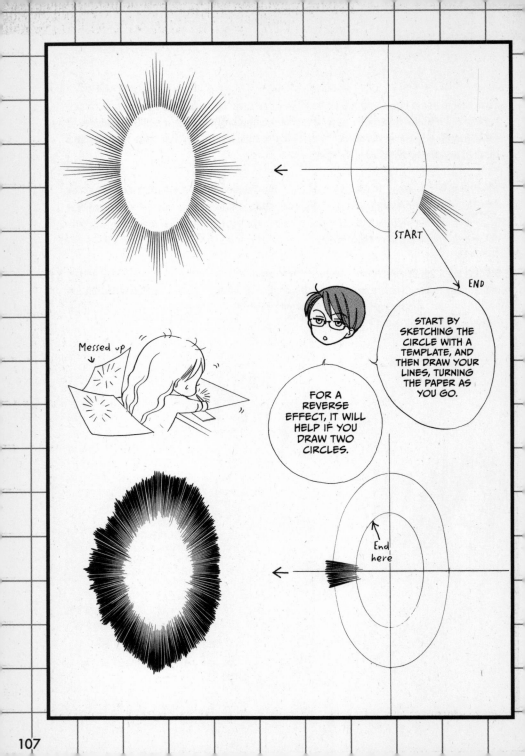

START

END

START BY SKETCHING THE CIRCLE WITH A TEMPLATE, AND THEN DRAW YOUR LINES, TURNING THE PAPER AS YOU GO.

FOR A REVERSE EFFECT, IT WILL HELP IF YOU DRAW TWO CIRCLES.

Messed up

End here

Filling in Spot Blacks

Most people use a brush and inkpot to fill in large areas of solid black, called spot blacks, but you can also use a brush pen, magic marker, or anything that will paint the area black—it doesn't matter. However, for work you're going to submit to a manga contest, please make sure not to use diluted ink or gray markers.

When blacking in areas, if you carefully paint the detailed areas around the outside of the area first, you can prevent momentum from taking your brush outside the lines. A great way to achieve nice details is by using a G pen or micron pen for the edges and then filling the bulk of the area with a brush or brush pen.

Ink and sumi ink evaporate and coagulate over time, so we recommend buying small bottles and keeping your stash fresh. Also, any ink that's left to dry on your brush will stiffen the brush's bristles. If you want to avoid damaging your brush, make sure to wash your brush thoroughly after you use it.

| Glossy Blacks |

IT WOULD BE WISE TO USE A BLUE PENCIL TO OUTLINE THE AREA YOU WANT TO PAINT BEFORE YOU START.

Ena just keeps adding to her pile of things she ↓ can't show him.

SPLAT

Using Erasers and Whites

Once you've finished filling in all the spot blacks, clean up your page with an eraser. The trick to using an eraser is to go slowly and carefully. If you try to rub out a large area in one go, you'll wrinkle your paper.

As for white, the general process is to wet your brush, then dip it in a small amount of white poster paint on the inside of a lid or a small plate. If your mixture gets too diluted, then the ink will dissolve; if it's too thick, it can dry out and peel. Try out your mixture on a different piece of paper before using it.

Poster paint will also harden as time passes; when it does, you should temper it with a little bit of hot water.

If you will be drawing in pen over where you used the white, correction fluid is the most convenient. There are water-based and oil-based correction fluids. If you use an oil-based correction fluid when correcting lines and blacks that were done with a water-based ink, then the two won't blend together.

Aside from correcting mistakes, white is also used to draw white outlines around people or hand-written text, and to put highlights in characters' eyes or on black areas. There happens to be white ink that you can use with a dip pen to draw thin lines too.

Eraser
White
I HEAR THAT IF I TAPE THE PAPER DOWN WITH MASKING TAPE, I WON'T HAVE TO WORRY ABOUT IT WRINKLING OR TEARING AS MUCH!
Gyaaa! My glasses! My glasses!
MAKE SURE TO CLEAN UP SMUDGES AND FINGERPRINTS, TOO
It still happens, even to people who are (supposedly) pros...

Tones

Tone, or "screentone," was originally a drafting tool. After becoming a staple of manga creation, tone has evolved into many new variations. The price has gone down too, and it has gotten easier to use.

Screentone is like a giant, transparent sticker with a pattern printed on it. You will eventually peel your tone "sticker" off the clear backing. First, clean the area where your tone will go by removing eraser droppings or pencil lines. If there are pencil lines under the tone, then the graphite particles will stick to the bottom of your tone, and it will show up in the printing.

When you need marks to show where the tone will go, such as a shadow outside of the characters or anything else that doesn't adhere to your manga's lineart, draw them with a light blue or yellow colored pencil.

Now, place the tone sheet over the paper and use a utility knife to cut a piece a little bit bigger than the area where you'll be laying it down. Peel off that piece and lay it lightly on your page, then cut off the extra bits. It's easy for tone to come off when it's very small, so use more tone than you need and scrape the pattern off the excess, making the remaining "sticker" invisible.

Thoroughly sweep away the scraped-off bits. Otherwise, they will stick to the cut edges of the tone and dirty your paper.

Types of Tone

FOR A BEGINNER, DOT TONES, GRADATIONS, AND CLOTHING PATTERNS SHOULD BE SUFFICIENT.

THEY HAVE SKY AND BUILDING BACKGROUNDS, TOO.

♪ How convenient.

DRAW THINGS YOURSELF.

...Yes, sir.

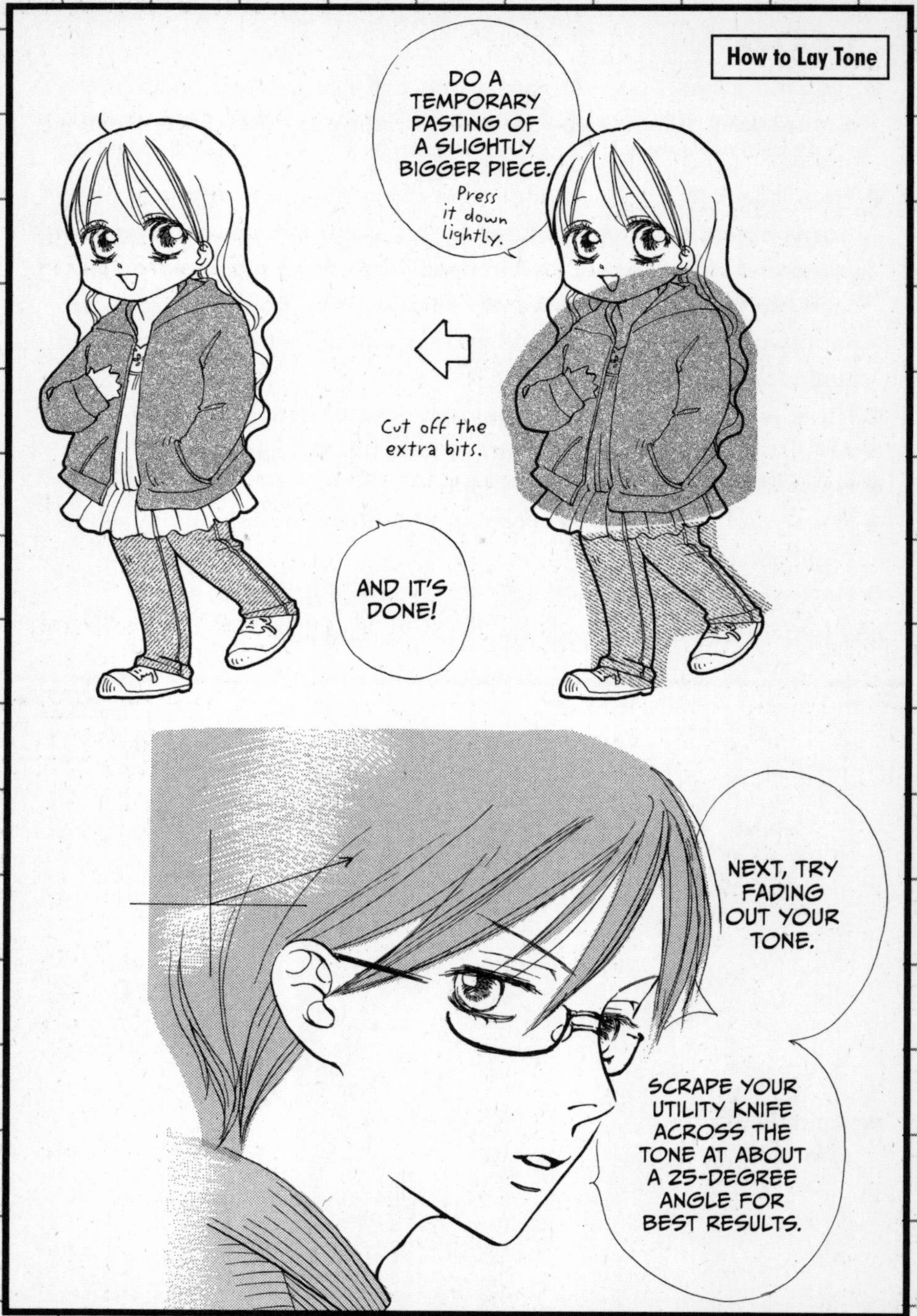
How to Lay Tone
DO A TEMPORARY PASTING OF A SLIGHTLY BIGGER PIECE.
Press it down lightly.
Cut off the extra bits.
AND IT'S DONE!
NEXT, TRY FADING OUT YOUR TONE.
SCRAPE YOUR UTILITY KNIFE ACROSS THE TONE AT ABOUT A 25-DEGREE ANGLE FOR BEST RESULTS.

Final Checklist

- First, put all your pages in order and make sure the numbers haven't disappeared. If they've become obscured by art, then write them in again.
- Next, check to make sure that none of the dialogue written in pencil has vanished. For text obscured by art, put tracing paper over your page and write the text on it in pencil. Use a big piece of tracing paper so that it doesn't move or come off. It's a good idea to trace nearby panel borders or word balloons onto the tracing paper as a guide for where it should go.
- Have you forgotten to erase any smudges or pencil lines?
- Are there any eraser droppings or tone bits still lingering?
- Have you forgotten to ink anything?
- Have you forgotten to fill anything with black, or left out any white highlights?
- Have you forgotten any tone?

Once you've completed the checklist, your manga is complete! Good work!

Final Check
PAGE ONE, PAGE TWO, PAGE THREE...
...PAGE FIFTEEN.
NO MATTER HOW MANY TIMES I COUNT IT, I'M ONE PAGE SHORT!
What'll I do?
Rejected drawings
"The Dish Mansion of Awajicho"

*Pun on the folk tale "Bancho Sarayashiki," in which a servant loses one of 10 valuable plates. Even unto death, she keeps counting, looking for the missing plate. "Awajicho," instead of Bancho, is where you can find the Hakusensha offices.

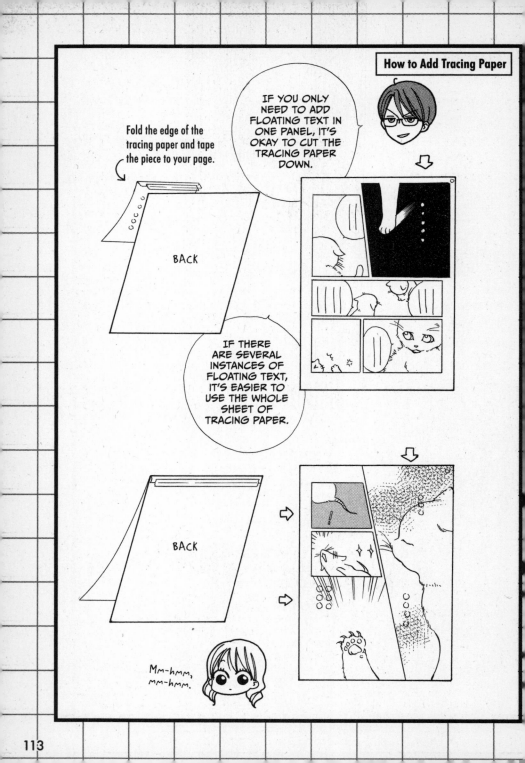

How to Add Tracing Paper

IF YOU ONLY NEED TO ADD FLOATING TEXT IN ONE PANEL, IT'S OKAY TO CUT THE TRACING PAPER DOWN.

Fold the edge of the tracing paper and tape the piece to your page.

BACK

IF THERE ARE SEVERAL INSTANCES OF FLOATING TEXT, IT'S EASIER TO USE THE WHOLE SHEET OF TRACING PAPER.

BACK

Mm-hmm, mm-hmm.

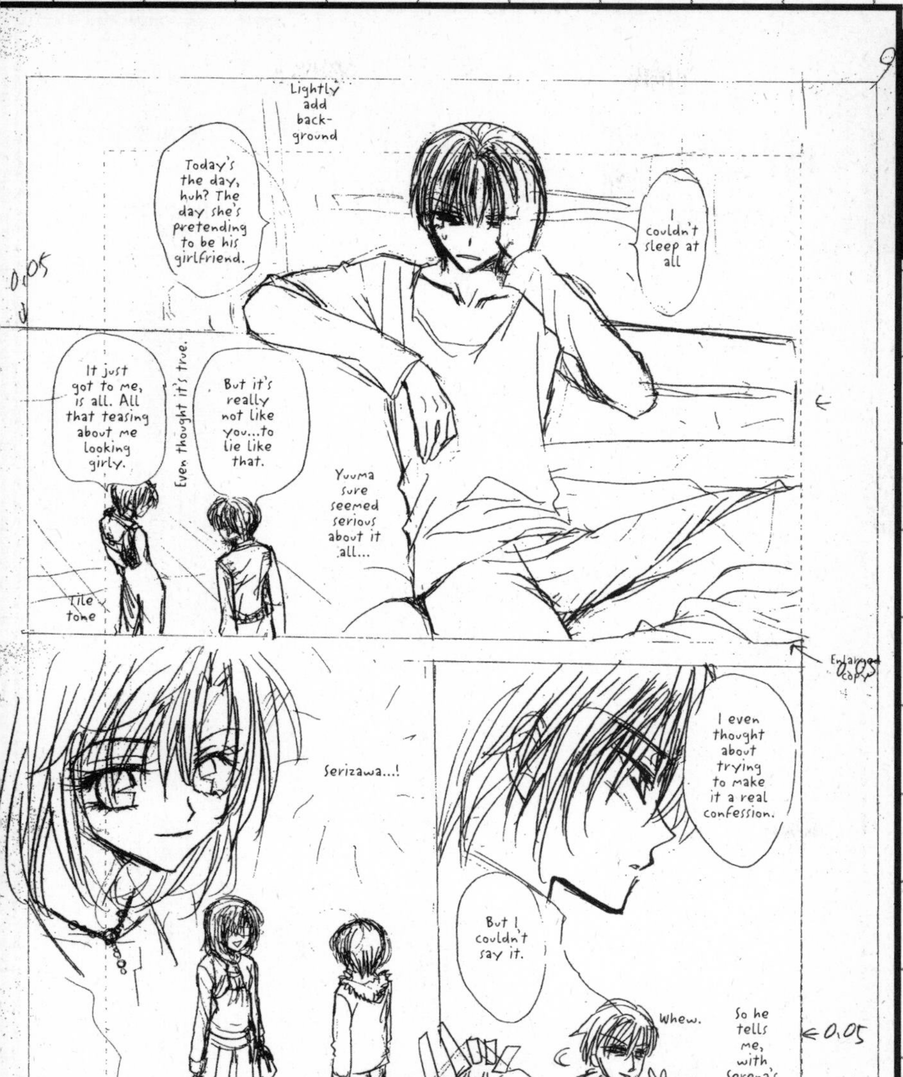
Lightly add background
I couldn't sleep at all
Today's the day, huh? The day she's pretending to be his girlfriend.
Yuuma sure seemed serious about it all...
But it's really not like you...to lie like that.
Even thought it's true.
It just got to me, is all. All that teasing about me looking girly.
Tile tone
0.05
I even thought about trying to make it a real confession.
But I couldn't say it.
So he tells me, with Serena's face...
Whew.
Yuuma-kun!
0.05
Serizawa...!
Tone

A scene richly woven from the use of the three shots—up, middle, and full—and overlap.

FINISHED PAGE

I COULDN'T SLEEP AT ALL.
TODAY'S THE DAY, HUH? THE DAY SHE'S PRETENDING TO BE HIS GIRL-FRIEND.
YUUMA SURE SEEMED SERIOUS ABOUT IT ALL.
BUT IT'S NOT REALLY LIKE YOU... TO LIE LIKE THAT.
IT JUST GOT TO ME, IS ALL. ALL THAT TEASING ABOUT ME LOOKING GIRLY.
Even though it's true.
I EVEN THOUGHT ABOUT TRYING TO MAKE IT A REAL CONFES-SION.
BUT I COULDN'T SAY IT.
SO HE TELLS ME, WITH SERENA'S FACE.
Huh!
YUUMA-KUUUN!
Pocky
SERI-ZAWA...!

NG Life (by Mizuho Kusanagi, from *Hana to Yume*)

She uses a template for word balloons, and her own inventive use of tone in the bottom right-hand panel.

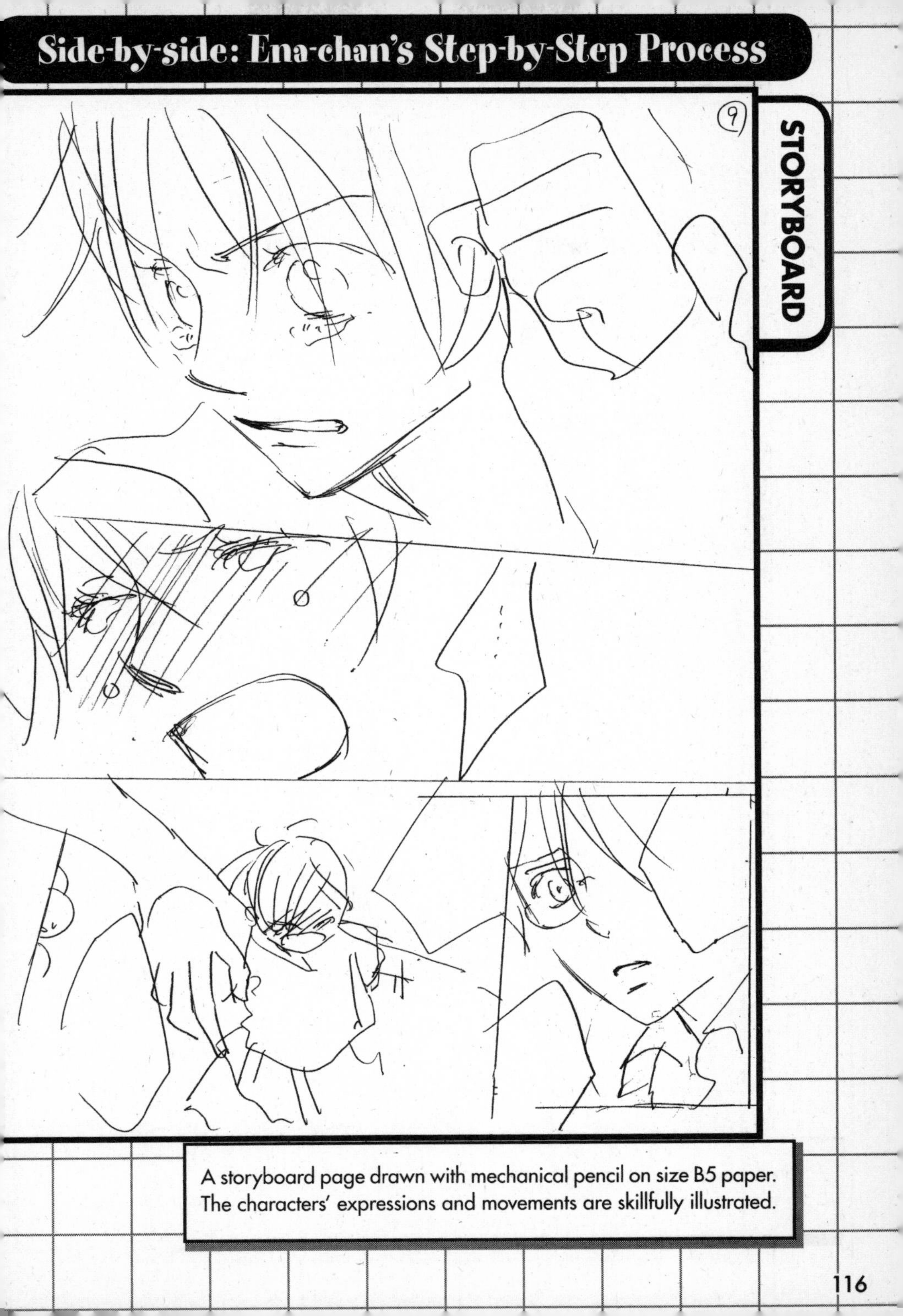
9

A storyboard page drawn with mechanical pencil on size B5 paper. The characters' expressions and movements are skillfully illustrated.

PENCIL

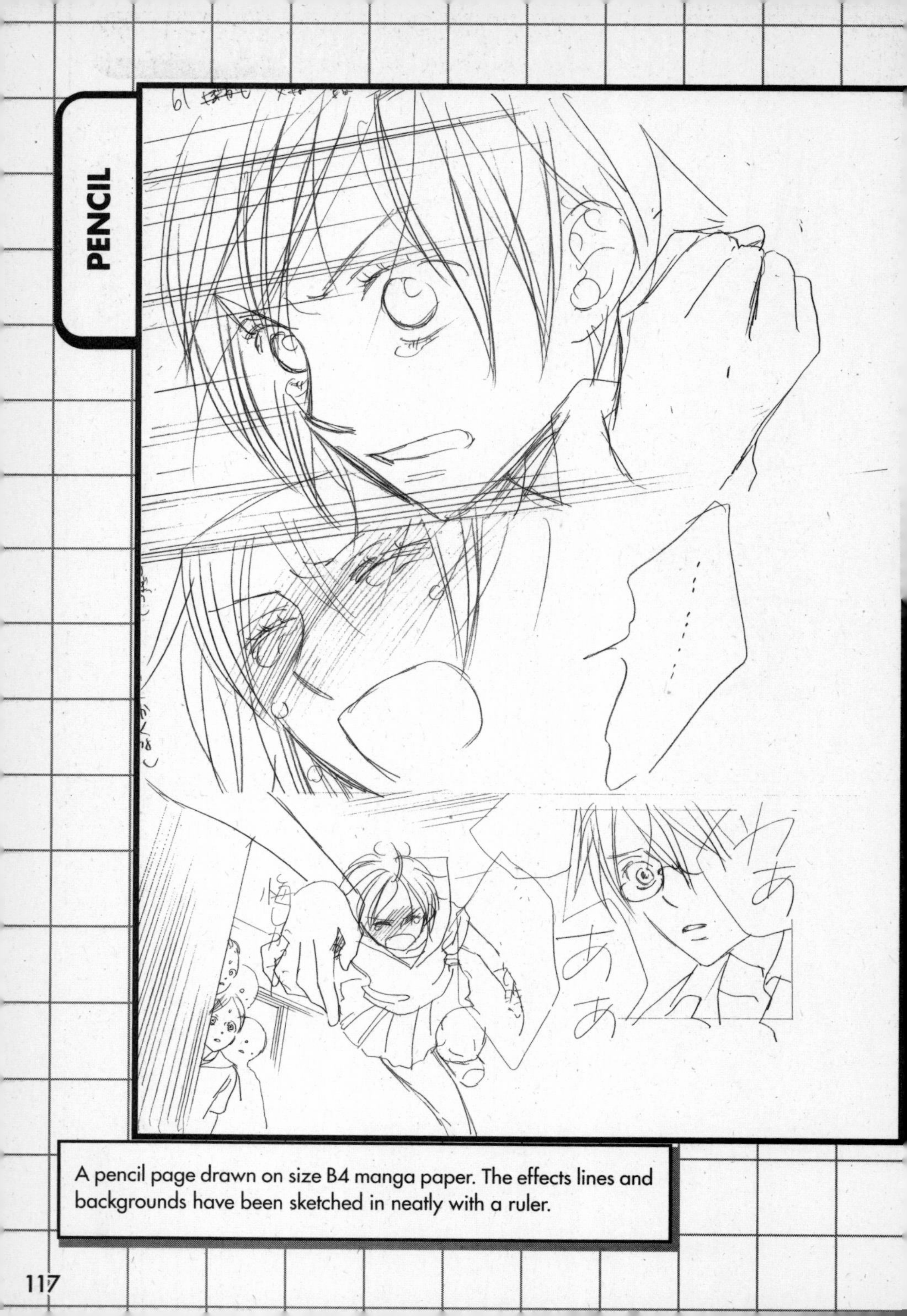
ああ
ああ

A pencil page drawn on size B4 manga paper. The effects lines and backgrounds have been sketched in neatly with a ruler.

INKING

1

A page where only the panel borders, word balloons and the characters have been inked. Smudges and stray lines will be corrected later.

A page with the effects lines inked in. If your pencils are precise, the inking of your effects lines and backgrounds will be clear and accurate.

FINISHING TOUCHES

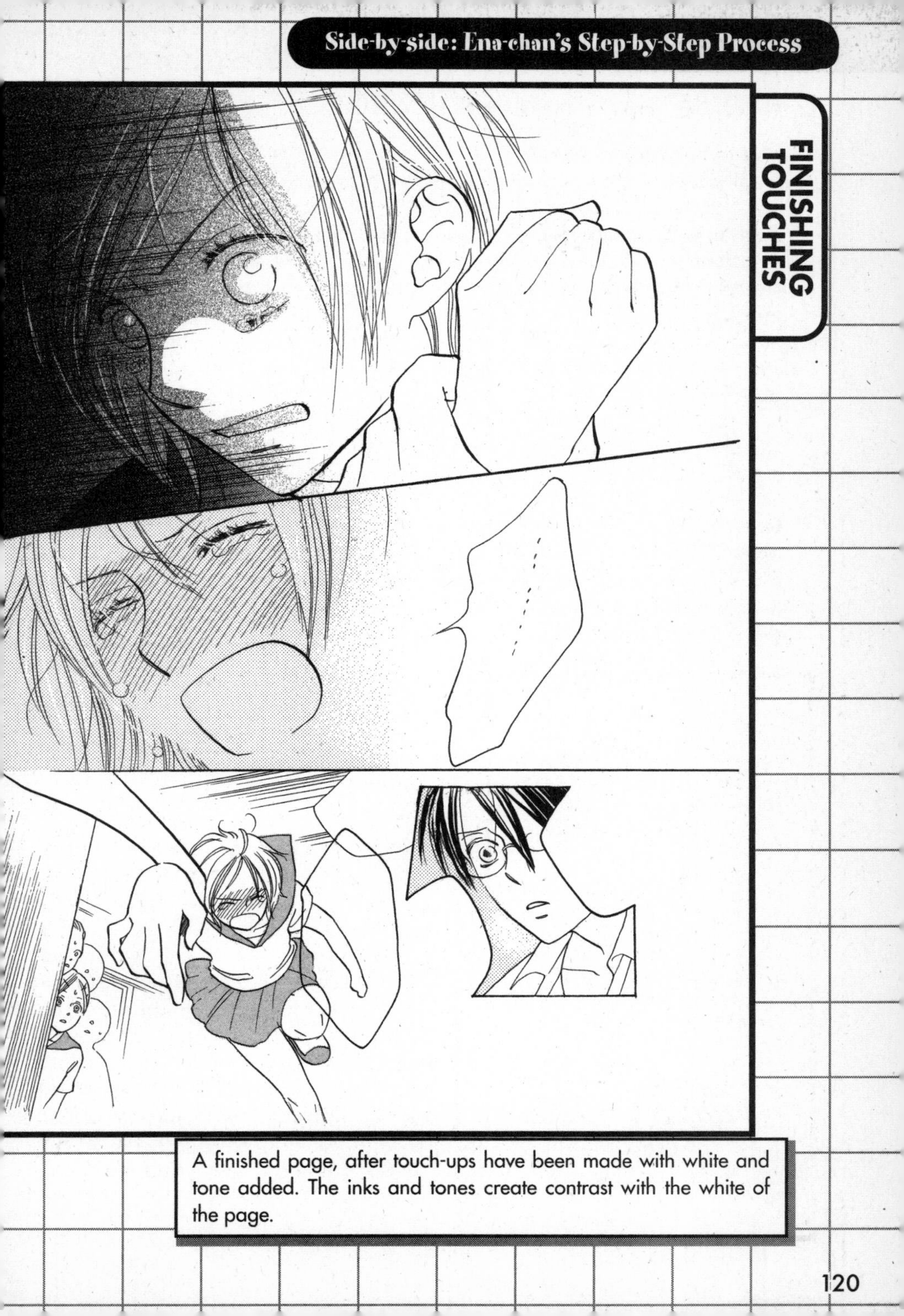

A finished page, after touch-ups have been made with white and tone added. The inks and tones create contrast with the white of the page.

Getting Your Manga Ready to Go

After you've completed your manga, and gone through with a final check, we encourage you to submit it to Hakusensha's *Hana to Yume, LaLa, Bessatsu Hana to Yume*, and/or *Melody* manga magazines.

There are two ways to submit your work: you can mail it to manga contests held by each editorial department, or you can bring your finished manga to an editorial department and give it to an editor in person for a personal evaluation. We'll talk more about bringing in your manga in person on the next page.

Each editorial department has their own manga contests, and the rules for submissions vary somewhat from magazine to magazine, so do your research carefully before entering. The rules for each contest are listed in the back of this book; please use that for reference. However, sometimes there are minor changes in the rules, so please check the latest issue of the magazine sponsoring the contest you wish to enter.

For each contest, we require you to include some basic information on the back of the first page of your manga. Please copy down the submission form, published on the contest pages of each magazine, and fill it in. You may also cut it out of the magazine or make a copy and attach that. Please be careful not to leave any fields blank. Sometimes, entrants leave their age and submission history blank, but we give advice based on your answers to those questions, so fill out the whole form.

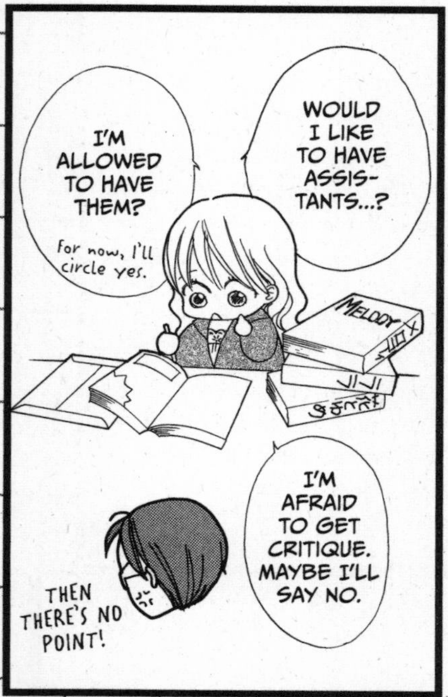
WOULD I LIKE TO HAVE ASSIS-TANTS...?
I'M ALLOWED TO HAVE THEM?
For now, I'll circle yes.
MELODY
I'M AFRAID TO GET CRITIQUE. MAYBE I'LL SAY NO.
THEN THERE'S NO POINT!

If mailing your submission, make sure you allot plenty of time for it to reach us by the contest deadline. If you think you might be late, please call the editorial department and discuss it with us.

Editor's note for English-speakers:
While this isn't explicitly called out in the contest instructions, please keep in mind that these contests are intended for Japanese speakers who are writing for a Japanese audience—a contest entry written in English is going to have some pretty big challenges ahead of it (also, having a Japanese mailing address is probably recommended). And particularly if you are interested in a one-on-one meeting with an editor, being a sufficiently fluent speaker of that editor's native language is a prerequisite, so that you can best understand and incorporate the invaluable feedback that will be provided. However, if you feel like your language skills are up to the task, give it a shot!

Bringing in Your Work

When you bring your work to us in person, you can get live critique and advice from an editor. You get the added bonus of the opportunity to hold a detailed question and answer session.

Here's a guide to the proper etiquette involved in traveling to an editorial department and bringing in your manga:

● **Always make an appointment.** Call the editorial department that you want to show your work to and make an appointment about a week in advance. The editorial departments get weekends and holidays off, so call on a weekday afternoon. Give your name to the editor who talks to you on the phone, and write down the date of your appointment and the name of that editor.

● **Don't be late.** Don't come late or more than 30 minutes early on the day of your appointment. If an unavoidable circumstance will make you late or cause you to cancel, then call the editorial department and let them know. If the editor you were going to see can't come to the phone, leave a message. When you get to Hakusensha, please give your name at the reception desk on the first floor, tell them the name of the editor and the department you will be seeing, and follow the instructions that they give you.

● **Bring your finished manga.** We cannot give you an accurate critique based on an incomplete manga or on storyboards. We cannot accept doujinshi or copies, either. As a rule, we only allow you to submit one finished manga. If you absolutely must get an opinion on more than one manga submission, then discuss that with the editor when making your appointment.

● **Come with questions.** This is your chance to hear what we really think. Get more than critique; come to us with the things that you have questions about. Any of the shojo manga editors at Hakusensha will answer your questions very nicely and politely, so don't hesitate to ask. If you would like to submit your manga for a contest, then leave it with the editor.

Please keep all of that in mind when you come to see us. Also, keep in mind that when our editorial departments are extremely busy, we will decline appointments. For those of you who live far away and/ or can't find a good opportunity to see us, we recommend that you attend the moving classroom that we hold all over the country. You will be able to hear not only from our editors, but from professional manga artists. Each magazine will inform you when and where one of these will be held.

Editor's note for English-speakers:

A more common opportunity in the U.S. is to do a portfolio review at an anime or comic convention—the same general advice is applicable, though. Finished work and good questions always get editors particularly excited about you and your manga!

BRING US YOUR MANGA!

How to Find Hakusensha

Address:
2-2-2 Kanda Awaji-cho, Chiyoda-ku, Tokyo, 101-0063

Phone Numbers:

- *Hana to Yume* Editorial Department (6F) **03-(3526)-8025**
- *Bessatsu Hana to Yume* Editorial Department (6F) **03-(3526)-8030**
- *LaLa Editorial Department* (5F) **03-(3526)-8035**
- *Melody* Editorial Department (5F) **03-(3526)-8045**

BY TRAIN

- Tokyo Metro Marunouchi Line, get off at Awajicho Station or Toei Shinjuku Line, get off at Ogawamachi Station. We're a two-minute walk from exit A3.
- Tokyo Metro Chiyoda Line, get off at Shinochanomizu Station. We're a five minute walk from exit B3.

Kandagawa
Ochanomizu Station
(Japan Railways)
Ochanomizubashi
Hijiribashi
Shoheibashi
Akihabara Station
(Japan Railways)
Police
WE ARE HERE
Chiyoda Line:
Shinochanomizu Station
Kanda Post Office
Manseibashi
Exit B3
Awajicho
Exit A5
Exit A3
Sudacho
Yasukuni Dori
Exit A2
Marunouchi Line:
Awajicho Station
Surugadai Shita
Ogawamachi
Toei Shinjuku Line:
Ogawamachi Station
Ginza Line:
Kanda Station
Sotobori Dori
Kanda Station
(Japan Railways)
Hakusensha Map

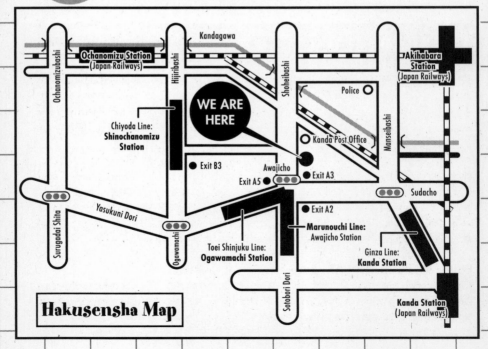

How to Use Digital Tools

In recent years, it's become much more popular for manga artists to go digital. They create their manga on the computer with the aid of graphics software such as ComicStudio or Photoshop. We still almost never see digitally-created submissions, but there's no denying that digital can be convenient and helpful.

The most common use of digital tools is for finishes—that is, to scan in and add finishing touches to the work after it's been inked. There are some manga artists who do everything digitally, including the storyboards, pencils, and inks, but in this book, we will give a simple introduction of how to add finishing touches to an already-inked page.

WHAT YOU'LL NEED

(1) Computer
You'll want at least 1GB of memory.

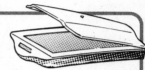

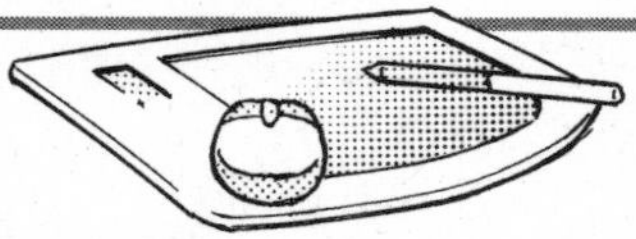

(2) Drawing tablet
Complete with stylus and mouse.

(3) Scanner
You will need at least size A4, capable of scanning a resolution of at least 600dpi.

(4) Graphics software
(In this book, we will be using ComicStudio EX3.0)

(5) Media
(Storage media—CD-R, magneto-optical drive, etc.)

FOR THE DIGITAL MANGA ARTIST...

With ComicStudio, published as MangaStudio in the U.S., you can not only do finishes (as we will show you), but you can also build your manga from the ground up, from storyboards to final check, with your computer.

COMIC STUDIO EX 3.0
CELSYS

ComicStudio offers...

● A natural pen stroke

It will correct subtle pen wobbles, and preserves the fade as you lift your pen at the end of a stroke.

● You can try anything!

You can redraw lines, change tone, and shuffle around blacks and whites. You can correct any part of the process, as many times as you want, until it looks exactly the way you want it to. And it's packed with all kinds of useful functions that you can only get with digital.

Check it out on the web at http://www.comicstudio.net/ or http://manga.smithmicro.com

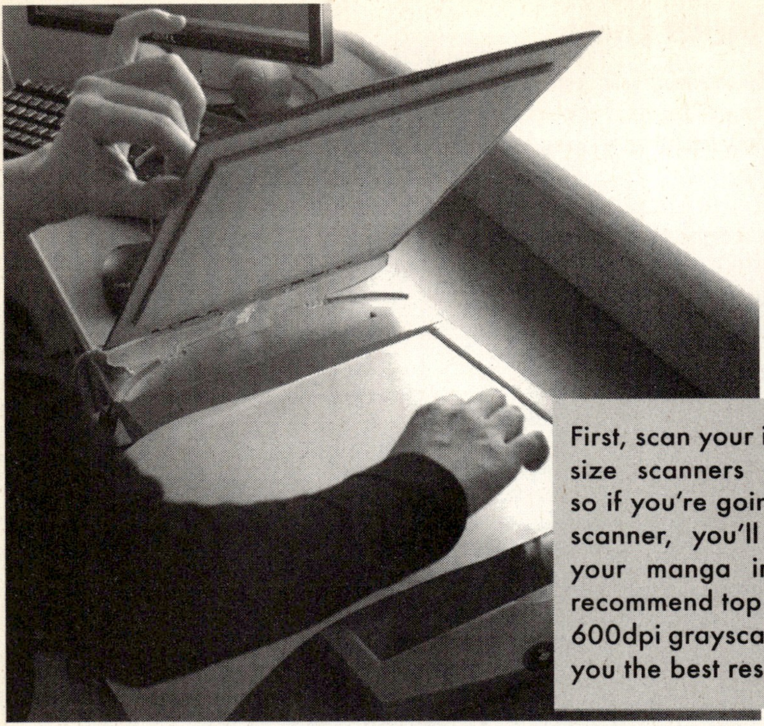

1 SCAN YOUR PAGE

First, scan your inked page. B4-size scanners are expensive, so if you're going to use an A4 scanner, you'll have to scan your manga in sections (we recommend top and bottom). A 600dpi grayscale scan will give you the best resolution.

2 STITCH THE IMAGES

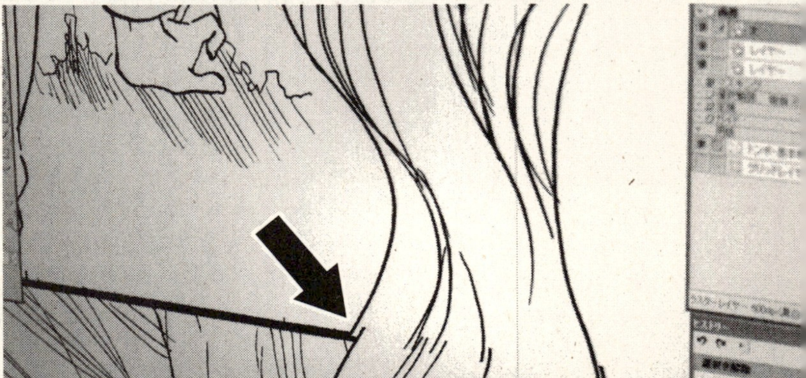

Connect the top half and the bottom half of your scanned page. When doing this, it's a good idea to zoom up close on the image.

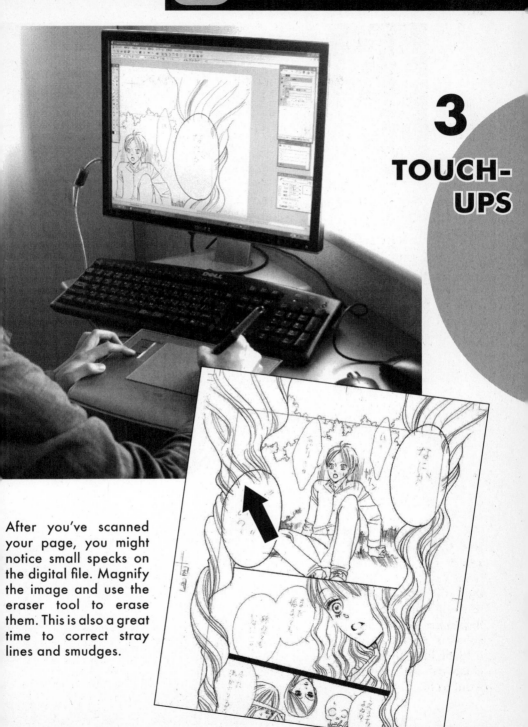

3 TOUCH-UPS

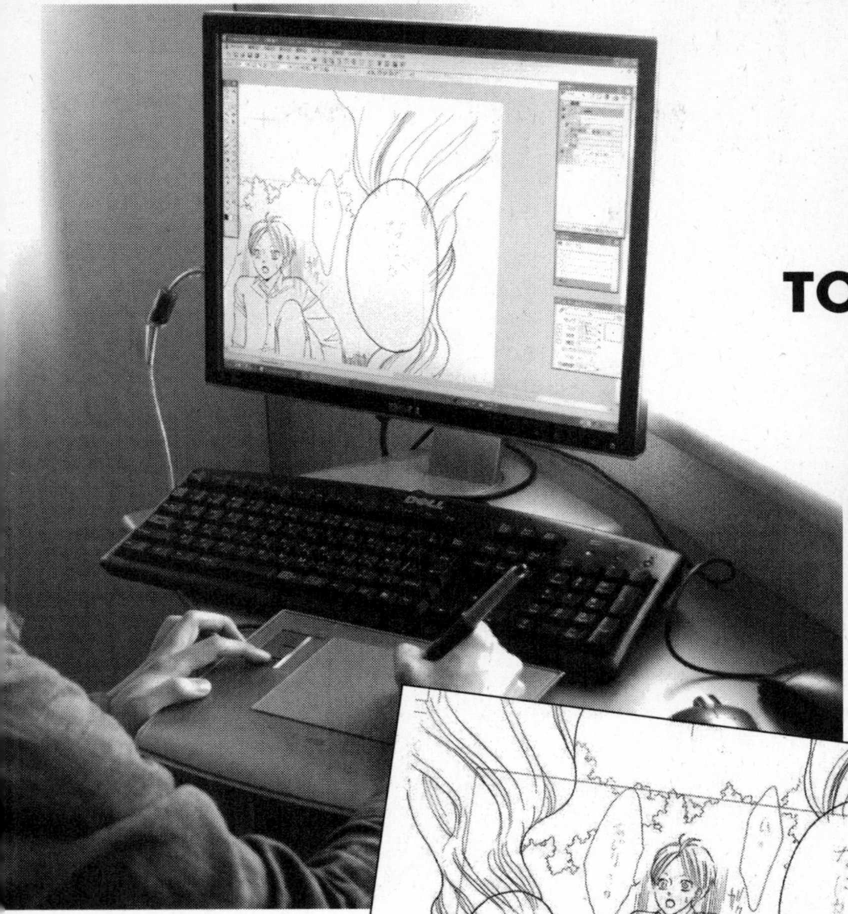

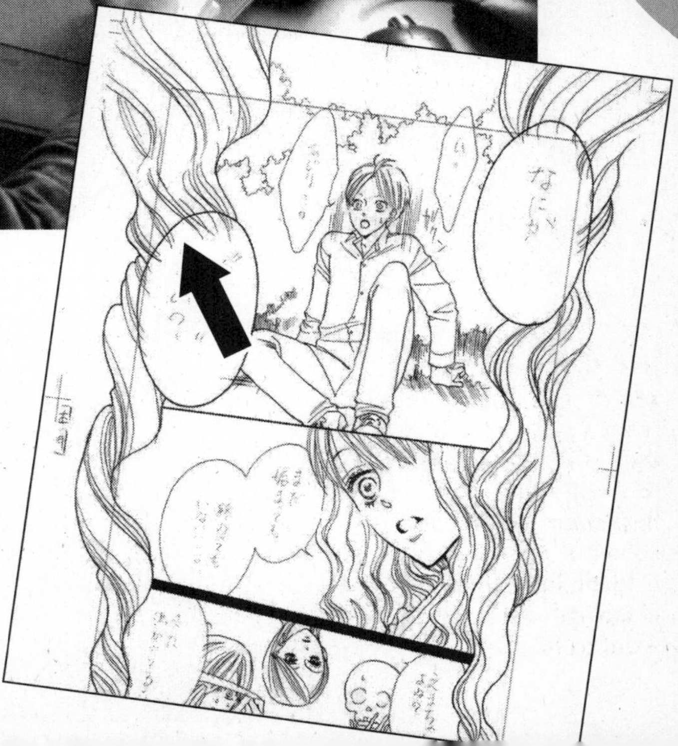

After you've scanned your page, you might notice small specks on the digital file. Magnify the image and use the eraser tool to erase them. This is also a great time to correct stray lines and smudges.

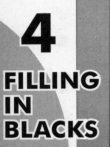

4 FILLING IN BLACKS

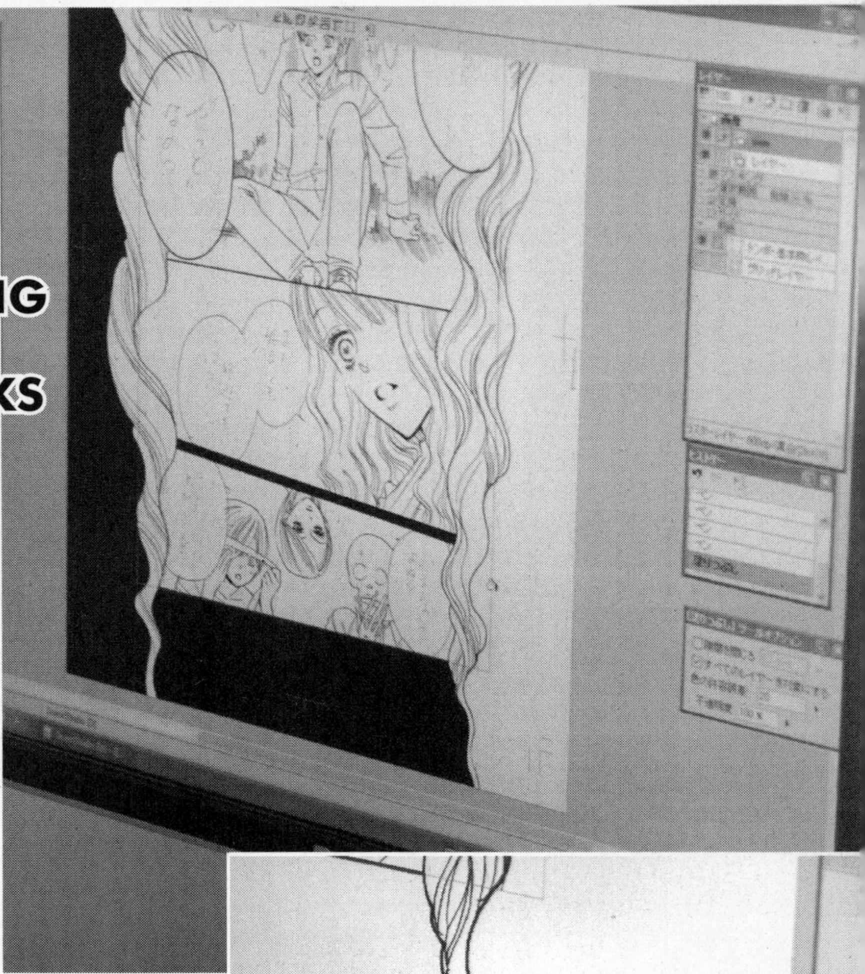

Use the select tool to select the area you want to fill with black, then fill it. The select tool will select any area that's bound by lines, so you may need to add or firm up lines to close off the area you want to fill.

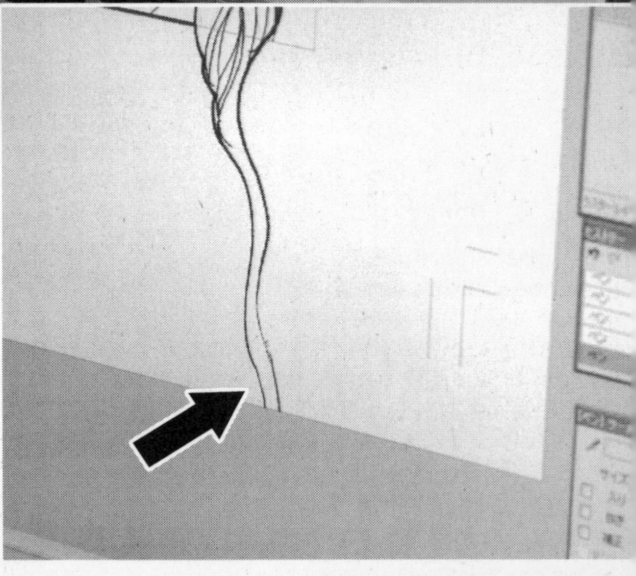

5 LAYING TONE

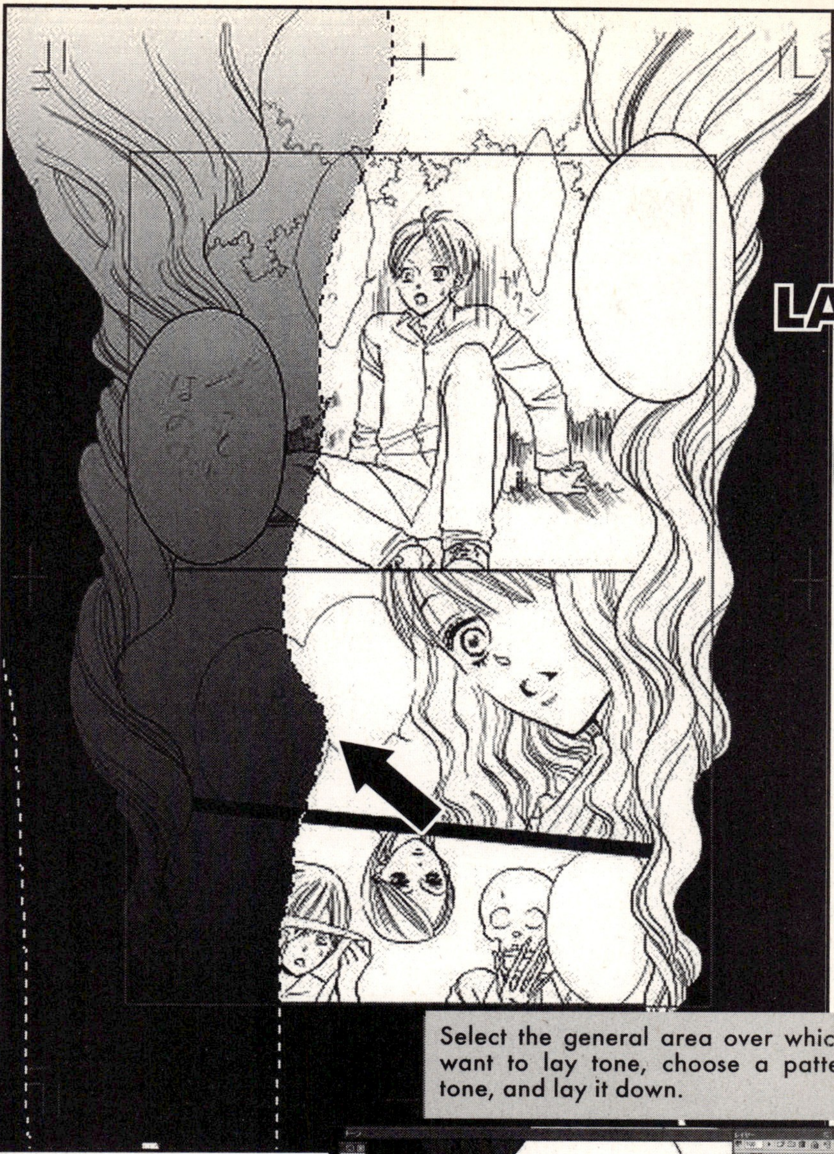

Select the general area over which you want to lay tone, choose a pattern of tone, and lay it down.

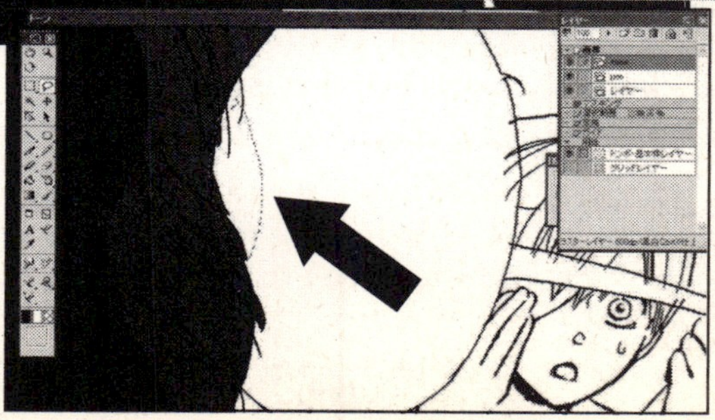

ɪxt, select the areas ɪere you don't need tone ɪd delete them. If there e still small pieces left ɪt you want to shave off, ɪn zoom in and delete the cess.

6 ADDING EFFECTS

Using a thick brush for the pen tool, you can draw tone patterns as if they were paint. That's how the tone was added for these hair shadows.

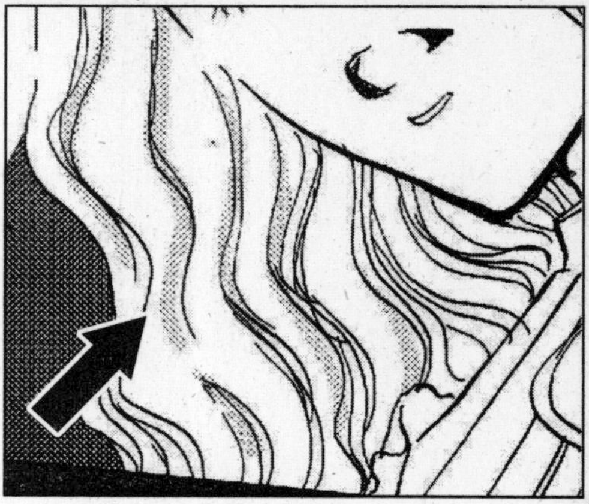

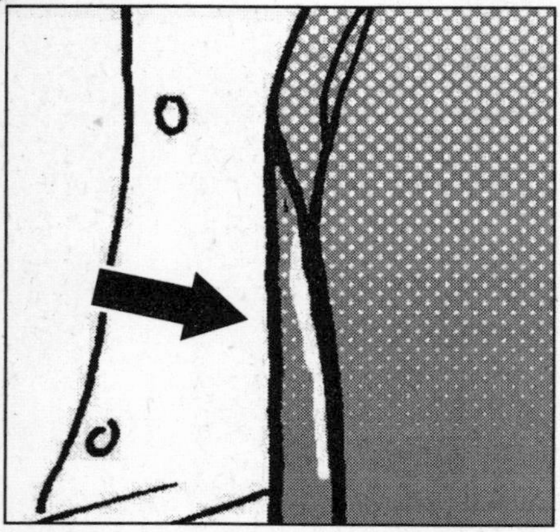

7 ADDIN HIGHLIGH

You can use the eraser tool (or white pen tool) to add highlights just as if it were white paint. The eraser tool also "scrapes away" tone just like a tone scrubber.

Save your work! If you plan to submit a digitally-created or finished manga to a contest, you'll need to complete this additional step: Save your manga to a CD; we recommend saving as .PSD files. Next, print out your manga on B4 paper, add the dialogue in pencil, and submit both the hard copy and your disc.

Aside from the tools we've already mentioned, ComicStudio has handy functions such as t line tool (to draw speed lines and such), and a function that alters scanned photographs ir manga-like backgrounds. Also, there are a few 3D objects and backgrounds included in t program, which you can pose and re-size to fit your needs. There's also a set of filters to a various digital effects. For more information, check out the software manual.

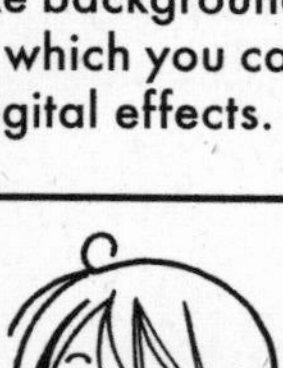

ComicStudio was developed specifically to create black-and-white comics, and it is the software that can recreate the various pen strokes from G pens and maru pens, an techniques such as line fades. It's quite an investment, and will take time to get used t if you can master it, then it will save on the time and money it takes to create manga.

ComicStudio (Celsys)	http://www.comicstudio.net

ENA-CHAN'S DIGITAL EXPERIENCE

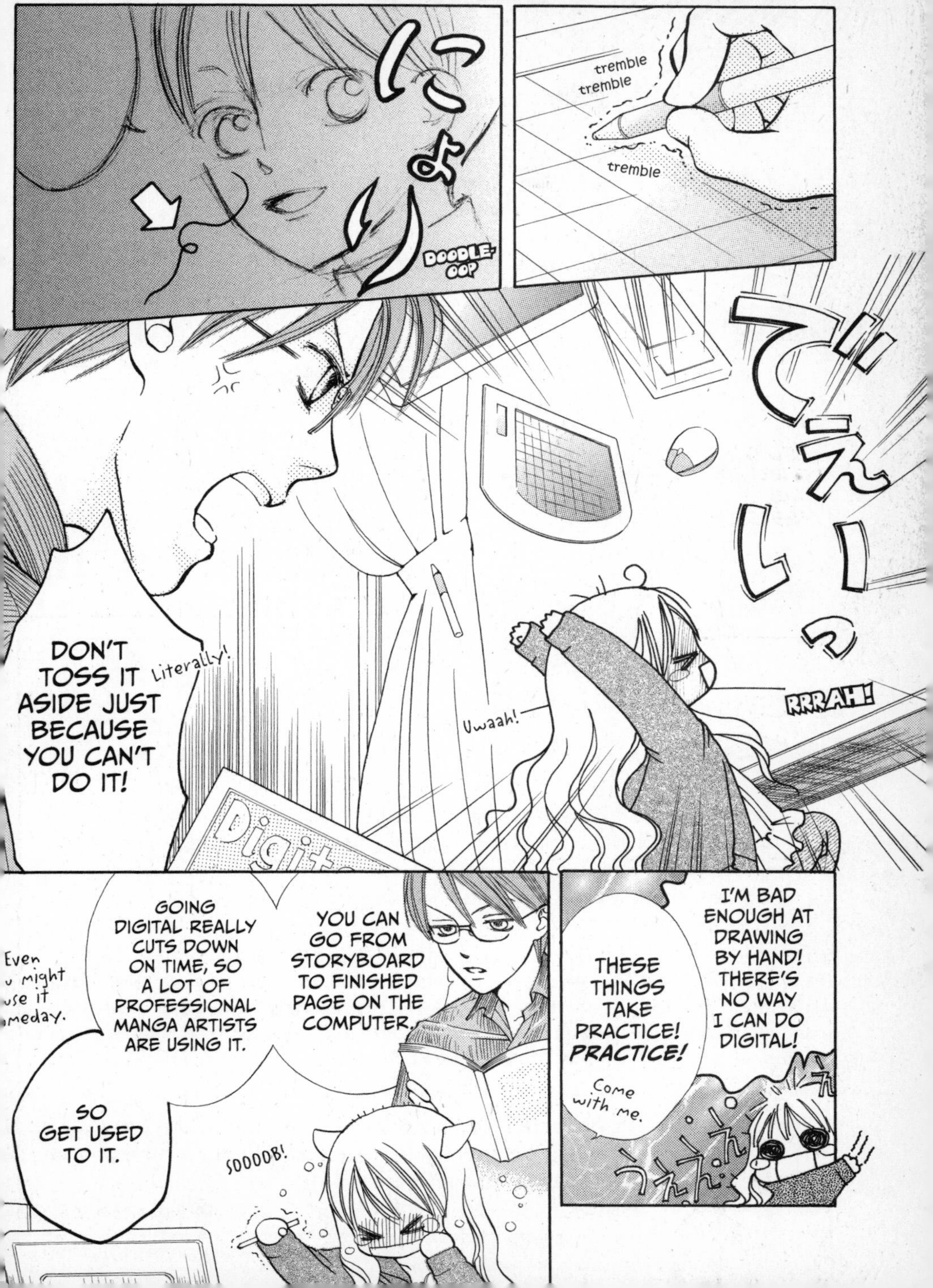

tremble
tremble
tremble
にょり
DOODLE-OOP
でぇいっ
RRRAH!
Uwaah!
DON'T TOSS IT ASIDE JUST BECAUSE YOU CAN'T DO IT!
Literally!
I'M BAD ENOUGH AT DRAWING BY HAND! THERE'S NO WAY I CAN DO DIGITAL!
THESE THINGS TAKE PRACTICE! PRACTICE!
Come with me.
YOU CAN GO FROM STORYBOARD TO FINISHED PAGE ON THE COMPUTER.
GOING DIGITAL REALLY CUTS DOWN ON TIME, SO A LOT OF PROFESSIONAL MANGA ARTISTS ARE USING IT.
SO GET USED TO IT.
SOOOOB!

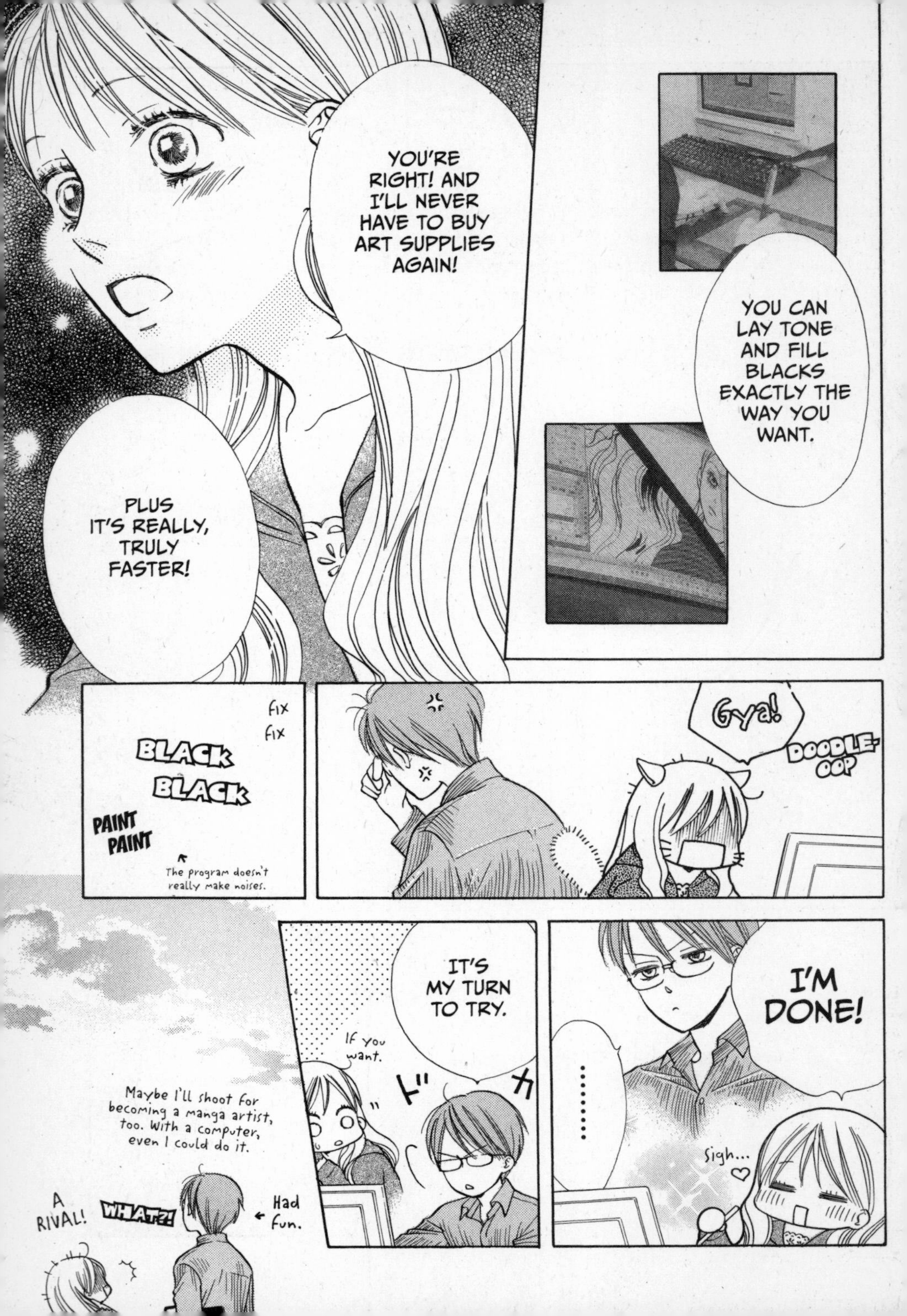
YOU CAN LAY TONE AND FILL BLACKS EXACTLY THE WAY YOU WANT.
YOU'RE RIGHT! AND I'LL NEVER HAVE TO BUY ART SUPPLIES AGAIN!
PLUS IT'S REALLY, TRULY FASTER!
Gya!
DOODLE-OOP
FIX
FIX
BLACK
BLACK
PAINT PAINT
The program doesn't really make noises.
I'M DONE!
......
Sigh... ♡
IT'S MY TURN TO TRY.
If you want.
ド
カ
Maybe I'll shoot for becoming a manga artist, too. With a computer, even I could do it.
Had fun.
WHAT?!
A RIVAL!

FINAL PRODUCT ● ENA-CHAN'S MANGA SUBMISSION! ●

Ena-chan's manga training began with gathering her supplies. Now, the work she wants to submit to a manga contest is finally complete! We will have editors from *Hana to Yume* and *LaLa* critique her finished manga. Everyone, do her the favor of being a good reader. Compare the final product to her outline on page 52 and the storyboards on page 78—you'll see the finished manga is the product of many revisions!

Submission Time!

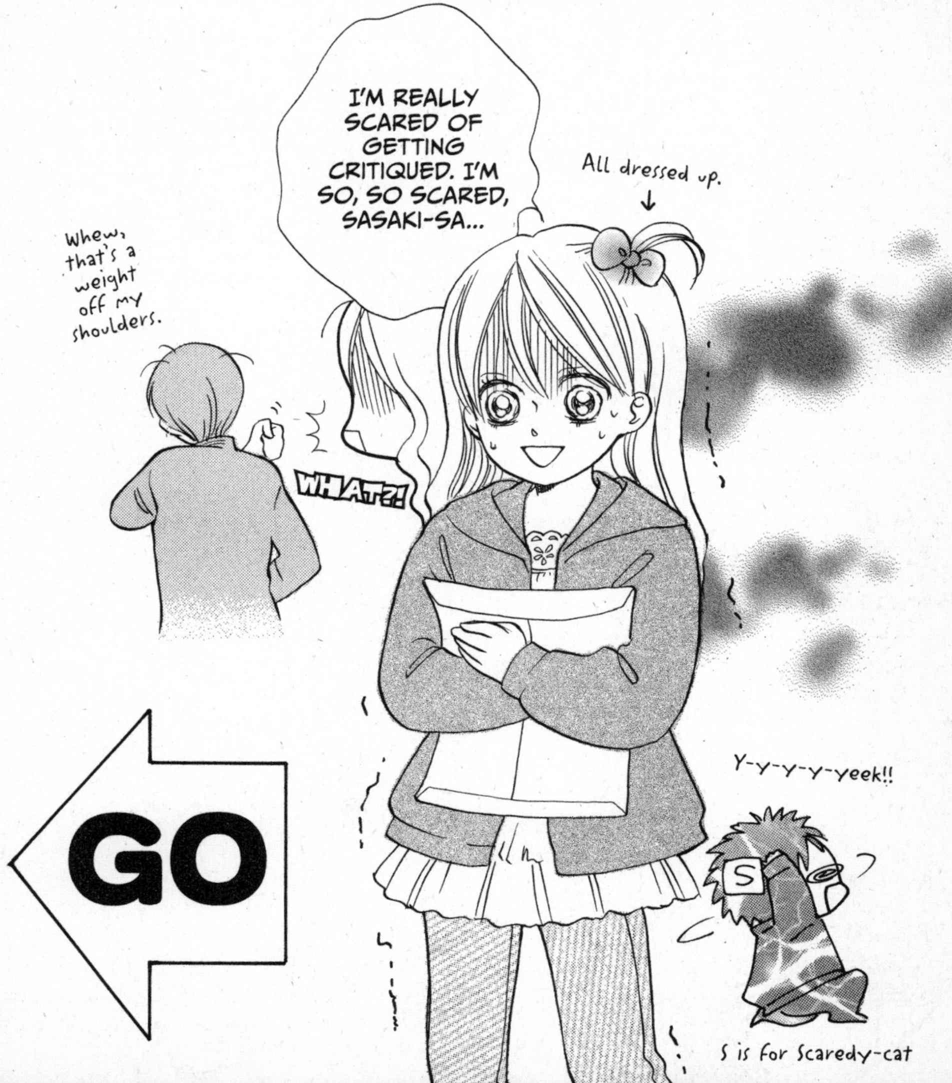
I'M REALLY SCARED OF GETTING CRITIQUED. I'M SO, SO SCARED, SASAKI-SA...
All dressed up.
Whew, that's a weight off my shoulders.
WHAT?!
Y-y-y-y-yeek!!
S
S is for Scaredy-cat
GO

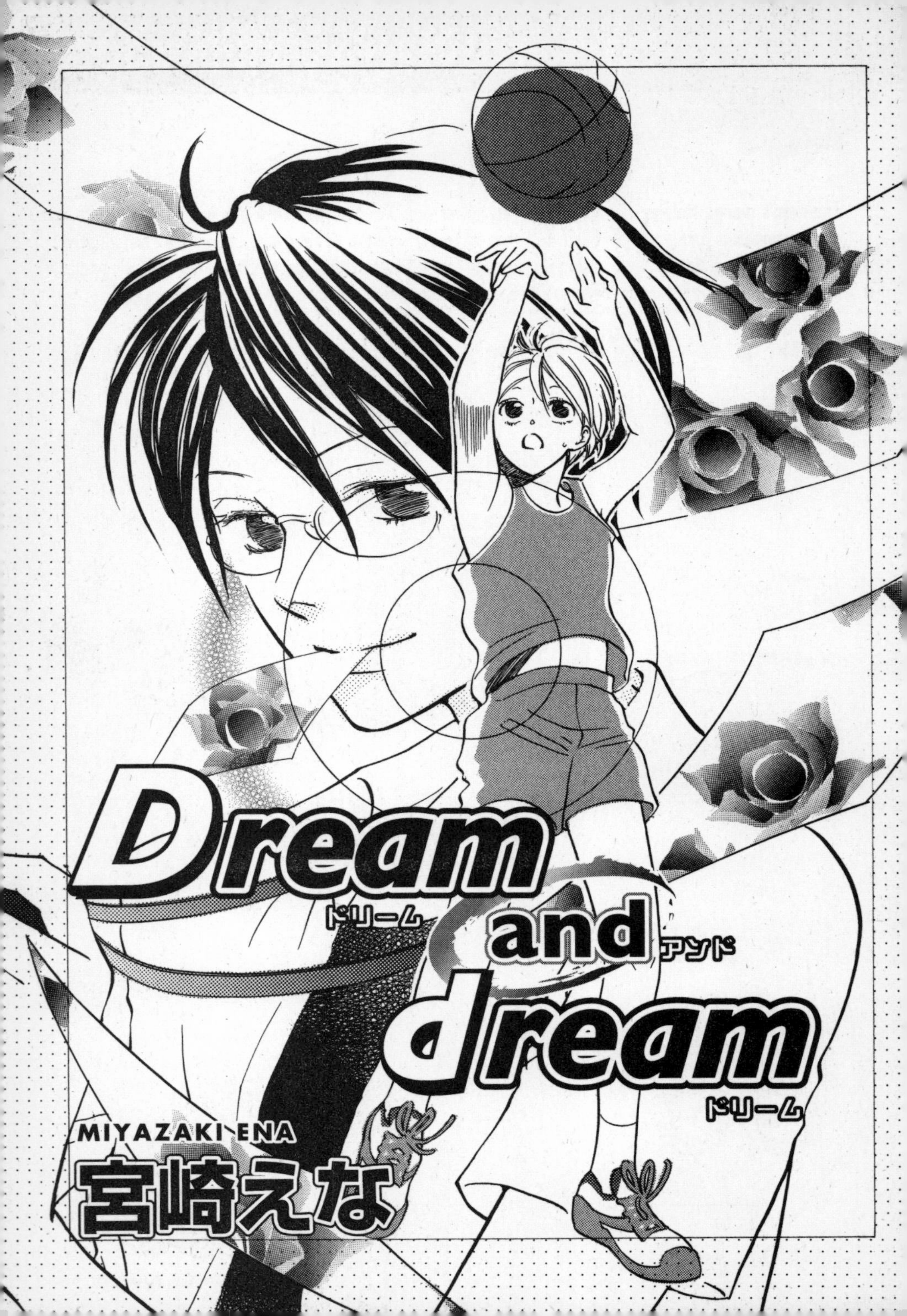
Dream
ドリーム
and
アンド
dream
ドリーム
MIYAZAKI ENA
宮崎えな

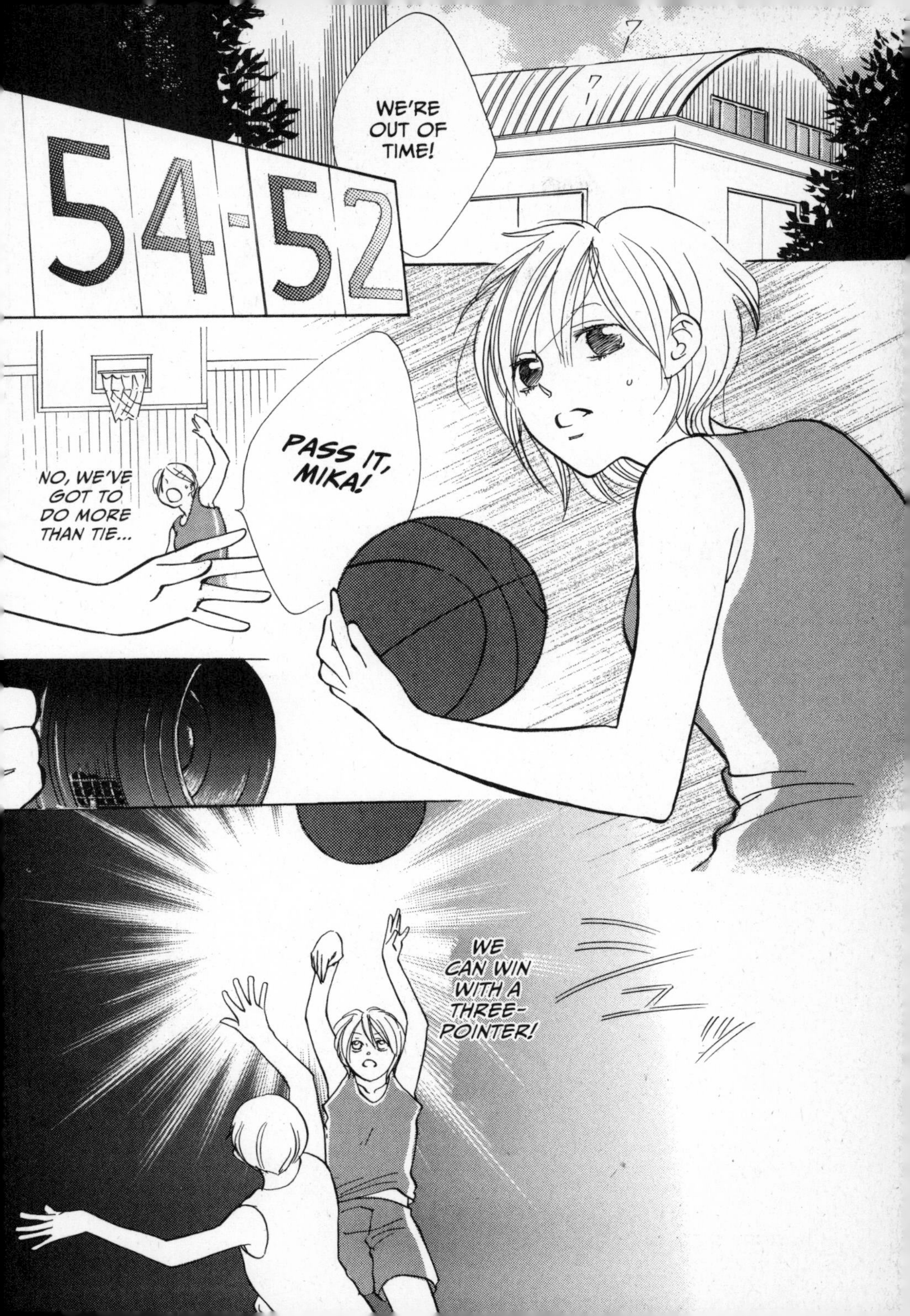

54-52
WE'RE OUT OF TIME!
PASS IT, MIKA!
NO, WE'VE GOT TO DO MORE THAN TIE...
WE CAN WIN WITH A THREE-POINTER!

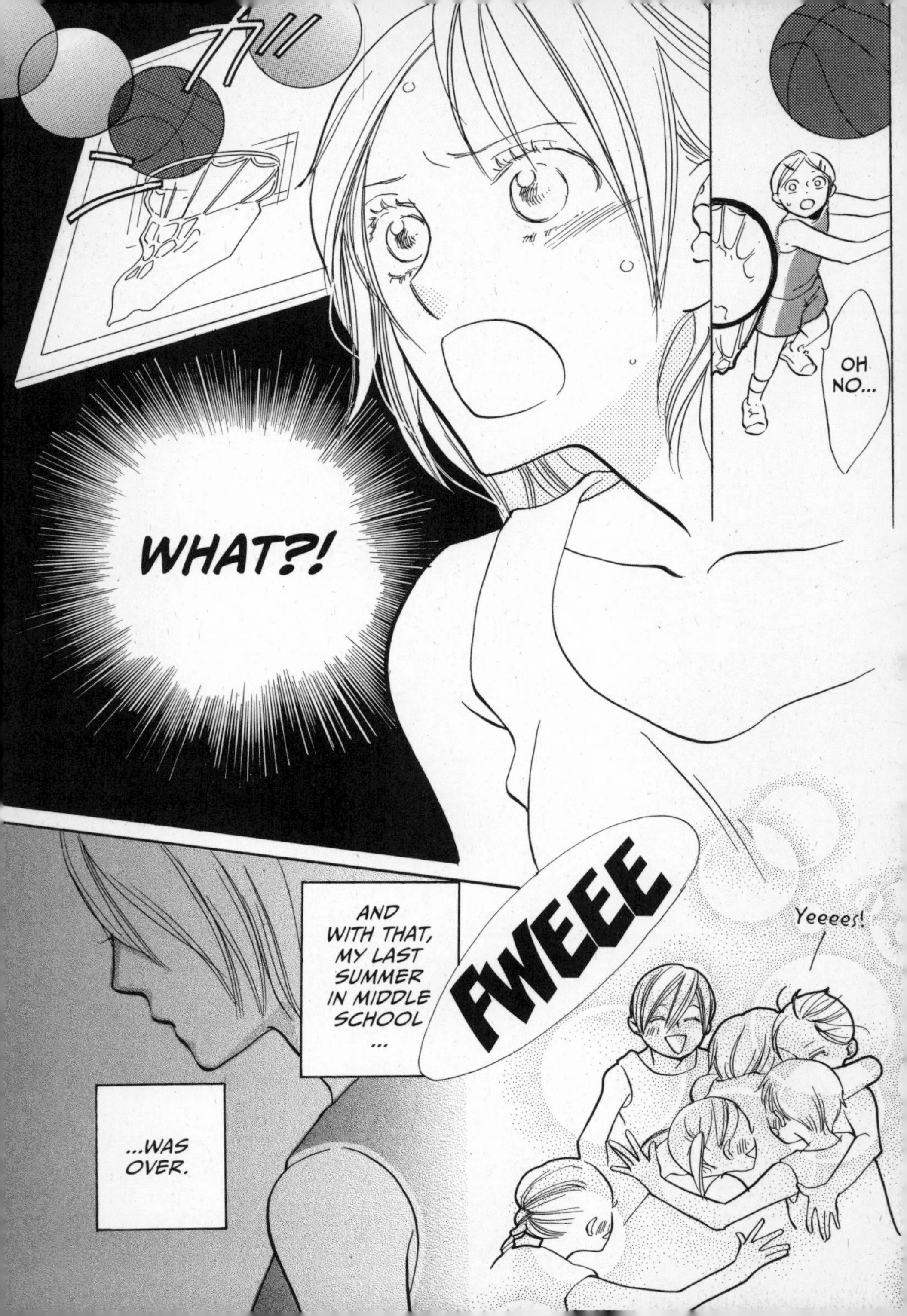
OH NO...
WHAT?!
FWEEE
Yeeees!
AND WITH THAT, MY LAST SUMMER IN MIDDLE SCHOOL ...
...WAS OVER.

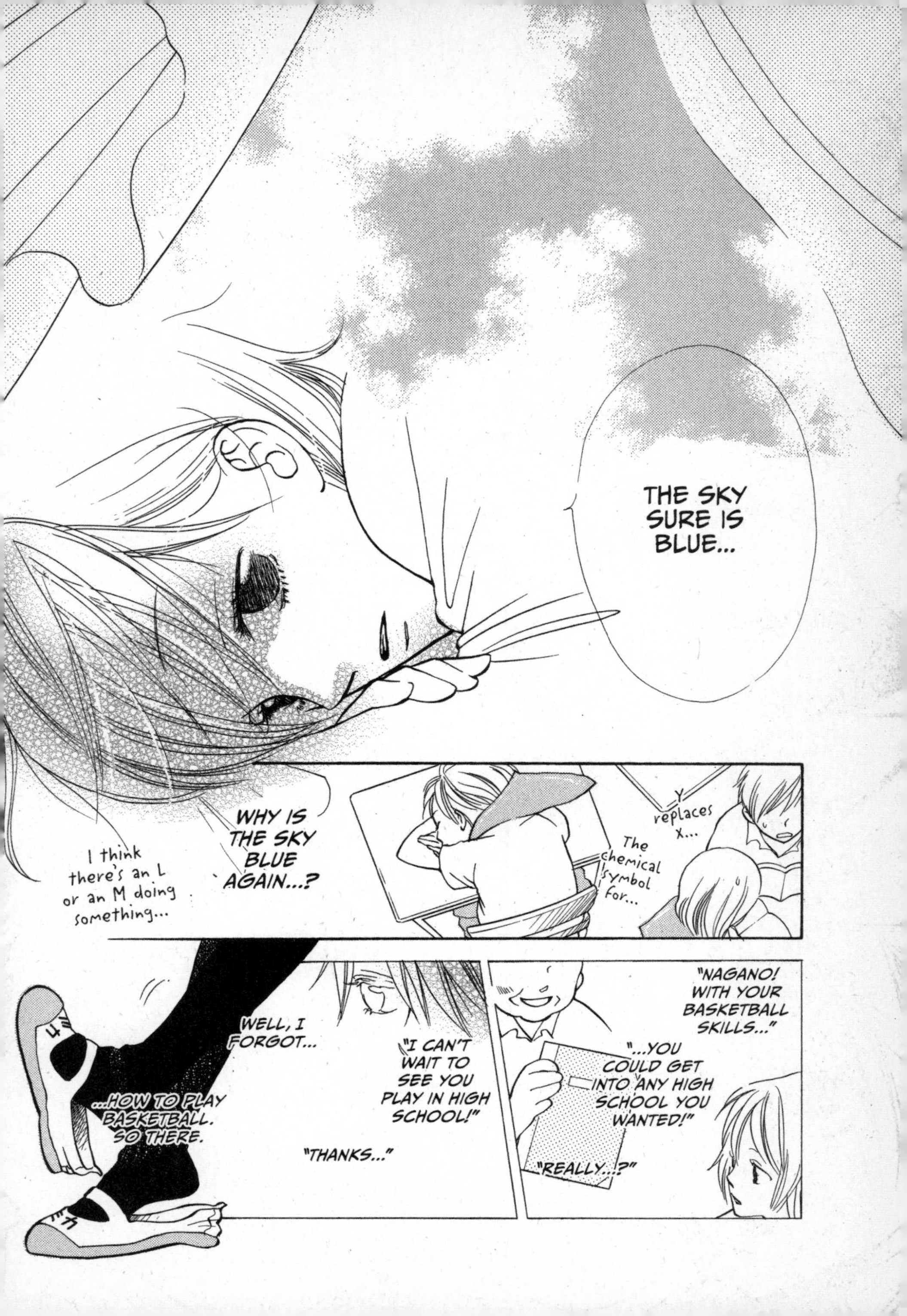
THE SKY SURE IS BLUE...
Y replaces x...
The chemical symbol for...
WHY IS THE SKY BLUE AGAIN...?
I think there's an L or an M doing something...
"NAGANO! WITH YOUR BASKETBALL SKILLS..."
"...YOU COULD GET INTO ANY HIGH SCHOOL YOU WANTED!"
"REALLY...?"
"I CAN'T WAIT TO SEE YOU PLAY IN HIGH SCHOOL!"
"THANKS..."
WELL, I FORGOT...
...HOW TO PLAY BASKETBALL. SO THERE.

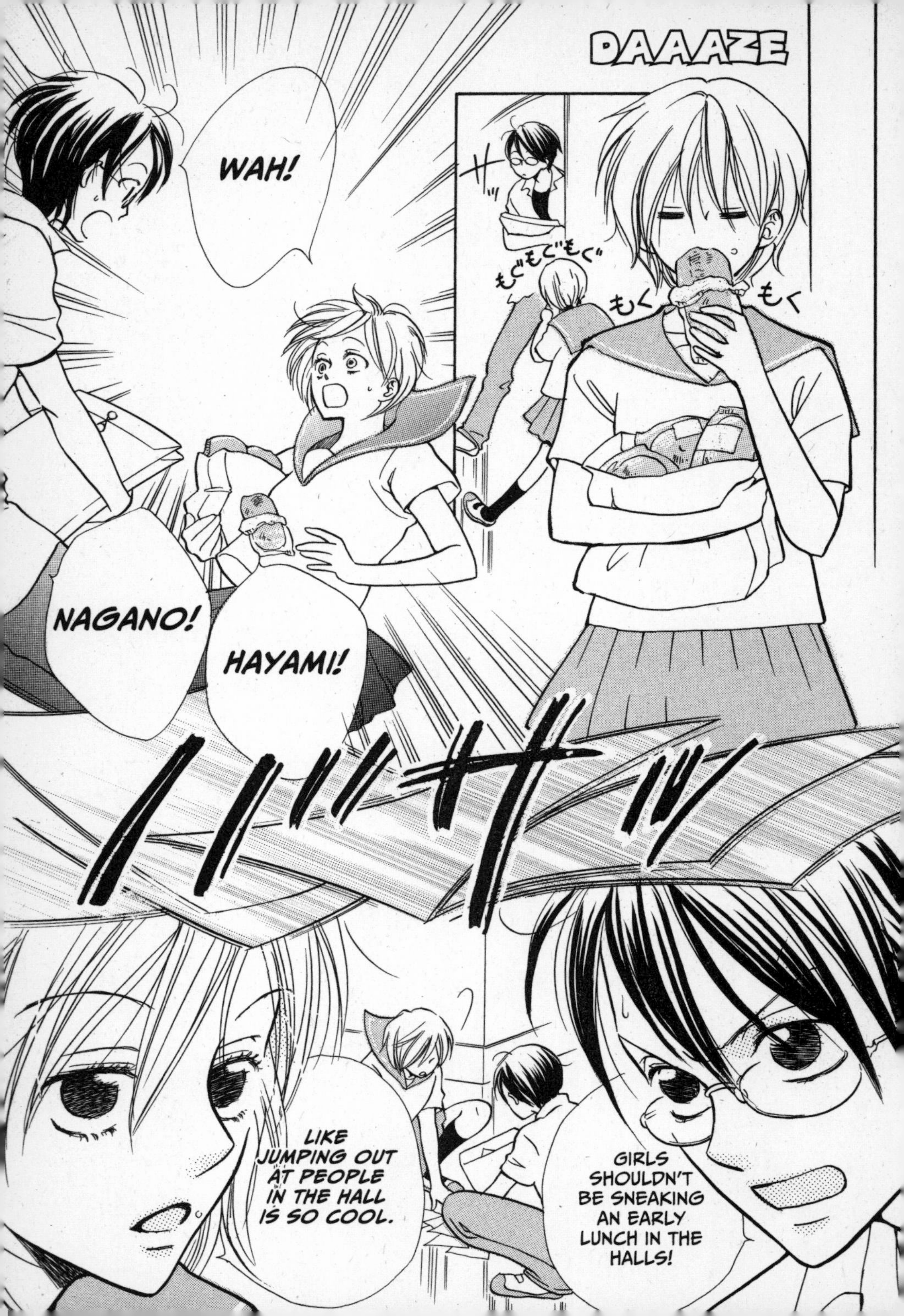
DAAAZE
もぐもぐもぐ
もく
もく
WAH!
NAGANO!
HAYAMI!
GIRLS SHOULDN'T BE SNEAKING AN EARLY LUNCH IN THE HALLS!
LIKE JUMPING OUT AT PEOPLE IN THE HALL IS SO COOL.

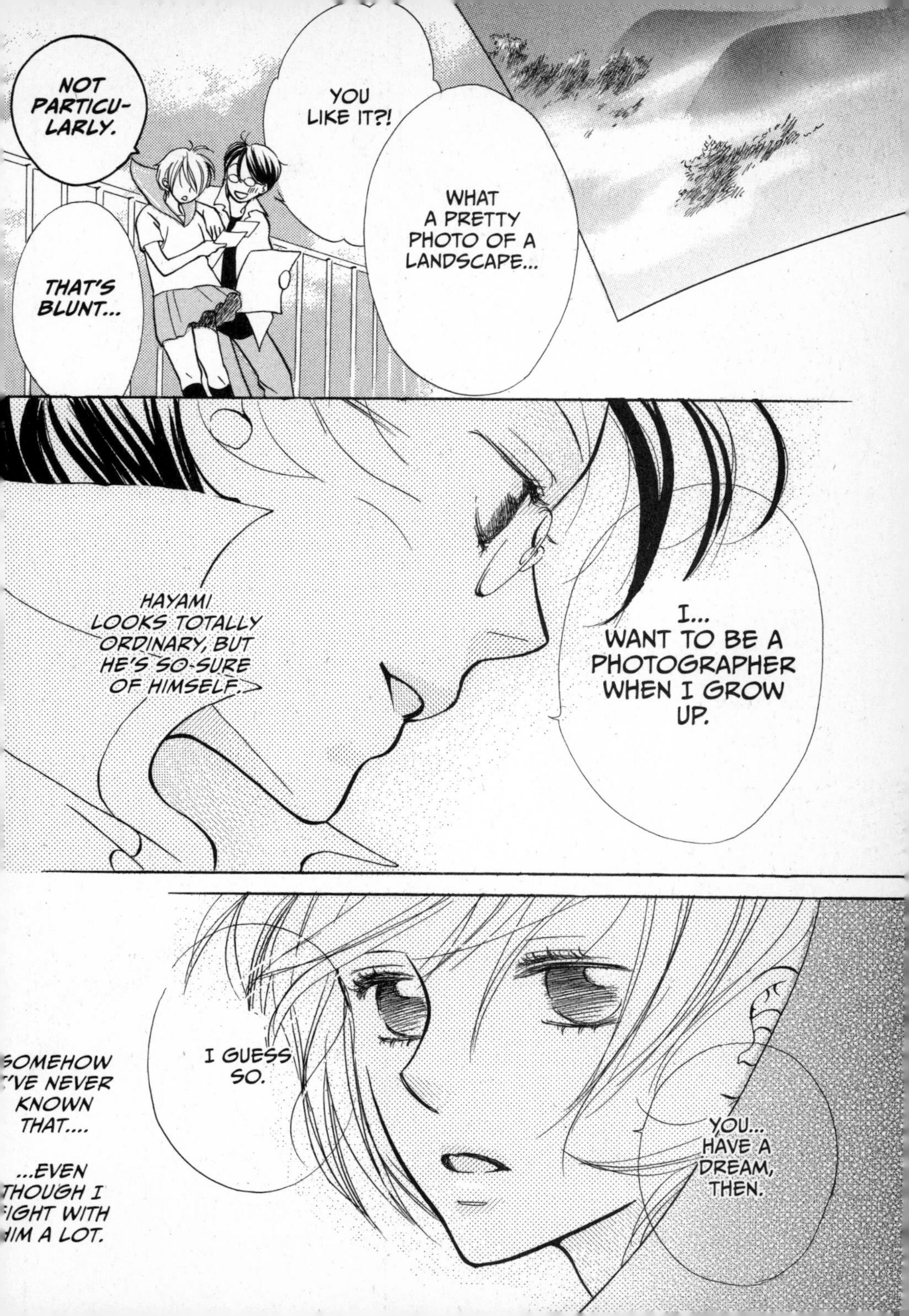
WHAT A PRETTY PHOTO OF A LANDSCAPE...
YOU LIKE IT?!
NOT PARTICU-LARLY.
THAT'S BLUNT...
I... WANT TO BE A PHOTOGRAPHER WHEN I GROW UP.
HAYAMI LOOKS TOTALLY ORDINARY, BUT HE'S SO SURE OF HIMSELF.
YOU... HAVE A DREAM, THEN.
I GUESS SO.
SOMEHOW I'VE NEVER KNOWN THAT....
...EVEN THOUGH I FIGHT WITH HIM A LOT.

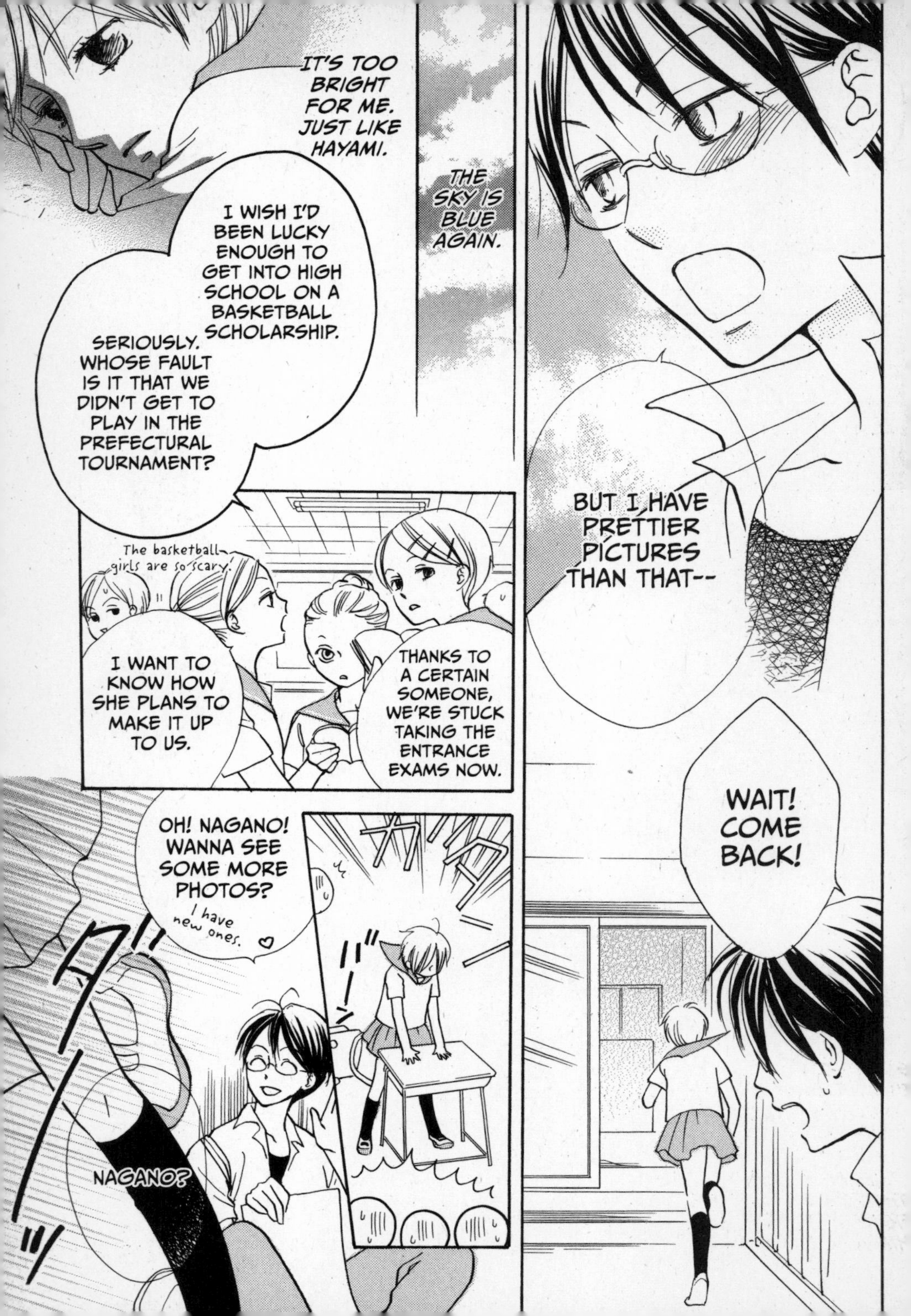
BUT I HAVE PRETTIER PICTURES THAN THAT--
WAIT! COME BACK!
THE SKY IS BLUE AGAIN.
IT'S TOO BRIGHT FOR ME. JUST LIKE HAYAMI.
I WISH I'D BEEN LUCKY ENOUGH TO GET INTO HIGH SCHOOL ON A BASKETBALL SCHOLARSHIP.
SERIOUSLY. WHOSE FAULT IS IT THAT WE DIDN'T GET TO PLAY IN THE PREFECTURAL TOURNAMENT?
THANKS TO A CERTAIN SOMEONE, WE'RE STUCK TAKING THE ENTRANCE EXAMS NOW.
I WANT TO KNOW HOW SHE PLANS TO MAKE IT UP TO US.
The basketball girls are so scary.
OH! NAGANO! WANNA SEE SOME MORE PHOTOS?
I have new ones. ♡
NAGANO?

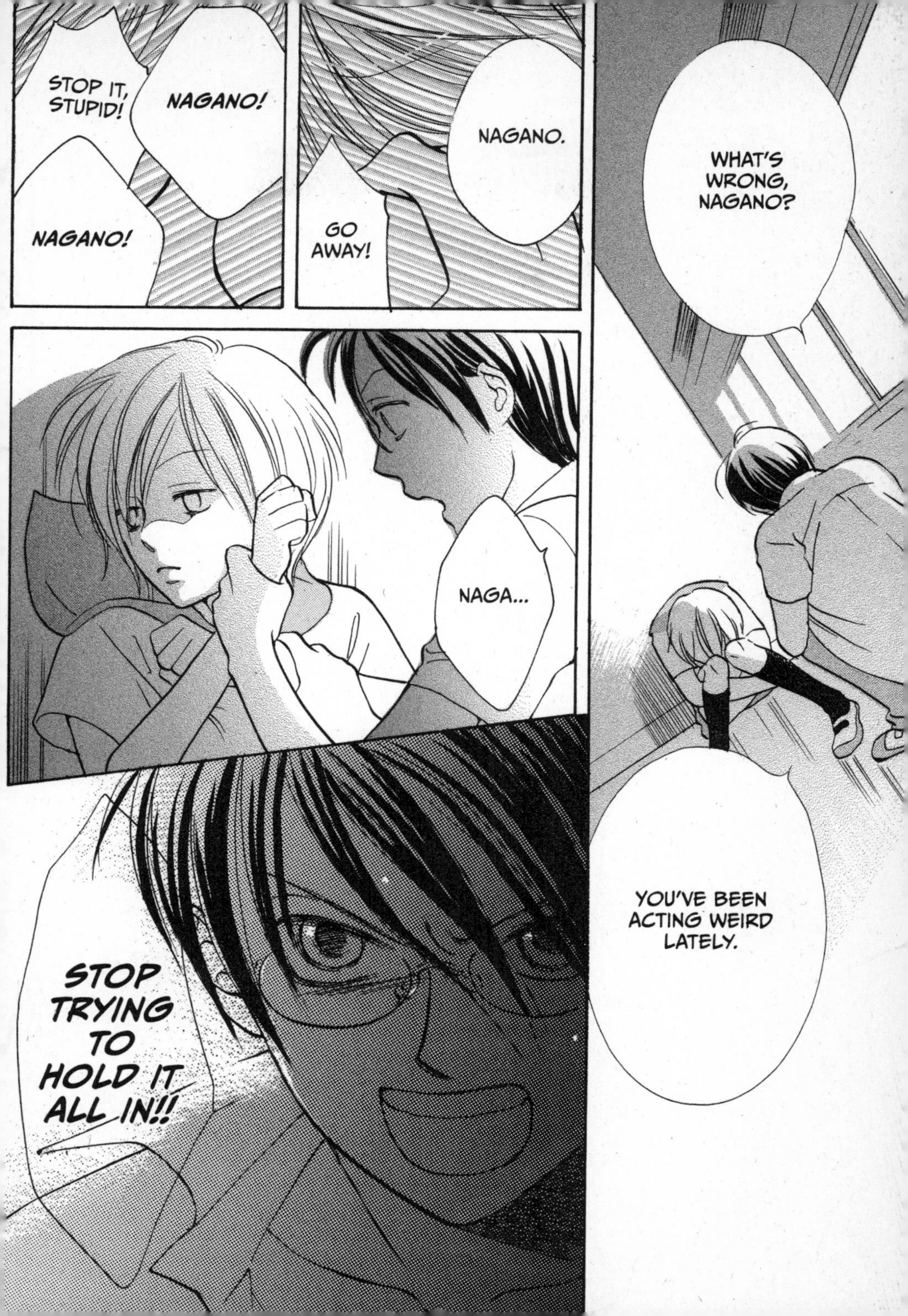
WHAT'S WRONG, NAGANO?
YOU'VE BEEN ACTING WEIRD LATELY.
NAGANO.
GO AWAY!
NAGANO!
STOP IT, STUPID!
NAGANO!
NAGA...
STOP TRYING TO HOLD IT ALL IN!!

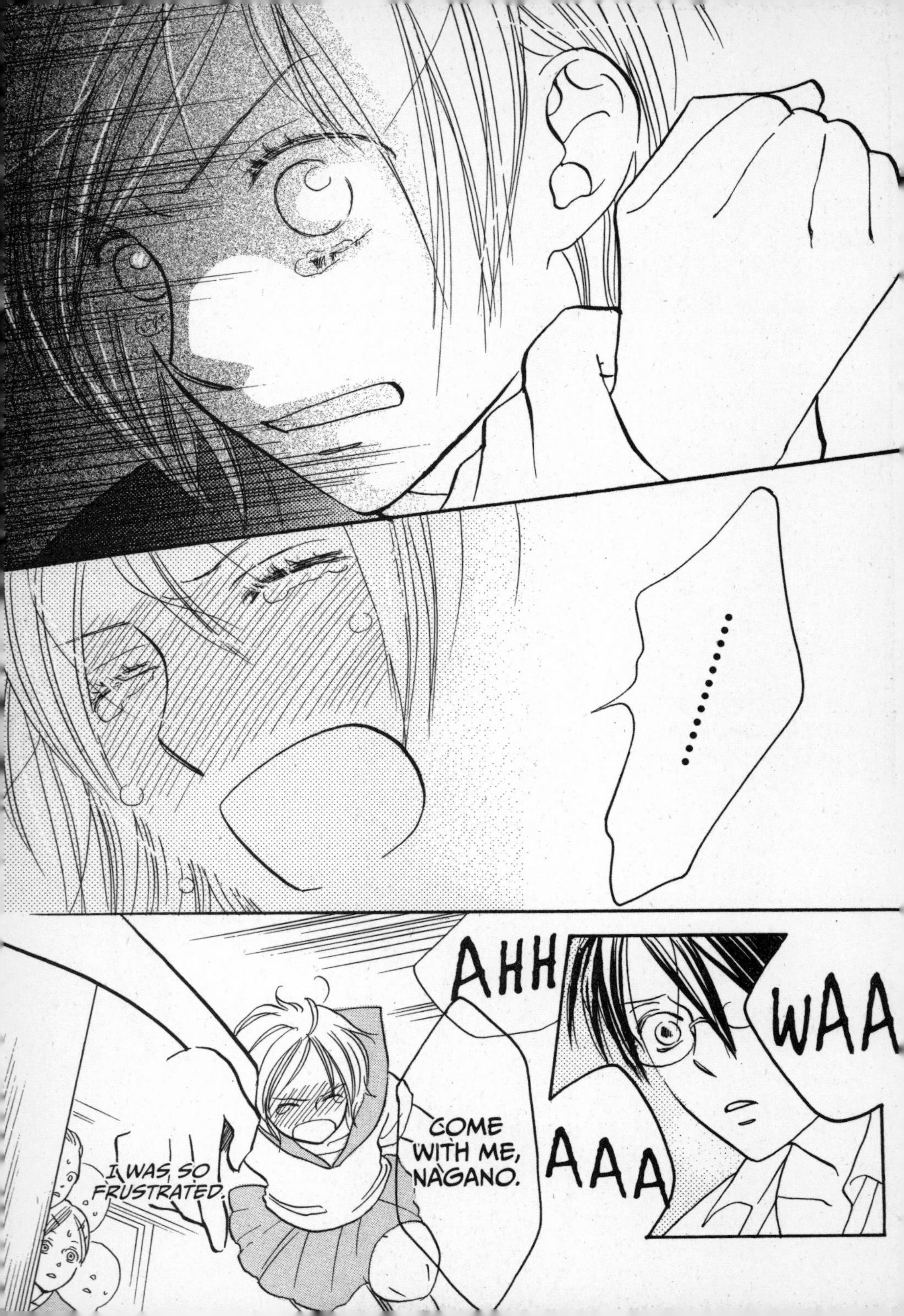
……
AHH WAA AAA
COME WITH ME, NAGANO.
I WAS SO FRUSTRATED.

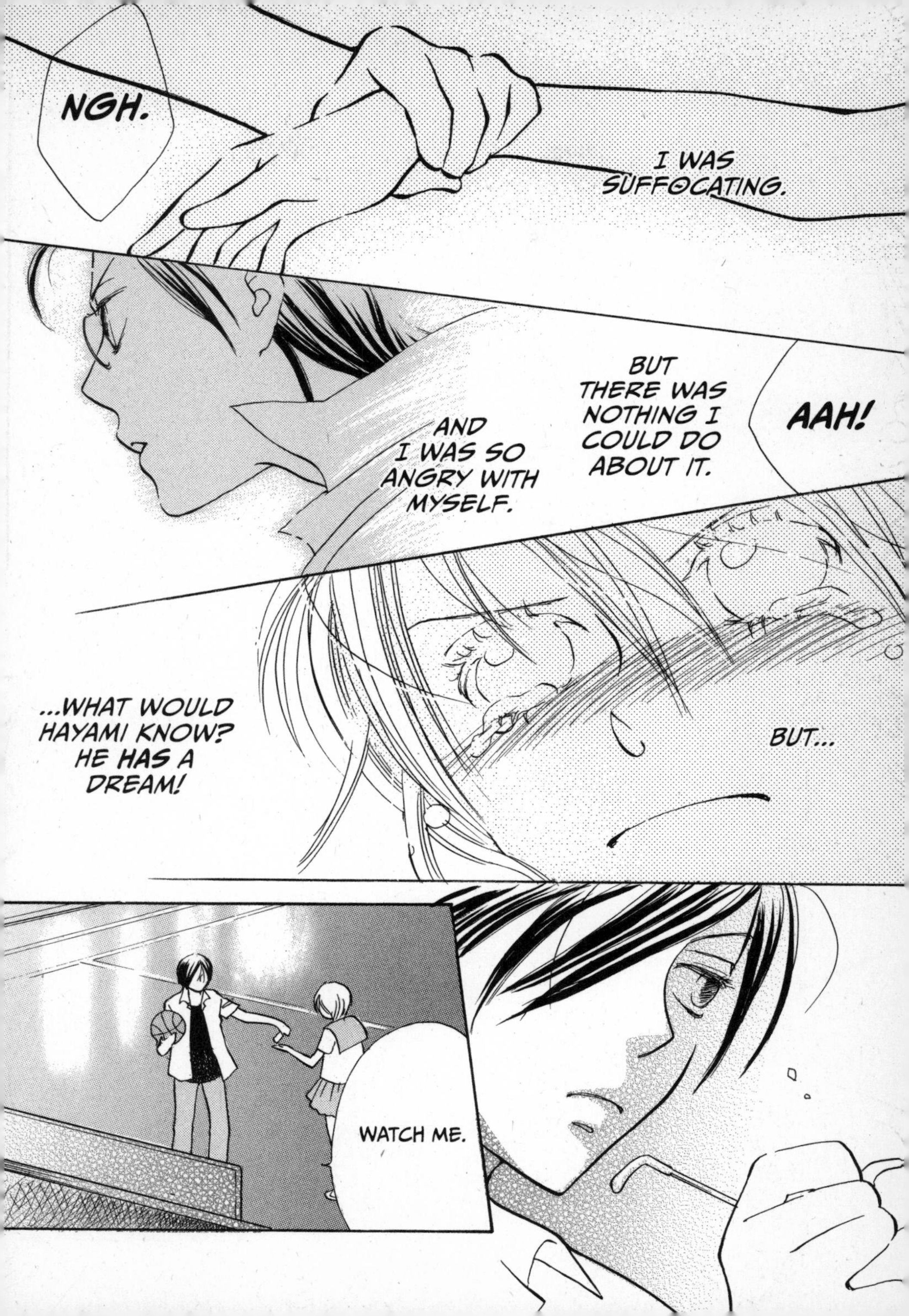
I WAS SUFFOCATING.
NGH.
AAH!
BUT THERE WAS NOTHING I COULD DO ABOUT IT.
AND I WAS SO ANGRY WITH MYSELF.
BUT...
...WHAT WOULD HAYAMI KNOW? HE HAS A DREAM!
WATCH ME.

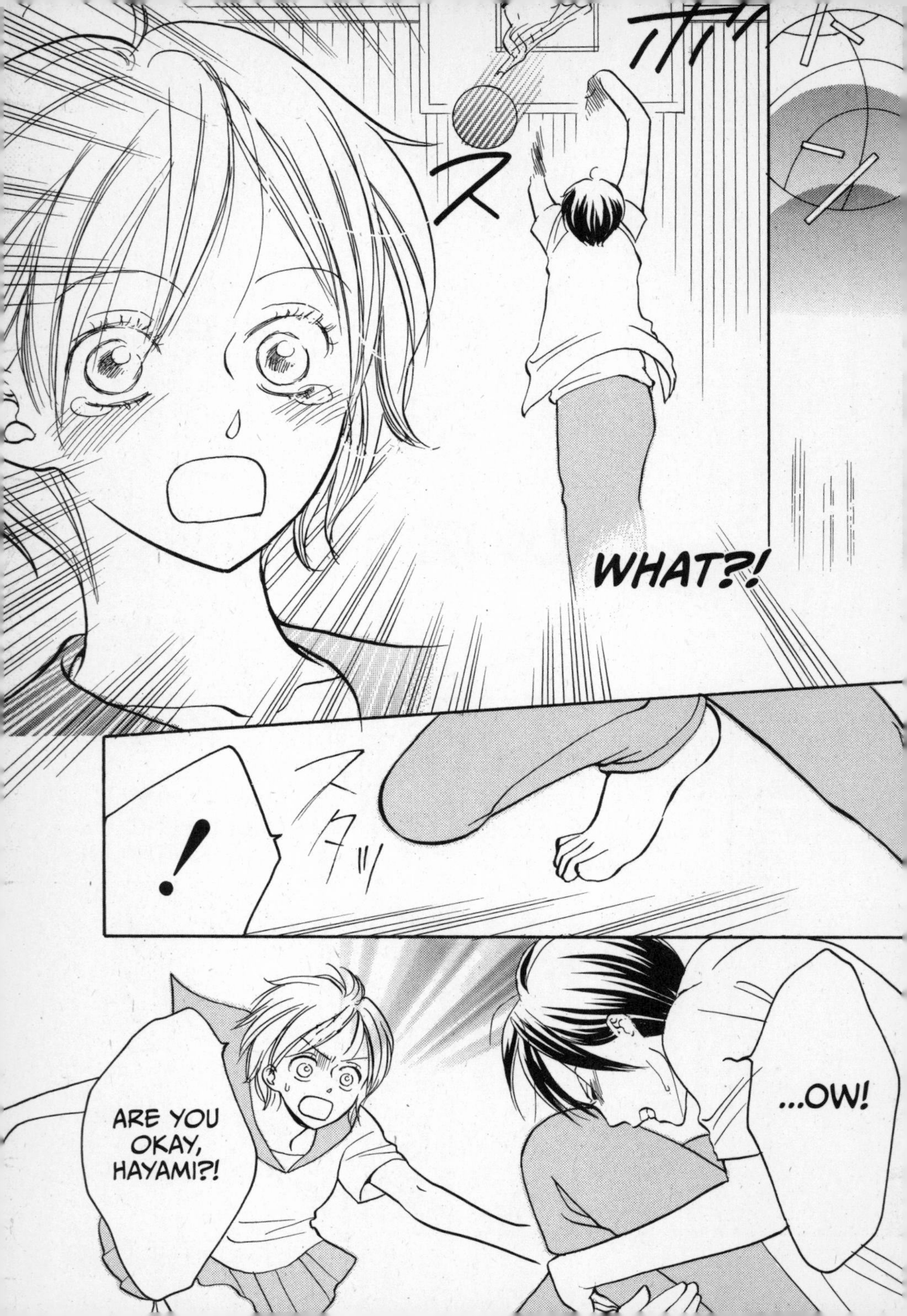
WHAT?!
!
スタッ
...OW!
ARE YOU OKAY, HAYAMI?!

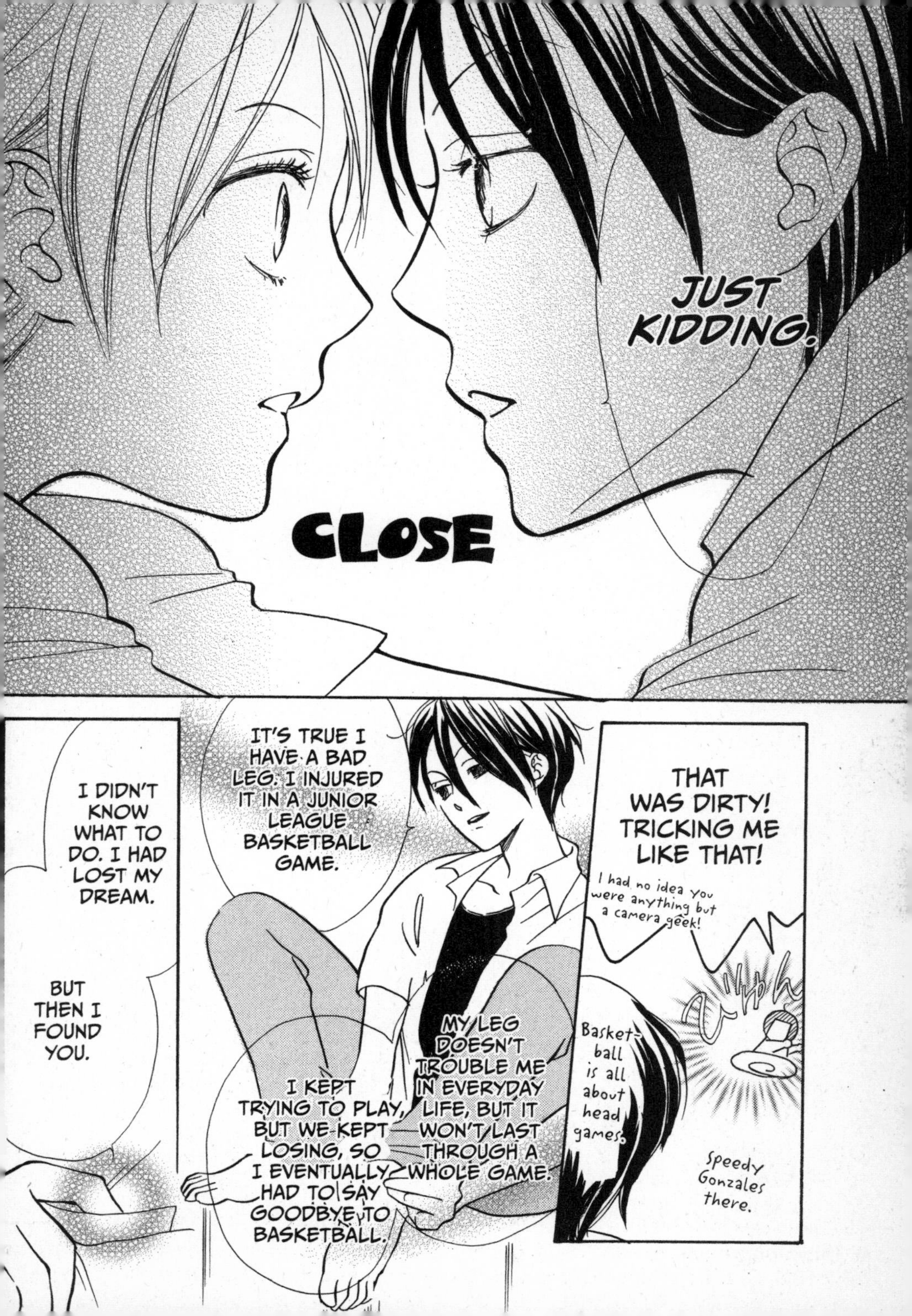
JUST KIDDING.
CLOSE
THAT WAS DIRTY! TRICKING ME LIKE THAT!
I had no idea you were anything but a camera geek!
Basketball is all about head games.
Speedy Gonzales there.
IT'S TRUE I HAVE A BAD LEG. I INJURED IT IN A JUNIOR LEAGUE BASKETBALL GAME.
I DIDN'T KNOW WHAT TO DO. I HAD LOST MY DREAM.
MY LEG DOESN'T TROUBLE ME IN EVERYDAY LIFE, BUT IT WON'T LAST THROUGH A WHOLE GAME.
I KEPT TRYING TO PLAY, BUT WE KEPT LOSING, SO I EVENTUALLY HAD TO SAY GOODBYE TO BASKETBALL.
BUT THEN I FOUND YOU.

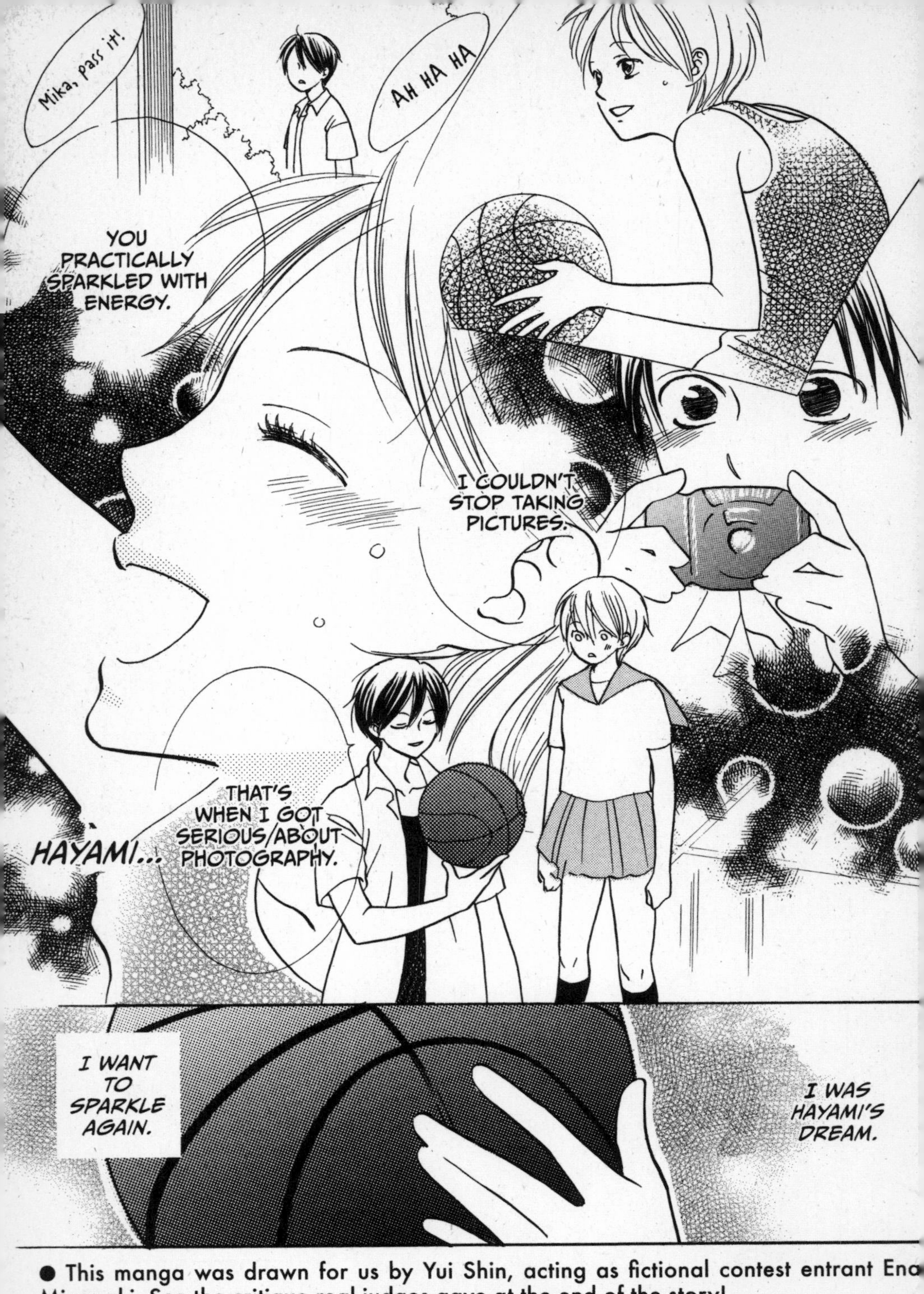

AH HA HA
Mika, pass it!
YOU PRACTICALLY SPARKLED WITH ENERGY.
I COULDN'T STOP TAKING PICTURES.
THAT'S WHEN I GOT SERIOUS ABOUT PHOTOGRAPHY.
HAYAMI...
I WAS HAYAMI'S DREAM.
I WANT TO SPARKLE AGAIN.

● This manga was drawn for us by Yui Shin, acting as fictional contest entrant Ena Miyazaki. See the critique real judges gave at the end of the story!

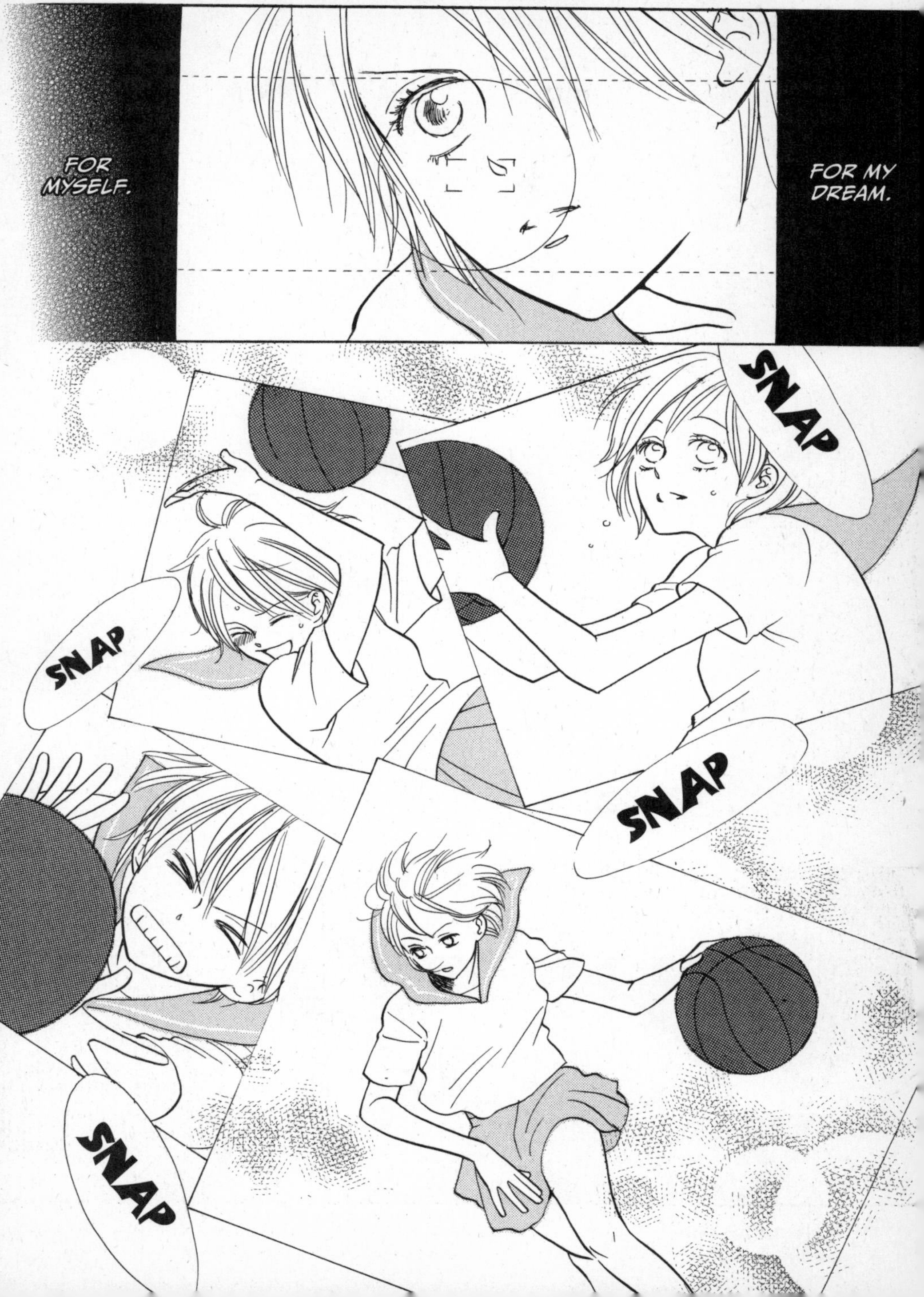
FOR MY DREAM.
FOR MYSELF.
SNAP
SNAP
SNAP
SNAP

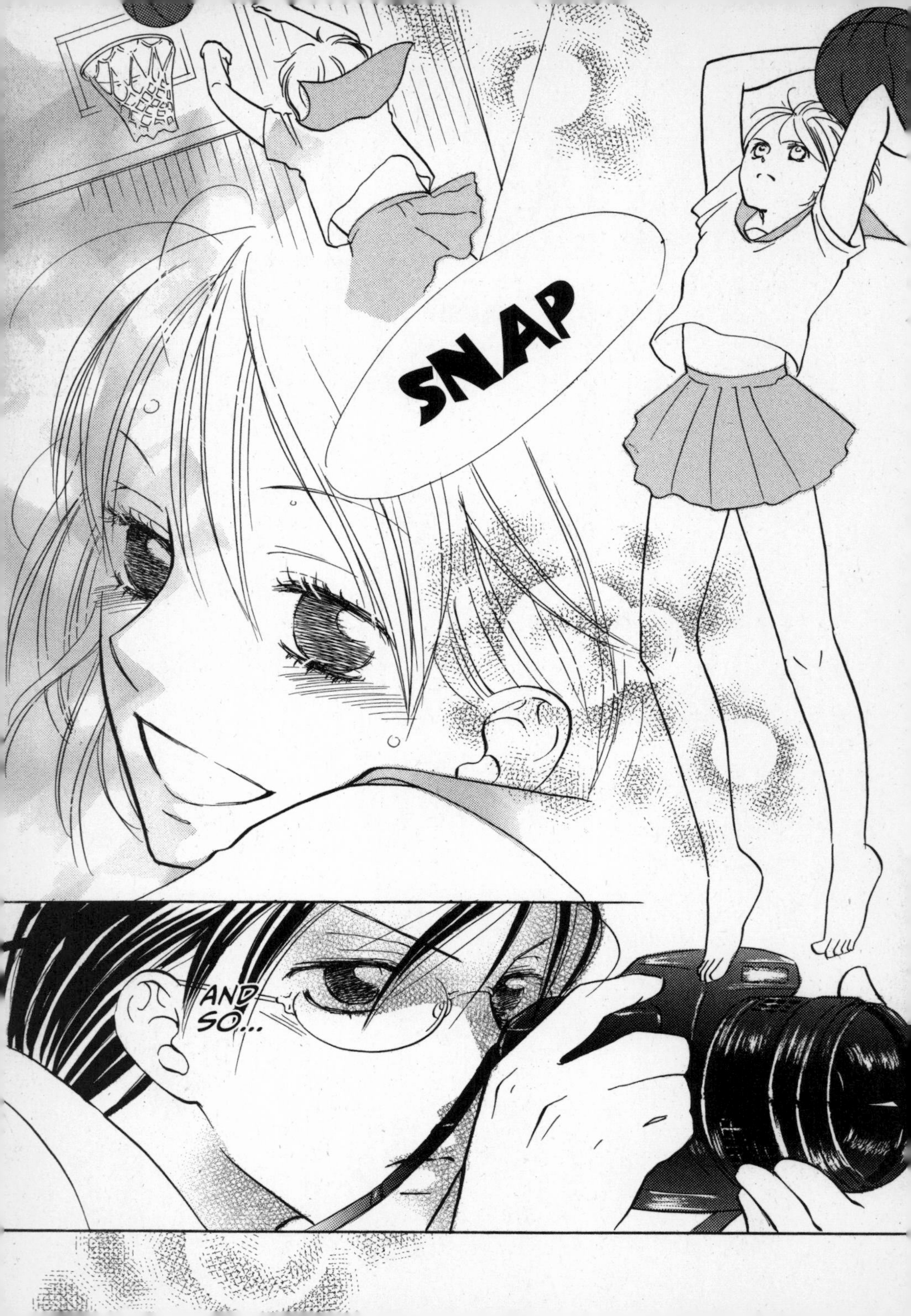
SNAP
AND SO...

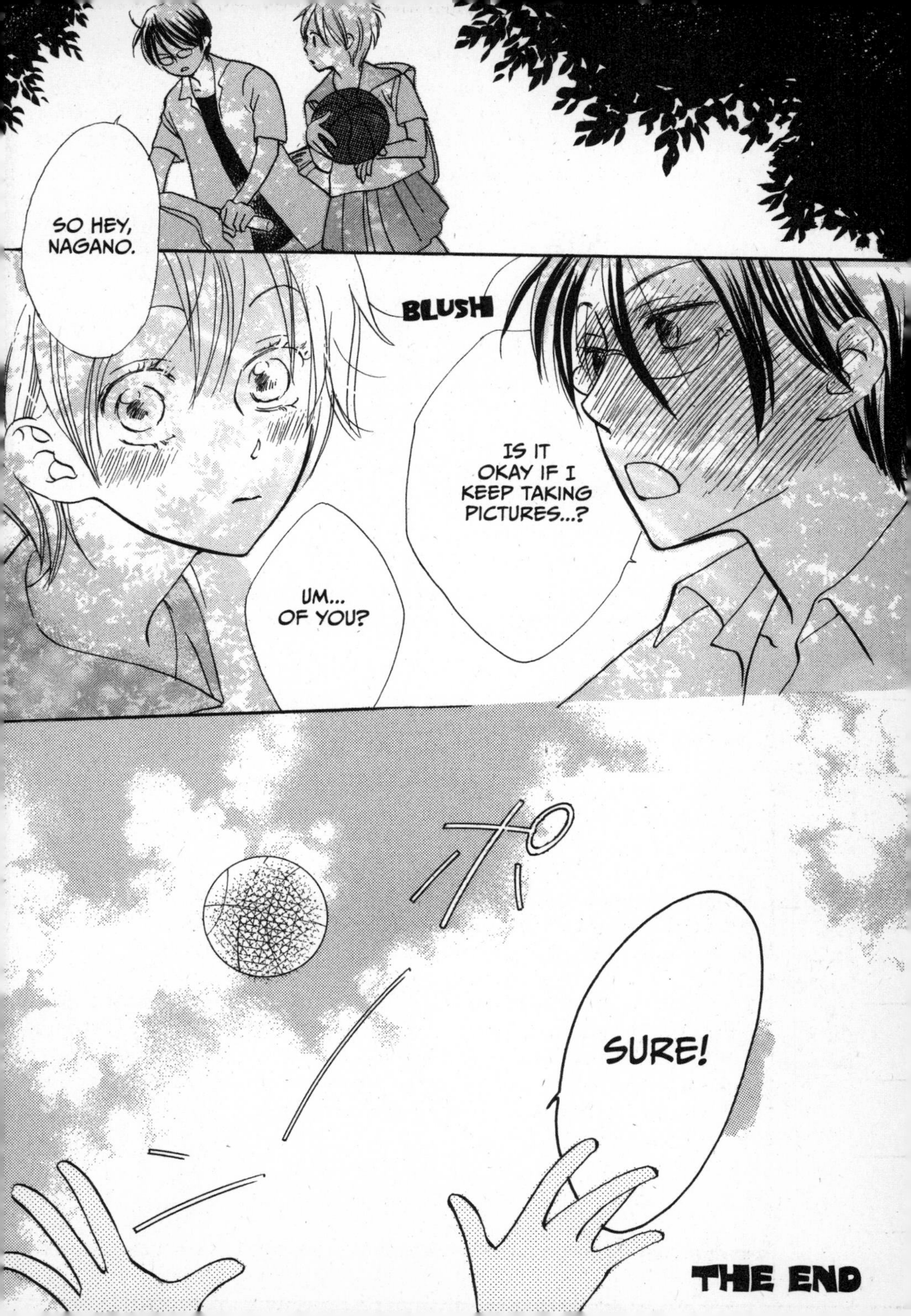
SO HEY, NAGANO.
BLUSH
IS IT OKAY IF I KEEP TAKING PICTURES...?
UM... OF YOU?
SURE!
THE END

Critique from Manga Contest Judges

We asked editors of the HMC (Hana to Yume Manga-ka Course) and LMS (LaLa Manga-ka Scout Course) to critique Ena-chan's manga.

Hana to Yume Editorial Department, Head of HMC, Takashi Sakuma

You did a great job making Hayami come across as dependable and encouraging by showing us how dedicated he is to watching over Mika when she's lost sight of her dream. You also succeeded in showing the cute sides of the characters, like when Hayami blushes on page seven, and when Mika starts sobbing in spite of herself on page nine.

You paced the story well, tracing the arc of Mika's frustration and come-back, but I felt that the whole thing was lacking tension and drama. Also, I would have liked to delve a little deeper into the mentality that made Mika think, "I want to sparkle again," "I want to play basketball," after she learns that she was the reason Hayami got into photography.

On the art side of things, you used a variety of camera angles, like the bird's-eye and the worm's-eye view, so I didn't get bored while reading. But it's a shame that the picture of the camera in the middle of page two doesn't stand out more, because it's an important piece of foreshadowing. It would be better to pull back a little, and really show us that it's a camera. Your inking is a little too heavy-handed, and the thinner lines in the character's hair and clothes come off looking overly sketchy; both these areas need improvement.

LaLa Editorial Department, Head of LMS, Akihito Masui

The discouragement Mika feels after the basketball game and her growing resilience as she gets back on her feet all comes together nicely.

It's a shame that both the main characters, Mika and Hayami, are a little dull. They're not exciting enough. In particular, there aren't enough scenes where Mika acts on her own; you need more incidents that show us why she's an interesting character. Consider giving her some defining personality trait, like, "She's dull, but extremely sure of herself." This is even more nitpicky, but I was concerned about how you depicted the friendship between Mika and Hayami. In particular, how come she didn't know he had a bad leg? How come she never knew he wanted to be a photographer? It's just not clear whether these two are as close as they're supposed to be.

As for the art, you have strong character designs, and you depict your characters' movements well. But your overall finishes suffer from being too sloppy. Practice inking so that you can make your lines smoother, particularly in the hair. Also, when laying tone, be careful not to accidentally go outside of the lines. Furthermore, do some research to find out how to use tone to give clothes and backgrounds more texture, in order to make your scenes more vivid.

DEALING WITH CRITICISM
THINKING ABOUT YOUR NEXT MANGA

Editor Sasaki (later referred to as Sasaki): Ena-san, you've gotten critique for your work from the editors in charge of the *Hana to Yume* and *LaLa* manga contests. What are your thoughts?

Applicant Ena (later referred to as Ena): Sakuma-san and Masui-san are way too harsh! They didn't say anything nice!

Sasaki: What are you talking about? They pointed out your flaws and told you areas to improve. That means all you have to do is fix those things, and you'll definitely get better.
Ena: Will they ever want to see work from me again?

Sasaki: Of course they do! They give such stern critiques because they want you to submit your next work to their contest. It doesn't make any sense to read the critique, throw up your hands, and decide you're done. Take their criticism as a means to improve your future work.
Ena: Yeah. I'll do my best. They both said, "It's not exciting enough."

Sasaki: The story starts with your main character Mika thinking, "I don't want to do anything," and so they were suggesting that there should be more dramatic tension that leads to her changing her thoughts to " I want to sparkle again."
Ena: But a lot of manga starts out that way.

Sasaki: In a series, you can get away with a main character being passive, because there's a lot more space to show them grow. In a one shot, though, we like to see some instant character development and choices from the main character. Mika lets other people determine her actions. We don't even know what attracts the two main characters to each other.
Ena: Is that what makes the main characters so dull?

Sasaki: Yes. The characters and story are dull, but the art is pretty dull, too.
Ena: Well, they're not flashy types.

Sasaki: She's a spirited athlete—that should give you plenty of material you can use to make her more interesting. You can make her face and eyes more unique, and you can also make her seem more athletic by picking shots that emphasize her height, or her long, pale limbs as they stick out of her uniform.
Ena: Oh, so that's your type? What a pervert!

Sasaki: What I'm saying is that the deeper the impression your characters leave, the easier it is for your readers to get into the story!!
Ena: You don't have to get mad. What should I do about Hayami?

Sasaki: Speaking as a fellow bespectacled guy, I'd like to see you show that even though Hayami appears to be kind of a doof, he's actually intelligent and active.
Ena: Yeah, yeah. What do they mean about the finishing touches being sloppy?

DEALING WITH CRITICISM

THINKING ABOUT YOUR NEXT MANGA

Sasaki: There are a lot of frames where the only tone is on the clothes and the ball. And that tone goes outside the lines.
Ena: I laid the tone on a little big on purpose to make it feel softer, but I guess that backfired.

Sasaki: It's okay to use techniques like that to your advantage. The problem is that your art isn't very sophisticated yet, so it ends up looking like a mistake. If you want your tone to look softer, scrape off some tone to fade it. That will look more professional. Also, your pen strokes are thick and rough, so be more delicate.
Ena: I've got to be more careful making manga, don't I?

Sasaki: You've only got 16 pages, so you don't have many panels in which to show off your characters. Use the panels you do have in service of advertising your character's appeal. If those panels charm your readers, you'll win them over more thoroughly than any dialogue could hope to.
Ena: I'll do my best! But it will be hard to get it all.

Sasaki: Even if you can't fix everything all at once, improve little by little, and apply what you've learned to your next work! There's no doubt in my mind that if you keep improving, you'll end up winning a contest or even going pro.

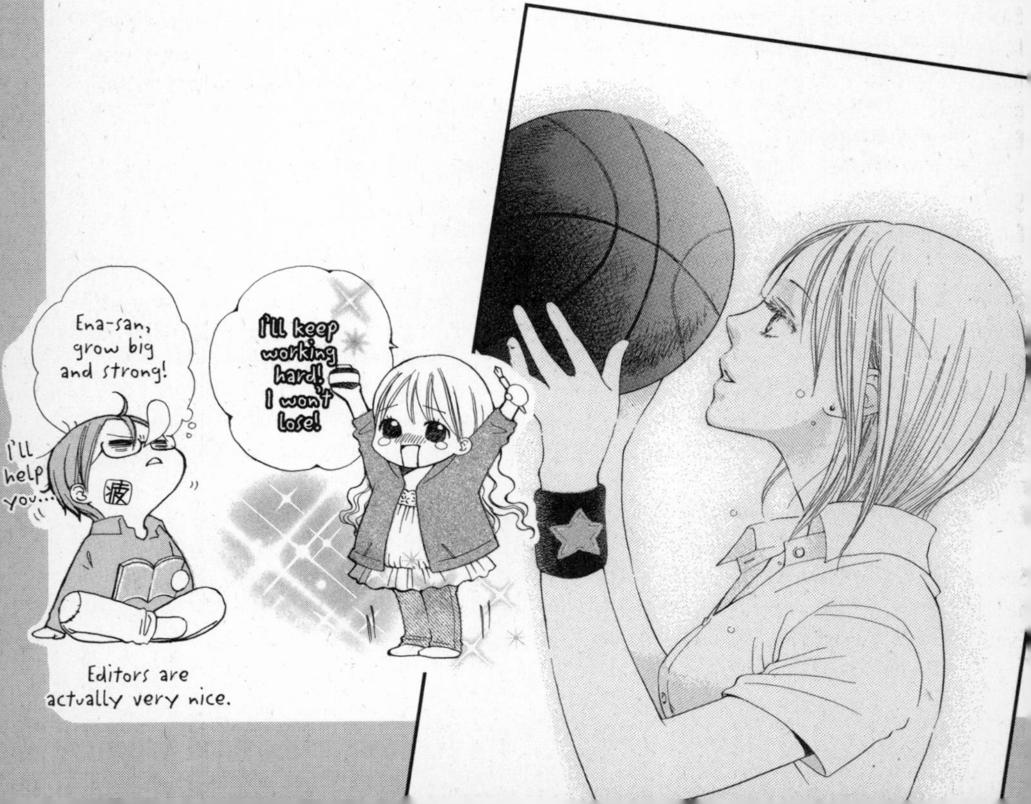

I'll keep working hard! I won't lose!
Ena-san, grow big and strong!
I'll help you...
Editors are actually very nice.

About Supplies

Q: When I ink, the ink bleeds all over the place.

A: There's a problem with your paper quality. Are you using paper that absorbs ink too easily, like sketchpad paper? Check the front and back of your manga paper to make sure the ink doesn't bleed through.

Q: My pen gets caught, and I can't draw clean, thin lines.

A: The quality of a pen stroke is determined by the relationship between your pen nib, your ink, your paper quality, and the pressure you exert on your pen. If there's nothing wrong with your pen or your paper, then adjust the positioning of the pen in your hand until you can repeat clean, thin lines.

Q: How often should I change my pen nibs?

A: There's no rule about this. Pens nibs split open while you use them, and so an older nib will open and stay open more easily. If your lines are thicker than you meant for them to be, then change the nib. If the nib's otherwise in good, usable condition, then save it for when you want to draw thicker lines. If it becomes hard to use, or if it rusts, then throw it away.

Q: I've heard that it's good to use a blue pencil for marking off areas where I want to put tone on the page. Won't that show up in the printing?

A: Most artists use light blue or pale yellow pencils, and those will not show up. Recently, deep blue pencils (such as Prussian blue) have shown up in printing.

Q: I've seen published manga that look like some of the pictures were created with diluted ink or gray markers.

A: You cannot use diluted ink or gray markers for submissions to contests.

Q: There are places where I want to use pencil drawing.

A: Pencil lines will not show up well in print. If you absolutely must have a pencil touch in places, then make a dark photocopy of your pencil drawing and paste it in.

Q: I've read that it's not good to use too much tone. About how much tone should I use?

A: You've been reading old manga tutorials, haven't you? As long as it doesn't make the picture dark and hard to see, we don't mind how much you use. On the other hand, if you use too much crosshatching, then your work will look old-fashioned. On top of that, poorly-drawn crosshatching will ruin your work.

Q: When I paint large areas in black, my page gets bumpy.

A: Are you using a wide brush? If you load up your page with sumi ink, the influx of moisture will cause the paper fibers in the page to swell. You'll also run into bumpiness issues if you paint over blacks that haven't yet dried. The trick is to use a small brush and paint over small parts at a time. For larger areas, it's also handy to use a quick-drying magic marker.

About Art and Character Design

Q: I want to use a photocopy for a flashback scene.
A: There's no problem with that. But don't use copies too much.

Q: I can't draw faces looking to the left.
A: Right-handed people have a hard time drawing faces and bodies facing right, and left-handed people have a hard time making them face left. The best thing you can do is practice it out of your system, but there are a lot of artists who will pencil out a face one way on the back of their page and trace it onto the front.

Q: I like how I drew my face, but it doesn't look right on the body.
A: You need more practice. That tends to happen when the balance is off, such as when the facial design looks very three-dimensional, but the body is flat. Try practicing drawing whole bodies, not just faces.

Q: I can't draw men very well.
A: This, too, comes from lack of regular observation and practice. Don't practice just the kinds of characters you're good at, but all kinds—old, young, male, female. You can look to published manga for inspiration, but also check out men's fashion magazines.

Q: My effects make my page look sloppy.
A: Are you going straight to the final draft without practicing? Don't go off of memory alone; look carefully at the effects pros use, then practice those techniques yourself on a different piece of paper. If you're still not confident, draw the effect in fully at the pencil stage so that all you have to do in the ink stage is trace.

Q: I can't get the things in my backgrounds to look three-dimensional. How do I create the right texture for glass and mirrors?
A: This goes for almost any concern you have about your art, but you can't draw anything well without observation and practice. Practice drawing whatever it is you need a couple of times after observing real objects, photographs, or professional manga drawings. But you can't copy photos from books or copy other artists' work. Make your own drawings original. As for ensuring three-dimensionality, pay close attention to thickening up lines in the foreground and making the lines of faraway objects thin. Don't draw from your memory or imagination.

FAQ ANSWERS TO FREQUENTLY ASKED QUESTIONS

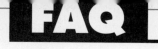

About Story

Q: I just can't come up with a story that will fit inside 16 pages.
A: 16 pages is industry standard. What part of your story do you want to draw the most? Try composing a short story that focuses on that moment.

Q: I can't create a snappy introduction. It takes too long to explain the setting and it starts out slow.
A: Trying to explain a complex world in 16 pages...that's way too tough. After all, you want to convey the situation your character is in with as few words as possible. Get your readers into the art as soon as possible. If you attract their attention with the opening scene, they'll be more likely to stick around for the explanation of the situation.

Q: Are there any themes I should avoid?
A: Stay away from subjects that unfairly discriminate or defame people or groups, or topics that make your readers uncomfortable for no reason. Deliberately inflammatory or off-putting works aren't suitable for submission to a manga contest.

Q: People often tell me my dialogue is too wordy.
A: Are you centering your story and scenes around the dialogue? Remember, brevity is the soul of wit.

About Characters

Q: I got a critique a while back that said my art style was old-fashioned.
A: It's the same with manga as with fashion--shojo manga goes through fads. The more popular a style, the more dated it will feel in a few years. Look over your characters' features, hairstyles, clothes and body shapes carefully. A little tweak here and there can go a long way.

Q: How do I make my characters more appealing? I'm told my art is pretty, but....
A: It's a given that the characters in a shojo manga are beautiful, but beauty alone doesn't make them appealing. It's the way you present your character moving, interacting with their background, gesturing, having habits, and living their goals that makes them appealing. Often, a character's flaws will bring out their appeal.

■ Other Questions

Q: How long does it take a professional manga artist to complete one chapter of manga?
A: That changes depending on the nature of the work, how regularly a story is published, how many pages are published at a time, and the help of assistants. You're not a professional yet, so you don't need to worry about how long it will take you to finish a manga for submission.

Q: Should I get experience as an assistant?
A: It would be a good experience for when you have assistants of your own someday. But it's a big mistake to think of it as an opportunity to learn techniques from professionals. Professionals hire assistants to help them meet their deadlines, so they're looking for people who are ready to get right to work. And your submission will never be at an advantage just because you were an assistant to a famous manga artist.

Q: I live out in the boondocks. Should I move to Tokyo?
A: Living in the country presents no obstacle to submitting work. There are many professional manga artists who continue to live out in the countryside.

Q: Can I submit a work I published as a doujinshi?
A: As a general rule, you should submit a new work that you drew specifically for the magazine contest that you're entering. You should also not resubmit a work. If you don't want to submit a work so much as get feedback, contact the editorial departments directly.

Q: What do they mean by "assigning editors"?
A: When an artist who has submitted a work gets the go-ahead to make a series, then an editor is assigned to her. Sometimes the editor who looked at your contest entry will become your editor until you go professional. The editor will give advice on how to rank high in the contests or how to get a published series.

Q: I'm taking college entrance exams, but should I quit school and focus on manga?
A: Your school records will have no effect on whether or not you can become a professional manga artist. And it is not true at all that graduates of a manga school are guaranteed to go pro. Education is a chance for you to broaden your horizons and gain a lot of valuable experience. There is no reference material better than real experience.

HAKUSENSHA'S EDITORIAL DEPARTMENTS

From *Glass Mask* and *Sukeban Deka* ("Delinquent Detective") to *Patalliro!*, *Touring Express*, *Please Save My Earth*, *Doubutsu no Oisha-san* ("Mr. Animal Doctor"), *Nante Suteki ni Japanesque* ("How Wonderfully Japaneseque"), *Baby & Me*, *Koucha Ouji* ("Tea Prince"), *Angel Sanctuary*, *Hana-Kimi*, and *Fruits Basket*, *Hana to Yume* has given life to a number of shojo manga masterpieces.

We pride ourselves on a broad approach to manga that bleeds beyond the borders of shojo and incorporates strong genre elements. The series mentioned above are from a variety of genres, including period romance, action, fantasy, history, sci-fi, suspense, gag, comedy, and school romance.

We also pride ourselves on being a place where for many years new manga artists have gotten their wings. All of our serialized artists were manga contest winners first, and we swear by our pledge to "discover, nurture, and promote new talent." If you've got what it takes, you could find yourself with a new series as soon as tomorrow.

Hana to Yume magazine is looking for new talent in every genre. Show us the future of manga, and we'll help you achieve it.

Hana to Yume Editor-in-Chief
Hideyuki Takada

Bessatsu Hana to Yume is a shojo manga magazine with a wide age-range of readers, home to a variety of genres and unique artists.

We publish long one-shots in every issue, so if you're an aspiring manga artist who has a big story you want to present, *Bessatsu Hana to Yume* is the place for you. Thrill our readers with that unique story and world you just can't stop thinking about!

Our supportive editorial department holds firmly to the stance that has always gotten Hakusensha results: "Find new artists and create hit manga." That may sound scary, but I swear we're not! Hakusensha editors are all great at giving compliments, and you'll get loads of advice. And we'll keep helping you grow through story meetings and experiences even after you get published.

Take the first step. We're waiting for your submissions!!

Bessatsu Hana to Yume Editor-in-Chief
Takeshi Yamaki

LaLa can say with confidence that we have the proven power to produce new talent. In the year 2006 alone, five new artists had their first graphic novels published through us. And almost all of our artists have multiple printings of their books.

All five of these artists started with the LMS (*LaLa* Manga-ka Scout Course)! From the monthly LMS, they progressed through the manga contest system though the thrice-annual long story LMG (*LaLa* Manga Grand-prix) or the Athena Newcomer Awards.

Now, this is the most important part! Almost 100% of artists currently drawing for *LaLa* started with the *LaLa* manga contests!! We would never take popular artists from other magazines for new titles here, because we are confident in our power to produce new rock stars.

Won't all of you submit your new hit manga to *LaLa*? Our motto is to make our strengths even stronger--we promise that we're just as excited as you to create your first professional manga!!

LaLa Editor-in-Chief
Ikuhide Ichikawa

Launched more than 20 years after the founding of Hakusensha (home of *Hana to Yume* and *LaLa*), *Melody* magazine is like the major leagues of shojo manga. We're a bi-monthly magazine that publishes once every two months, and because of that, we put more emphasis on creating worthwhile reading material with our manga artists.

If you want to be a professional manga artist for *Melody*, the first thing to keep in mind is that we only go on sale six times a year, so there are fewer opportunities to be published with us than with other magazines. The hurdles are that much higher, but the joy at overcoming them is also that much greater for artist and editor. That is the number one reason that we want to respond to those of you who bring in and mail us your manga, even now when we're not having regular manga contests.

As in all professions, it's harder be a manga artist after you've become a pro than when you're trying to become one. Our magazine often places priority on story over characters in its publications, which is somewhat different from the trends of recent mainstream manga. In some ways it will be even more demanding to be a pro here than at other magazines.

We welcome anyone looking for a lifetime career in manga.

Melody Editor-in-Chief
Takashi Iida

HMC HANA TO YUME MANGA-KA COURSE

SUBMISSION GUIDELINES

ELIGIBILITY: We welcome all ages and genders. We only accept unpublished original works.
PAGE COUNT: 16 pages for story manga. 8-10 pages is the general rule for gags and short manga. It's all right to go over or under the page count a little bit, but we will be judging your ability to fit the story into 16 pages.
DEADLINE: Once a month (send in by the 15th of each month)
RESULTS ANNOUNCED: Results will be announced in the issue of Hana to Yume that goes on sale on the 20th of the month after the deadline.
ADDRESS: Hakusensha, Attn: Hana to Yume HMC, 2-2-2 Kanda Awaji-cho, Chiyoda-ku, Tokyo, 101-0063
JUDGES: Manga artists published in any Hana to Yume magazine and the editor-in-chief of each magazine.
PRIZES:

- **Gold Rose Award:** ¥500,000, plus a MacBook
- **Gold Lily Award**: ¥300,000, plus a home copy machine
- **Award of Excellence:** ¥150,000, plus a digital camera or home fax machine
- **Effort Award:** ¥10,000, plus Copic Ciao Markers 36-color set
- **Best Ten Award:** Second Place, ¥30,000; Third Place, ¥20,000; Fourth through Tenth Place, ¥10,000

*The first place winner will get the Effort Award or higher.
**Anyone who ranked in the top ten will also be judged for one of the following three awards.

- **Editor-in-Chief's Most Promising Award:** ¥10,000
- **Newcomer Award:** (awarded to a first-time entrant who ranked in the top ten) ¥10,000
- **Pick-Up Award:** (one entrant will be selected every time) ¥20,000
- **Best 20 Award:** ¥6,000
- **Best 30 Award:** ¥3,000

Everyone ranking 30 or above will be presented with a three-sheet set of I.C. tone and 20 sheets of limited edition manga paper.

- **Special Gag Award:** (awarded every month to the funniest entry) ¥10,000

BONUS

- The first-place manga will be published in *Hana to Yume* or a special edition.
- Responses and critique will be given free of charge to all entrants.
- All entrants will be presented with a set of art prints.

***Winners will receive their prize money within a month after the release date of the issue announcing the results. Prizes of more than ¥100,000 are subject to taxes.

This information is current as of December 2006. Details such as prizes awarded and eligibility are subject to change, so when entering, we recommend you check the latest issue of the magazine.

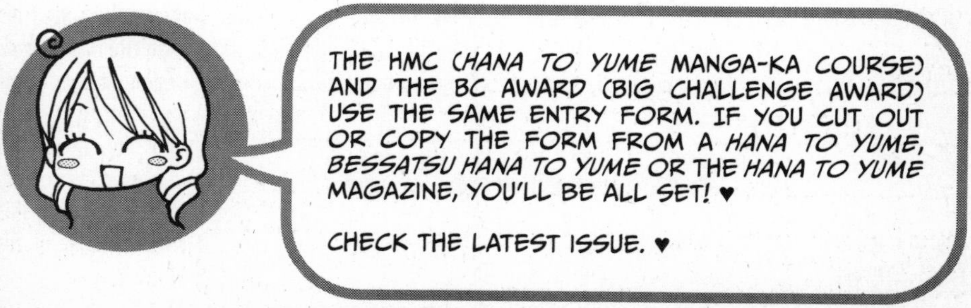
THE HMC (*HANA TO YUME* MANGA-KA COURSE) AND THE BC AWARD (BIG CHALLENGE AWARD) USE THE SAME ENTRY FORM. IF YOU CUT OUT OR COPY THE FORM FROM A *HANA TO YUME*, *BESSATSU HANA TO YUME* OR THE *HANA TO YUME* MAGAZINE, YOU'LL BE ALL SET! ♥
CHECK THE LATEST ISSUE. ♥

SUBMISSION GUIDELINES

BIG CHALLENGE AWARD

ELIGIBILITY: The Big Challenge Award is a manga contest that aims to produce many new shojo manga artists. We welcome all ages and genders. We only accept unpublished original works.

PAGE COUNT: As a general rule, 24, 30, 32, or 40 pages. Shorts should be 8-16 pages.

DEADLINE: Twice a year (on the 15th of March or September).

RESULTS ANNOUNCED: Results will be announced in the Hana to Yume published on the 20th, or the Bessatsu Hana to Yume published on the 25th, two months after the deadline.

ADDRESS: Hakusensha, Attn: Hana to Yume Editorial Department XXth Big Challenge Award, 2-2-2 Kanda Awaji-cho, Chiyoda-ku, Tokyo, 101-0063

JUDGES: Manga artists published in any Hana to Yume magazine and the editor-in-chief of each magazine.

PRIZES:
- **Big Challenge Grand Prize:** ¥1,000,000 and a coupon to travel overseas for research (worth ¥200,000)
- **Selected:** ¥500,000, plus a laptop computer
- **Runner-Up:** ¥300,000, plus a digital camera
- **Fine Work:** ¥150,000, plus a Copic marker set
- **Honorable Mention:** ¥50,000

*Winners of the above will also be judged for the following special awards.
- **Authors' Favorite:** ¥50,000
- **Editor-in-Chief's Most Promising Award:** ¥50,000
- **Special Gag Award:** ¥50,000

**Everything ranked above "Fine Work" will be published in either Hana to Yume, Bessatsu Hana to Yume, or The Hana to Yume. After that you will be assigned an editor who will support you in creating your next work.

ADDITIONAL PRIZES:
(1) 50 sheets of limited edition manga paper
(2) Set of Hana to Yume prints
(3) Big Challenge Award Special Submission Manual Sheet

The top 20 submissions will receive a thorough critique sheet. Manga will be returned free of charge upon request.

***Winners will receive their prize money within a month after the release date of the issue announcing the results. Prizes of more than ¥100,000 yen are subject to taxes.

HMC/BC AWARD ENTRY FORM

Applying for ____th HMC / ____th BC Award   Date sent: __/__/__ (day/month/year)

	Number of Pages	Age
TITLE		

PEN NAME	**REAL NAME**

Postal Code	
	ADDRESS

Phone (+ area code)	Would you like your entry returned? **Yes / No**	Would you like to receive critique? **Yes / No**	(For the BC Award, only those ranking 20 or higher will receive critique)	School Name / Place of Employment

E-mail address		Would you like to receive notices from each contest?	**No / Yes, by e-mail / Yes, by direct mail**

Experience submitting to this magazine **This is my ___th time.**	Highest score until now (When, which award, rank) (Leave blank if does not apply)		Submitted elsewhere? **Yes / No**	Highest score until now (When, which award, rank) (Leave blank if does not apply)

Please attach a sheet of paper with the information on this form to the back of the first page of your manga using clear tape. We will only use the personal information on this form for the purposes of this contest.

**This information is current as of December 2006. Details such as prizes awarded and eligibility are subject to change, so when applying, we recommend you check the latest issue of the magazine.

LALA MANGA-KA SCOUT COURSE

OBJECTIVE: The goal of the LaLa Manga-ka Scout Course is to train professional shojo manga artists.

ELIGIBILITY: As long as you submit a never-been-published work, we accept any age, gender, and experience level.

PAGE COUNT: 16 pages for story manga, 8-16 for gag manga.

DEADLINE: Once a month (turn in by the 10th of the month).

RESULTS ANNOUNCED: Results will be announced in the LaLa magazine published one month after the deadline.

ADDRESS: Hakusensha, Attn: LaLa Editorial Department LMS, 2-2-2 Kanda Awaji-cho, Chiyoda-ku, Tokyo, 101-0063

RETURN AND CRITIQUE: Return of entry and critique are free of charge.

JUDGES: *LaLa* editors and editor-in-chief

PRIZES:

● **LMS Grand Prize:** ¥500,000, plus a trip overseas for research (after you create a serialized manga)

● **Diamond Rookie Award:** ¥300,000, plus a fax machine

● **Best Rookie Award:** ¥150,000

● **Excellent Rookie Award:** ¥30,000

● **Rookie Award:** ¥10,000

Additionally, winners of the "Best/Excellent/Rookie" awards will receive 32 sheets of manga paper, plus a five-sheet set of tone, and an original tone designed by manga artist Meca Tanaka.

● **Best 30 Award:** ¥5,000 yen prize money

● **Special Gag Award:** ¥30,000

Additionally, winners of the "Best 30/Gag" awards will receive 32 sheets of manga paper, plus a three-sheet set of tone, and an original tone designed by manga artist Meca Tanaka.

*Those who do extremely well will be assigned an editor for guidance. The top work will be published in our magazine.

SPECIAL PRIZES:

● **Special Genre Award:** (additional award presented to exemplary works in their given genre, such as romance, sci-fi, etc.): ¥10,000

● **Pick-Up Award:** (additional award presented to the work selected as "This Month's Best XX Award"): ¥10,000

● **First Submission Award:** (additional award presented to a first-time submission that wins the Excellent Rookie Award or higher): ¥10,000

● **Grade-Up Award:** (for the person who shows the most improvement since their last submission): ¥3,000

SPECIAL PRIZES:

☆ Those who earn the Rookie Award or higher get a free pass in the first round of judging for the LMG (LaLa Manga Grand-Prix). Furthermore, in some cases, winners will receive a phone call directly from an editor to give them advice.

EXTRA BONUS!

☆ Those wishing to get their entry back will receive an original tone designed by a LaLa artist, a set of art prints, an envelope and numbered ticket to use for their next submission (your manga is returned free of charge).

☆ Those submitting for the first time will be presented with a manga scale, an official LMS Strategy Guide, and a collection of interviews with 10 LaLa artists.

**We aim to award prize money one month after announcing the results. Prize money of ¥100,000 or more is subject to taxes.

**This information is current as of December 2006. Details such as prizes awarded and eligibility are subject to change, so when applying, we recommend you check the latest issue of the magazine.

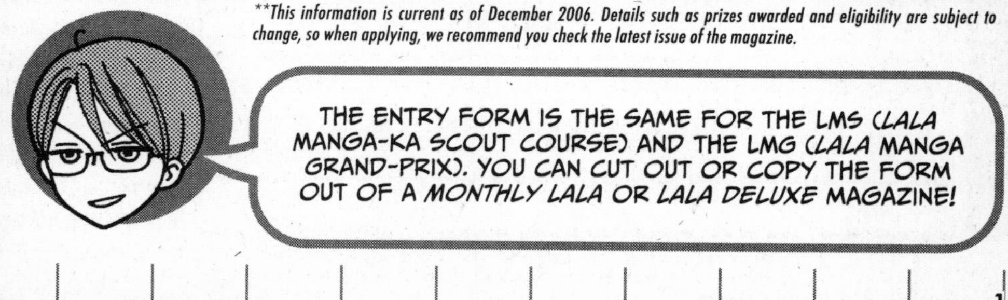

THE ENTRY FORM IS THE SAME FOR THE LMS (LALA MANGA-KA SCOUT COURSE) AND THE LMG (LALA MANGA GRAND-PRIX). YOU CAN CUT OUT OR COPY THE FORM OUT OF A *MONTHLY LALA* OR *LALA DELUXE* MAGAZINE!

OBJECTIVE: The LMG is a manga contest that aims to produce professional manga artists.

ELIGIBILITY: As long as you submit an unpublished, original work, we welcome professionals, amateurs, and anyone who wants to participate.

PAGE COUNT: 16, 24, 32, or 40 pages for story manga, 6-16 pages for gag manga.

DEADLINE: Three times annually (turn in by the end of April, August, or December)

RESULTS: Results will be announced in the Monthly LaLa magazine that will go on sale on the 24th, two months after the deadline.

ADDRESS: Hakusensha, Attn: Monthly LaLa Editorial Department LaLa Manga Grand-Prix, 2-2-2 Kanda Awaji-cho, Chiyoda-ku, Tokyo, 101-0063

RETURN AND CRITIQUE: We aim to return submissions by mail, free of charge, to those wanting them back, one month after the winners are announced. Please understand that we do not give critique on manuscripts.

JUDGES: LaLa artists and the LaLa editor-in-chief

PRIZES:
- **Grand-Prix:** ¥1,000,000, plus a laptop computer
- **Grand-Prix Runner-Up:** ¥70,000 plus a laptop computer
- **Platinum Debut Award:** ¥50,000, plus a laptop computer
- **Gold Debut Award:** ¥30,000, plus a digital video camera
- **Fresh Debut Award:** ¥15,000, plus a digital camera
- **Special Gag Award:** ¥50,000, plus a tone set
- **High-Level Award:** ¥5,000, plus a tone set
- **Special Judges' Award:** ¥30,000, plus a tone set
- **Special Editorial Department Award:** ¥30,000, plus a tone set

BONUS:
☆ Those who pass the final round of judging will receive grant money in the amount of ¥10,000.
☆ Those who pass the first round of judging will receive a special library card.
☆ All entrants will receive a set of art prints.

AMAZING LMG!

(1) Those who are awarded the Fresh Debut Award or higher have their winning entries published in LaLa, LaLa Deluxe, or a special edition published by LaLa. Naturally, the artist is also assigned an editor.
(2) All those who pass the final round of judging will be assigned an editor who will diligently follow up with them until they get a published work!
(3) Those who ranked in the Rookie Award or higher in the LMS will bypass the first round of judging. Please specify when entering.
(4) Promising artists will be among a select few invited to the special LMG Seminar lecture—a shortcut to getting your work published.

*We aim to award prize money one month after announcing the results. Prize money of ¥100,000 or more is subject to taxes.

APPLYING FOR THE __TH LMS/LMG.

Write in the number and circle which contest you're entering.

Please attach a sheet of paper with the information on this form to the back of the first page of your manga with clear tape. We will only use the personal information on this form for the purposes of this contest.

LALA MANGA CONTEST ENTRY FORM						
TITLE		Number of Pages		**REAL NAME**		
PEN NAME			SCHOOL NAME / PLACE OF EMPLOYMENT		Age	
ADDRESS	Phone (+ area code)					
		May we contact you by phone? Yes/No		Would you like critique over the phone? Yes / No (only for LMS)		
# of submissions	____ times for this magazine		Highest score until now:	LMS LMG	___ Contest	___ Award
Would you like a critique of your work?	Yes / No *No critique for LMG		Would you like us to return your entry?	Yes / No	Would you like us to introduce you to assistants?	Yes / No

**This information is current as of December 2006. Details such as prizes awarded and eligibility are subject to change, so when applying, we recommend you check the latest issue of the magazine.

Shortcut to getting your work published and getting a series! Melody happily welcomes hand-delivered manga!

OBJECTIVE: Melody is looking for works with a sense of originality and passion! Won't you publish your first work in Melody, a magazine full of works—such as *Himitsu: Top Secret* and *Ooku*—that challenge the conventions of traditional shojo manga? There is no deadline. We accept walk-in hand-delivered submissions anytime.

ELIGIBILITY: We welcome both professionals and amateurs. However, we only accept original, unpublished works.

PAGE COUNT: As a general rule, we accept 16, 24, 32, or 40 pages. More pages are okay, too. Gags and shorts should be six pages or more.

APPOINTMENTS: Please make an appointment at least a day before you come in. Call: 03-3526-8045 (Melody editorial department). *We're not in on Saturdays, Sundays, or holidays.

**Please see page 120 for details on delivering your manga in person, and page 121 for a map to Hakusensha.

We also accept mailed-in submissions from those living far from Tokyo.

● When submitting by mail, please make sure to let us know by phone ahead of time. The editor who takes your call will not only look over your work, but also give you critique over the phone.

● When you send your manga, keep a copy of it on hand. You will need this when receiving critique over the phone.

● Address: Hakusensha, Attn: [Name of Editor], Melody Editorial Department Manga Mochikomi, 2-2-2 Kanda Awaji-cho, Chiyoda-ku, Tokyo, 101-0063

Bonus: Everyone who brings in her work will receive a commemorative item (telephone card, library card, etc.).

MANGA ENTRY FORM					
TITLE		(__ pages)		**PEN NAME**	
PHONE NUMBER		EMPLOYMENT / SCHOOL NAME		**FULL NAME**	
ADDRESS					
Submission / Award history					
Favorite manga genres, artistic inspirations					

Please attach a sheet of paper with the information on this form to the back of the first page of your manga using clear tape. We will only use the personal information on this form for the purposes of this project.

**This information is current as of December 2006. When bringing in your work, we recommend you check the latest issue of the magazine.

SUBMISSION GUIDELINES **BC**

HANA TO YUME, BESSATSU HANA TO YUME, LALA, MELODY

ATHENA NEWCOMER AWARD

ELIGIBILITY: Anyone can participate. Even if you have been published in another magazine, if we have determined that you are new to the profession, we acknowledge your eligibility. Only submit original, unpublished, unsubmitted works.

PAGE COUNT: 16, 24, or 32 pages for story manga. In the case of a gag manga or other genre, please combine a few storylines to meet the page requirements.

DEADLINE: Once a year (turn in by October 1st).

ADDRESS: Hakusensha, Attn: Athena Newcomer Award, 2-2-2 Kanda Awaji-cho, Chiyoda-ku, Tokyo, 101-0063

RESULTS: Results will be announced in Hana to Yume issue 2, Bessatsu Hana to Yume February issue, Monthly LaLa February issue, Melody February Issue.

JUDGES: Artists currently published in any Hakusensha magazine and each magazine's editor-in-chief.

PRIZES:

● **Newcomer Grand Prize** (one winner): Main prize: certificate and commemorative medal; Additional prizes: ¥2,000,000, plus a laptop computer

● **Excellent Newcomer Grand Prize** (no limit to number of winners): Main prize: certificate and commemorative medal; Additional prizes: ¥1,000,000, plus a laptop computer

● **Newcomer Prize** (no limit to number of winners): Main prize: certificate and commemorative medal; Additional prizes: ¥500,000, plus DVD entertainment system

● **Fine Work** (no limit to number of winners): Main prize: certificate and commemorative medal; Additional prizes: ¥200,000, plus a home copy machine

● **Excellent Published Newcomer Award** (no limit to number of winners): Main prize: certificate and commemorative medal; Additional prize: ¥300,000

BONUS:

☆ All entrants will receive a library card signed by that year's judges and 32 sheets of limited edition manga paper.

☆ Those who pass the first round of judging will receive a grant of ¥10,000.

☆ Detailed critique and priority invitation to each magazine's moving classroom.

☆ All four magazines will combine to back you up! Because all four magazines sponsor this contest together, you have a lot of options as to where to go next. After you win the award, we will discuss with you and determine which magazine you will work to be published in, based on your interests and the nature of your manga.

☆ The award-winning manga will be published in a comic anthology! If you win the Athena Newcomer Award, your work will instantly be in a graphic novel. Not a bad way to commemorate your award and give you encouragement for the future.

☆ The "Excellent Published Newcomer Award" will be presented to excellent manga submitted by artists who have been professional for less than one year. Being published doesn't mean the fun of contests has to end!

*All prizes will be awarded at the award ceremony held at the end of the January following the deadline. Prizes of ¥100,000 or more are subject to taxes.

ATHENA NEWCOMER AWARD
ENTRY FORM

TITLE	(__ pages)			PEN NAME	
	Number of Pages				
ADDRESS INCLUDE POSTAL CODE AND PREFECTURE NAME				FULL NAME	
PHONE NUMBER		AGE		EMPLOYMENT / SCHOOL NAME	
Would you like us to return your entry?	Yes / No	Submission / Award history			
Favorite genres and artistic inspirations					

Please attach a shee of paper with th information on thi form to the bac of the first page o your manga usin clear tape. We wi only use the persona information on thi form for the purpose of this contest.

This information is current as of December 2006. Details such as prizes awarded and eligibility are subject to change, so when applying, we recommend you check the latest issue of one of the four magazines.

awing manga is a very fun job. Seeing a blank piece of paper come to
 with art and stories you created yourself is one of the most rewarding
periences you can have.

en though manga is fun, there are a lot of obstacles on the road to
coming a professional manga artist. Whenever you feel like you've hit a
adblock, crack open this book.

e two things editors think about most often while reviewing a submitted
nga are, "Why didn't they do research before drawing this?" and,
Why didn't they practice first?" We focused on addressing those two
ues as we wrote this book.

s book isn't really about "how to draw shojo manga." It's a guidebook
 becoming a professional shojo manga artist. The difference is subtle, but
st. Even while you're having fun drawing, keeping in mind an end goal
 getting published will actually bring you that much closer to achieving
blication.

ing able to share the manga you loved drawing with readers will magnify
 joy you experienced while drawing. We hope that this book has been,
d will continue to be, a helpful guide for making your dream of being a
ofessional manga artist a reality.

s book would not be possible without the artistic contributions of Yui
in. Not only did she take time out of her tight schedule to provide us with
taggering amount of art, but she also had to draw in a style completely
ferent from her own, in the role of aspiring manga artist. On top of that,
 even put her work before our judges! We are indebted to you.

o, a big thanks goes to our graphic designer, Saki Koyatsu, who so
tiently and untiringly laid out page after page for us. Truly, thank you
y much. Thanks also to all the artists who let us use their work in this
ok, starting with Reiko Shimizu. Thank you all so much.

d so, until we meet again, dear shojo manga artist!

m the editorial departments of *Hana to Yume, Bessatsu Hana to Yume,*
a, and *Melody.*

AFTERWORD

Hi, I'm Yui Shin. I drew the manga and the illustrations that go with the text in this book. Every time I drew something, I thought, "This isn't a good example..." "These aren't professional drawings..." and "Readers, I'm sorry. Master Hakusensha, forgive me."

Back when I was unpublished and submitting work to contests, I was pretty lost. I spent my days wondering, "What do I do now...? (cry)." But thanks to the goodwill of the editors, I have somehow ended up masquerading as a manga artist. Don't worry! If I was able to become a manga artist, then you can do it, too! Let's shoot for the moon, guys!

慎紀
Yui Shin

Yui Shin's Profile

■ First Work: "House of Flowers," 2003, published in The LaLa Melody
■ Hometown: Tokyo ■ Birthday: June 14 ■ Blood type: A
■ Favorite things: movies, oil paintings, cacti, cats, sake, Aya Kouda, Gorey, Chihiro Onitsuka, etc.
■ Least favorite things: sweet things, working digitally

Published by *Hana to Yume* Comics: *Walking with Papa, Ghost Only: Restaurant for Ghosts*

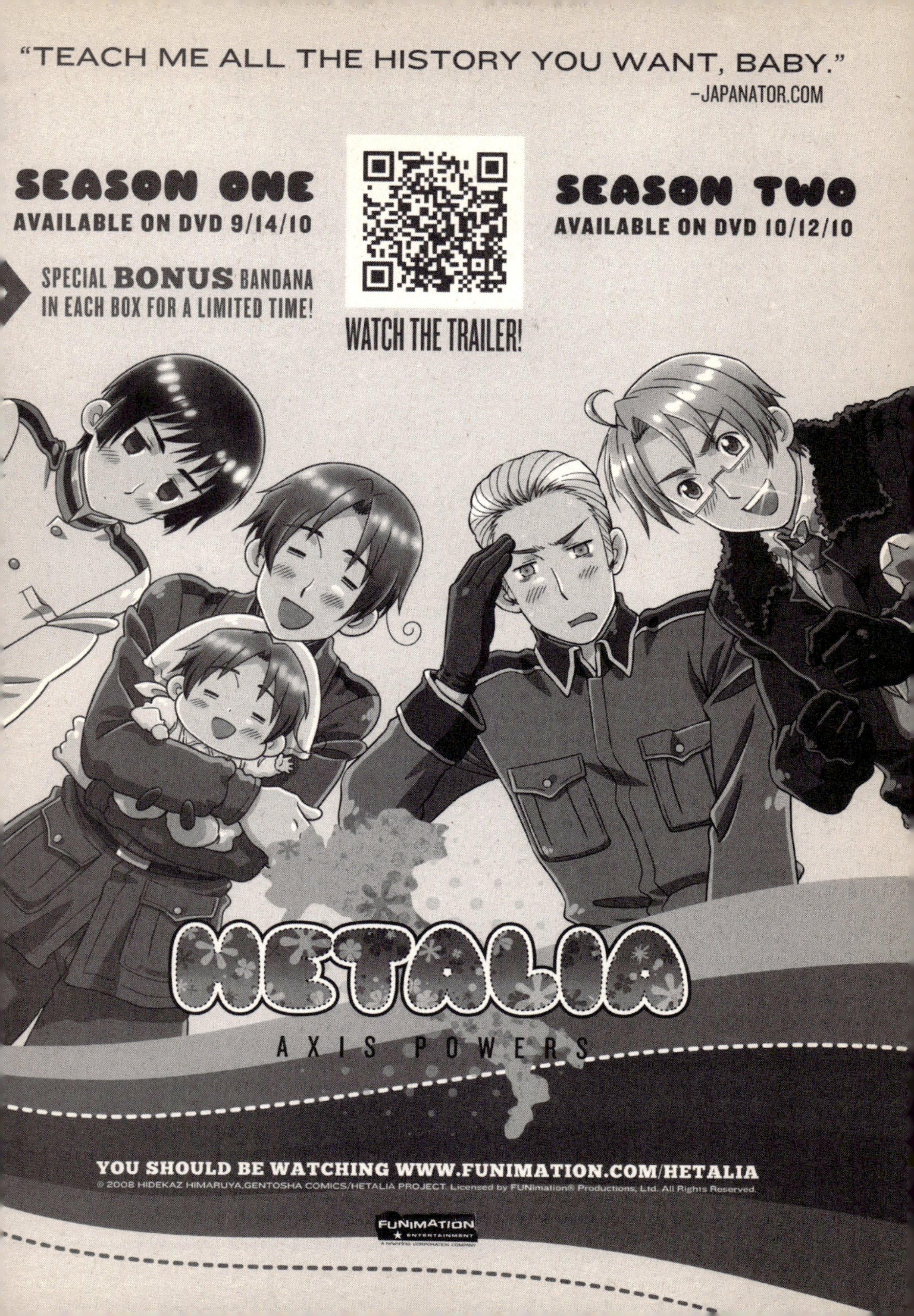
"TEACH ME ALL THE HISTORY YOU WANT, BABY."
–JAPANATOR.COM
SEASON ONE
AVAILABLE ON DVD 9/14/10
SPECIAL BONUS BANDANA IN EACH BOX FOR A LIMITED TIME!
WATCH THE TRAILER!
SEASON TWO
AVAILABLE ON DVD 10/12/10
HETALIA
AXIS POWERS
YOU SHOULD BE WATCHING WWW.FUNIMATION.COM/HETALIA
© 2008 HIDEKAZ HIMARUYA,GENTOSHA COMICS/HETALIA PROJECT. Licensed by FUNimation® Productions, Ltd. All Rights Reserved.
FUNIMATION ENTERTAINMENT

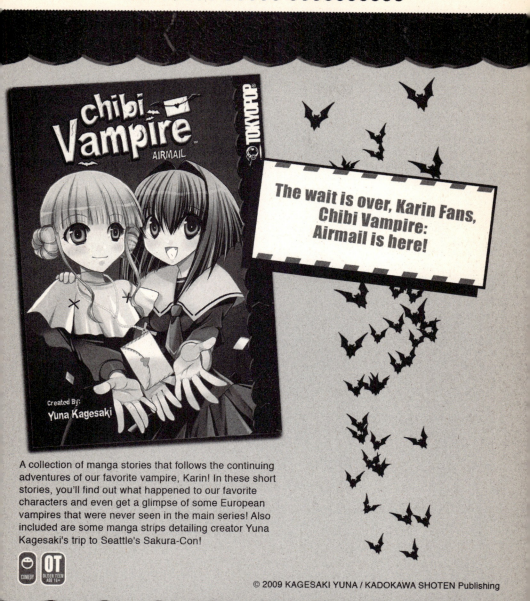

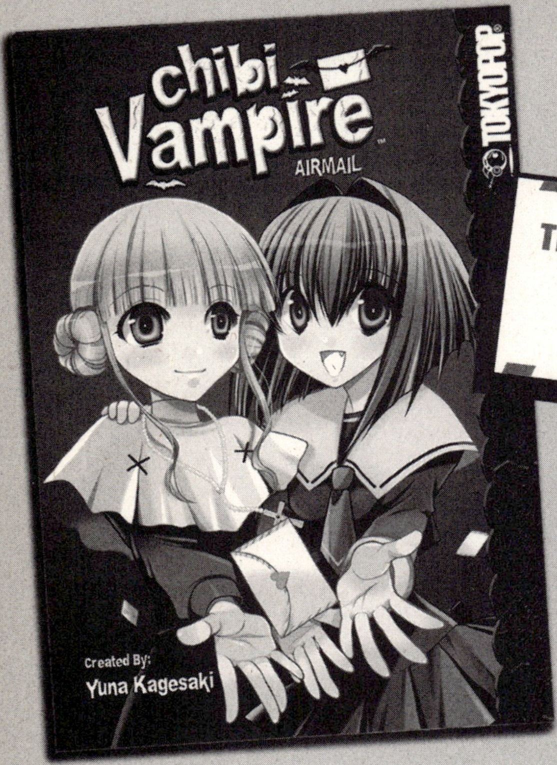
chibi Vampire
AIRMAIL
TOKYOPOP
Created By:
Yuna Kagesaki

The wait is over, Karin Fans, Chibi Vampire: Airmail is here!

A collection of manga stories that follows the continuing adventures of our favorite vampire, Karin! In these short stories, you'll find out what happened to our favorite characters and even get a glimpse of some European vampires that were never seen in the main series! Also included are some manga strips detailing creator Yuna Kagesaki's trip to Seattle's Sakura-Con!

COMEDY | OT OLDER TEEN AGE 16+

BE SURE TO VISIT WWW.TOKYOPOP.COM/SHOP FOR EVERYTHING YOU COULD EVER WANT!

Collect Them All!

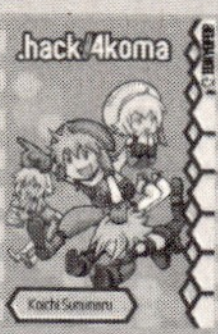
.hack//4Koma

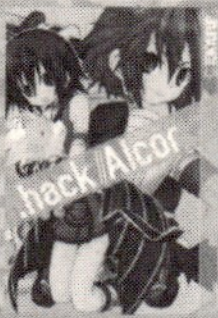
.hack//Alcor

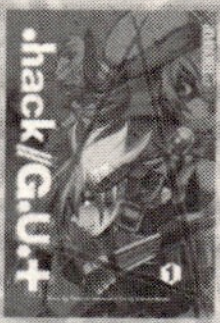
.hack//G.U.+
Volume 1

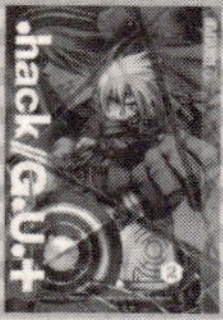
.hack//G.U.+
Volume 2

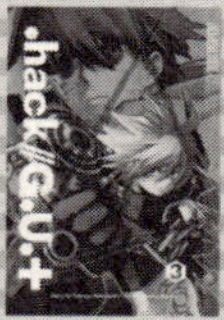
.hack//G.U.+
Volume 3

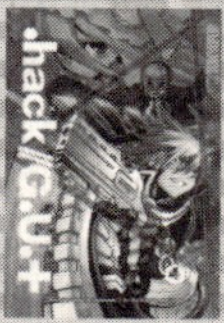
.hack//G.U.+
Volume 4

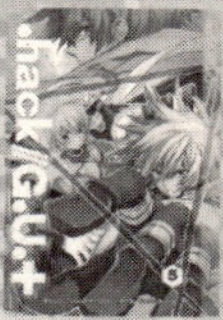
.hack//G.U.+
Volume 5

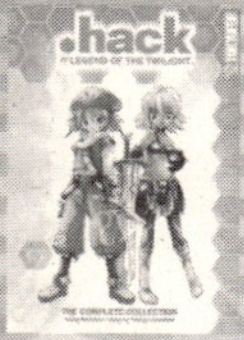
.hack//Legend of the Twilight:
The Complete Collection

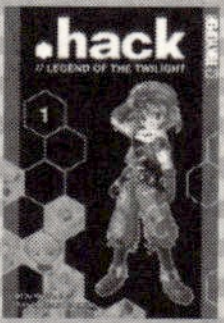
.hack//Legend of the Twilight
Volume 1

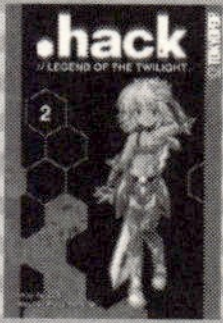
.hack//Legend of the Twilight
Volume 2

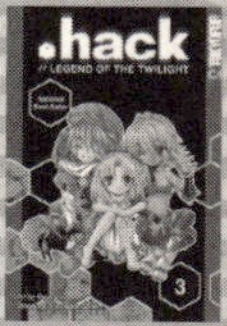
.hack//Legend of the Twilight
Volume 3

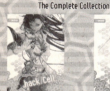

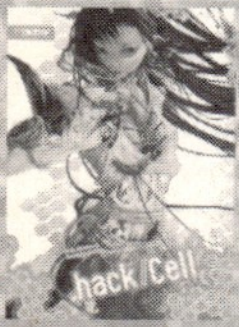
.hack//CELL
Volume 1

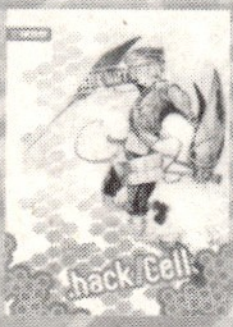
.hack//CELL
Volume 2

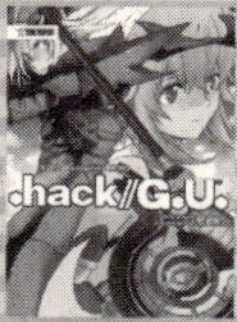
.hack//G.U. Novel
Volume 1

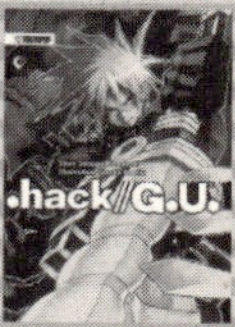
.hack//G.U. Novel
Volume 2

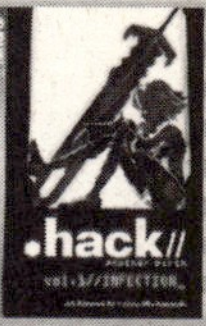
.hack//Another Birth
Volume 1

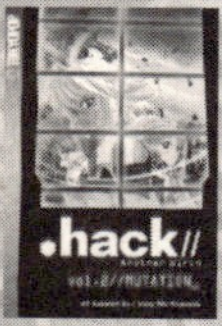
.hack//Another Birth
Volume 2

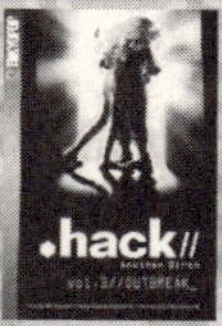
.hack//Another Birth
Volume 3

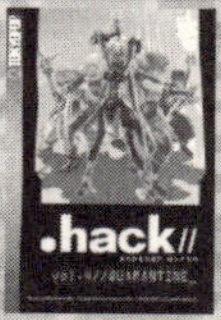
.hack//Another Birth
Volume 4

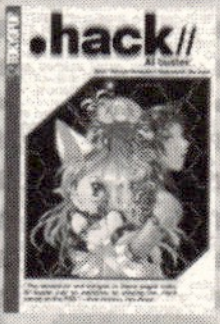
.hack//AI buster
Volume 1

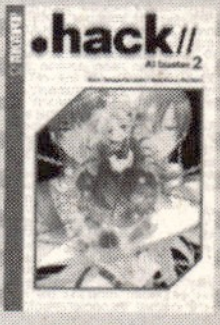
.hack//AI buster
Volume 2

T TEEN AGE 13+

BUY THEM ALL AT WWW.TOKYOPOP.COM/SHOP

The World Is Back, and It Will Surprise You!

Two years after the popular video game The World was shut down, Tokio Kuryuu cannot wait for The World R:X to come out. Unfortunately for him, he forgets to reserve a copy and finds himself without access. That is, until a beautiful new transfer student suddenly and mysteriously forces Tokio into the game and makes him her servant!

Preview at www.TOKYOPOP.com/hack_Link

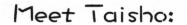

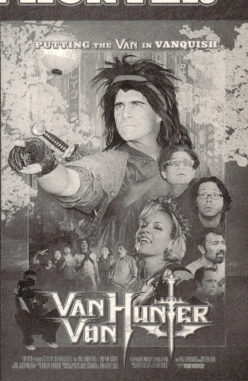

STOP!

This is the back of the book.
You wouldn't want to spoil a great ending!

This book is printed "manga-style," in the authentic Japanese right-to-left format. Since none of the artwork has been flipped or altered, readers get to experience the story just as the creator intended. You've been asking for it, so TOKYOPOP® delivered: authentic, hot-off-the-press, and far more fun!

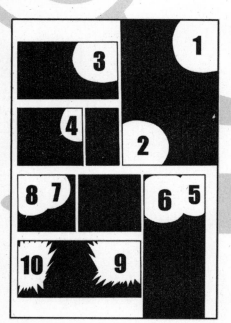

DIRECTIONS

If this is your first time reading manga-style, here's a quick guide to help you understand how it works.

It's easy... just start in the top right panel and follow the numbers. Have fun, and look for more 100% authentic manga from TOKYOPOP®!